TENTH EDITION

OFF THE BEATEN PATH® ALABAMA →

A GUIDE TO UNIQUE PLACES

GAY N. MARTIN
Revised and updated by Jackie Sheckler Finch

gpp®
travel

Guilford, Connecticut

All the information in this guidebook is subject to change. We recommend that you call ahead to obtain current information before traveling.

To buy books in quantity for corporate use
or incentives, call **(800) 962-0973**
or e-mail **premiums@GlobePequot.com.**

Project Editor: Alexandra Singer
Layout: Joanna Beyer
Text design: Linda R. Loiewski
Maps: Equator Graphics © Morris Book Publishing, LLC

ISSN 1535-8291
ISBN 978-1-4930-0382-2

Printed in the United States of America

My gratitude to my family for their encouragement:
Kelly Rose; Sean, Devin, Dylan, and Emma Rose; Stefanie, Will,
Trey, and Arianna Scott; and Logan, Olivia, and Grayson Peters.
And a special remembrance to my husband, Bill Finch,
who taught me how to value every day on this earth.

—Jackie Sheckler Finch

Florence

Huntsville

NORTHWEST
ALABAMA

NORTHEAST
ALABAMA

Birmingham

CENTRAL ALABAMA

Montgomery

SOUTHWEST
ALABAMA

SOUTHEAST
ALABAMA

Mobile

Contents

About the Author

Gay N. Martin, who lives in Alabama, enjoys writing about travel in the Southeast. Her articles and travel pieces have appeared in *Modern Bride,* the *Boston Herald, Kiwanis,* the *Atlanta Journal-Constitution,* the *London Free Press,* the *San Antonio Express-News,* the *Seattle Post-Intelligencer, Far East Traveler,* the *Birmingham News,* the *Times-Picayune,* the *Grand Rapids Press, Upscale Living Magazine,* and other publications. She has won numerous writing awards for fiction and nonfiction in state, regional, and national competitions. She is also the author of Globe Pequot's *Off the Beaten Path Louisiana* and *Alabama's Historic Restaurants and Their Recipes,* published by John F. Blair.

Before embarking on her writing career, Martin taught high school for 11 years, served as resource coordinator of her school's program for gifted and talented students, and sponsored the school newspaper.

About the Revisor

An award-winning journalist and photographer, Jackie Sheckler Finch has covered a wide array of topics—from birth to death, with all the joy and sorrow in between. She has written for numerous publications and is the editor of a nationally award-winning regional magazine. She is also the author of more than a dozen books and has been named the Mark Twain Travel Writer of the Year by the Midwest Travel Writers Association a record five times, in 1998, 2001, 2003, 2007, and 2012. She also belongs to the Society of American Travel Writers and the National Federation of Press Women. She shares her home with resident guard and entertainer, a rescued pooch named Pepper. One of her greatest joys is taking to the road to find the fascinating people and places that wait over the hill and around the next bend.

Acknowledgments

As I crisscrossed Alabama while researching this book, many people offered suggestions and provided information. I want to thank everyone who helped me with the birthing of the previous nine editions as well as this one. My appreciation to the excellent team of public relations officials who promote the awesome aspects of Alabama, as well as to the residents, volunteers, and business owners who took the time to share what makes Alabama special. Gratitude to Tracee Williams, Amy Lyons, Alexandra Singer, and the friendly and professional staff at Globe Pequot Press for allowing me the pleasure of revising this book.

Introduction

As a vacation destination, Alabama surprises most first-time visitors. With its varied and splendid geography, moderate climate, and Southern hospitality, the state makes an ideal year-round getaway. From its craggy Appalachian bluffs to sugar-sand beaches on the Gulf of Mexico, Alabama's wealth of natural beauty offers a happy (and uncrowded) vacation choice for everyone.

Alabama's link with sports is legend—think Bear Bryant, Joe Namath, Bo Jackson, Pat Sullivan, John Hannah, Hank Aaron, Joe Louis, Willie Mays, Jesse Owens, LeRoy "Satchel" Paige, Bobby Allison—and the list goes on. Although racing fans throng Talladega's speedway and Birmingham's Alabama Sports Hall of Fame represents diversity, visitors soon discover that football reigns supreme here. The first Alabama–Auburn clash dates to February 22, 1893, and loyalty lines continue to divide families, friends, and lovers. The stirring words "Roll Tide" and "War Eagle" enter the typical childhood vocabulary early on.

Designed by Robert Trent Jones, the largest golf course construction project ever attempted winds its way through Alabama. The world-famous golf architect, who died in 2000, called this project the greatest achievement of his career; the *New York Times* calls it "some of the best public golf on Earth." Unless you agree with Mark Twain that golf is a good walk ruined, you can't pass up the **Robert Trent Jones Golf Trail**, which tests the skills of all golfers from scratch handicappers to hopeless duffers. Beginning in the mountains and lakes of the Appalachian foothills and continuing southward to the white sands and wetlands of the Gulf Coast, this group of PGA tour–quality courses, ranging from 36 to 54 holes each, provides superb golfing and splendid scenery.

The Trail continues to shine, and the two top public golf courses in the US await you here, according to *Golf World* readers, who recently ranked Opelika's Grand National site #1 and Prattville's Capitol Hill #2. Also, out of roughly 13,500 public-access courses, Mobile earned #32. "With rankings like this one and being named the top golf value destination in the country by *Golf Digest,*" said Dr. David Bronner, "we hope to introduce even more people to golf in Alabama." Conceived by Bronner and funded by the Retirement Systems of Alabama (RSA), the Trail has transformed Alabama into a golfing mecca. So come on down and play.

To learn more about all 11 locations on the RTJ Golf Trail or to settle into one of the nearby upscale resorts along the way, call (800) 949-4444 or visit rtjgolf.com or pchresorts.com.

And while you're at it, check out the new RTJ Spa Trail, part of the Robert Trent Jones Golf Trail's Resort Collection at Four-Diamond-rated properties in Point Clear, Mobile, Montgomery, Birmingham, Opelika, and Florence. After all, who doesn't need a little pampering, particularly in these trying times?

Speaking of trails, anglers will want to follow their bliss on the *Alabama Bass Trail.* Developed by the state Department of Conservation and Natural Resources and the first of its kind in the country, this trail consists of 11 premier bass fishing lakes across the state with plenty of outstanding bass tournaments on the agenda. And that's not all. *Audubon* magazine named the Alabama Coastal Birding Trail, which stretches through Baldwin and Mobile Counties, one of the country's best viewing sites. Birders will find directional and interpretive signs all along the way.

> ## alabamatrivia
>
> Alabama's Robert Trent Jones Golf Trail is the world's largest golf-course construction project.

Stars still fall on Alabama, and visitors can dip into a rich musical heritage throughout the state. Depending on your own particular penchant, you may catch a classical music concert at the Birmingham Civic Center or a swinging jazz session during Florence's yearly tribute to the "Father of the Blues," W. C. Handy. The *Alabama Music Hall of Fame,* near Tuscumbia, features memorabilia of Nat King Cole, Hank Williams, Sonny James, Lionel Richie, the Commodores, Emmylou Harris, Dinah Washington, the Temptations, and many other musicians with Alabama connections.

This guide book spotlights some of the state's special places—not only major sites such as the United States Space & Rocket Center in Huntsville but also small towns frozen in time and tucked-away treasures occasionally overlooked by the natives. In the state's northern section, Huntsville makes a handy launching pad from which travelers can easily loop both east and west to take in north Alabama's unique attractions. Heading south, the Birmingham area serves as a convenient base from which to branch out into the state's central section. From there you can sweep farther south to

Montgomery to see the state capital area and southeastern section, which includes the historic Chattahoochee Trace. This account concludes with the beaches of Gulf Shores and one of the state's most beautiful cities, Mobile. In his book *A Walk Across America,* Peter Jenkins describes being captivated by Mobile, calling it a fantasy city. "Even more than by the psychedelic azaleas," he said, "I was moved by the great-grandfather live-oak trees."

Alabama's surprises start as soon as you cross the border, and the following sneak preview will give you an idea of what to expect. Huntsville, while playing a strategic role in the nation's space program, also preserves its past at EarlyWorks and at Alabama Constitution Village, a living-history museum. Delegates drafted Alabama's first constitution here in 1819, and when you enter the village, you may smell bread baking and see aproned guides dipping beeswax candles or carding cotton—quite a contrast to the future-focused Space & Rocket Center. By the way, if you've harbored a secret yen to taste the astronaut's life but always thought Space Camp was just for kids, you're in for another surprise: The Space & Rocket Center offers programs for all who dare to delve into space technology, from fourth graders to grandparents. You might even participate in a simulated space-shuttle mission. If you're not ready for such a challenge, you can still stop by the gift shop and sample some freeze-dried astronaut ice cream.

Heading east gets you to Scottsboro, home of the "First Monday" market, one of the South's oldest and largest "trade days." Also known for its many caves, this area attracts spelunkers from around the world. Russell Cave, located at Jackson County's northeastern tip, could be called Alabama's first welcome center. Some 9,000 years ago bands of Native Americans began occupying the large cave; archaeologists, using carbon dating, have determined it to be the oldest known site of human occupancy in the southeastern US.

At DeSoto State Park, also in the northeast region, visitors can view Little River Canyon National Preserve, the largest and one of the deepest gorges east of the Mississippi River. Near the charming mountain hamlet of Mentone, Cloudmont Resort features a dude ranch and ski slopes (albeit with Mother Nature getting some assistance from snow machines).

Lakes Guntersville, Wheeler, and Wilson make northern Alabama a haven for water sports enthusiasts. Lake Guntersville State Park hosts *Eagle*

Awareness Weekends in January through the first weekend in February, a good time of the year to spot bald eagles. Many visitors report being surprised by Alabama's state parks, which offer a sampling of some of the state's most spectacular vistas, such as the awe-inspiring Cathedral Caverns, plus a host of recreation options—and at bargain prices.

At Cullman, visitors can take a Lilliputian world tour at Ave Maria Grotto, a unique garden filled with more than 125 miniature reproductions of famous buildings. The reproductions were made by a gifted Benedictine monk named Brother Joseph Zoettl. And nearby Hanceville has become a mecca for pilgrims who want to visit the Shrine of the Most Blessed Sacrament of Our Lady of the Angels Monastery.

In Blount County you can see three of the state's covered bridges. Master-and-slave team John Godwin and Horace King built a number of Alabama's early bridges. After gaining his freedom, King joined Godwin as a business partner, later erecting a monument in "lasting remembrance of the love and gratitude he felt for his lost friend and former master." The monument can be seen at a Phenix City cemetery.

Each summer visitors can witness the reenactment of a miracle in northwest Alabama at Ivy Green, home of America's courageous Helen Keller.

As Alabama's major metropolis, Birmingham's paths are well trampled. Still, the Magic City offers some not-to-be-missed treats, such as the historic Five Points South area with its boutiques and outdoor eateries and the 740-acre *Barber Motorsports Park* near Irondale. On the somber side, the Birmingham Civil Rights Institute and nearby complex re-creates a journey through the darkness of segregation.

Farther south you'll find Montgomery, a backdrop for sweeping drama since Jefferson Davis telegraphed his "Fire on Fort Sumter" order from here and the Civil War proceeded to rip the country apart. Less than a century later, the Civil Rights Movement gained momentum in this town, paving the way for overdue national reform. The interpretative Rosa Parks Library and Museum offers an in-depth look at the Montgomery bus boycott and pays tribute to the "Mother of the Civil Rights Movement." Also located here, the *Alabama Shakespeare Festival* provides top dramatic entertainment.

Don't miss Selma, a quintessential Southern city, but one that preserves its drama-filled past—from Civil War to civil rights. Spring Pilgrimage events include home tours, a reenactment of the Battle of Selma, and a grand ball on Sturdivant Hall's lovely lawn. Selma also stages an annual Tale Tellin' Festival honoring Alabama's first lady of folk legends and ghost stories, Kathryn Tucker Windham, who died in June 2011.

Traveling down to Monroeville, the Literary Capital of Alabama, you'll see the courthouse and surrounding square where Truman Capote and Harper Lee, author of *To Kill a Mockingbird,* roamed as childhood friends.

Still farther south, the Gulf Shores and Orange Beach area, with glistening white beaches, sea oats, and sand dunes, lures many visitors. The coastal area also offers historic forts, grand mansions, a multi-rooted (French, British, and Spanish) heritage, and superb cuisine.

On Mobile Bay's eastern shore, a strange spectacle known as "Jubilee" sometimes surprises visitors. Spurred by unknown forces, shrimp, flounder, crab, and other marine creatures suddenly crowd the shoreline, usually several times a summer. When the cry of "Jubilee!" rings along the beach, people rush to the water's edge to fill containers with fresh seafood.

Alabama's colorful celebrations run the gamut from Mobile's Mardi Gras (which preceded New Orleans's extravaganza) and Gulf Shores's National Shrimp Festival to Opp's Rattlesnake Rodeo, Dothan's National Peanut Festival, and Decatur's hot-air balloon gala called the "Alabama Jubilee."

When making travel plans, call ahead because dates, rates, and hours of operation change from time to time. Unless otherwise stated in this guide, all museums and attractions with admission prices of $5 or less per adult are labeled modest. A restaurant meal (entree without beverage) classified as economical costs less than $10; moderate prices range between $10 and $25; and entrees $25 and above are designated expensive. As for accommodations, those that cost less than $85 per day are described as standard; an overnight price between $85 and $150 is called moderate; and lodging costing more than $150 is designated deluxe.

Director of tourism Lee Sentell and the Alabama Bureau of Tourism & Travel encouraged everyone to eat their way around the state by creating the coveted brochure *100 Dishes to Eat in Alabama Before You Die.* "This is the largest brochure we have ever printed and it's full of exciting places to discover and experience," Sentell said.

General Alabama Trivia

- In 1540 Hernando de Soto traveled through much of what is now Alabama.

- On December 14, 1819, Alabama became the 22nd state in the Union.

- Alabama seceded from the Union on January 11, 1861, and rejoined on June 25, 1868.

- Montgomery has served as the state capital since 1846. Former capitals included St. Stephens, Huntsville, Cahaba, and Tuscaloosa.

- In 1959 the camellia became Alabama's state flower, replacing the goldenrod, which held that honor from 1927.

- The tarpon was designated as Alabama's official saltwater fish in 1955.

- Red iron ore, scientifically known as hematite, is the state mineral.

- Distinguished educator and humanitarian Julia Tutwiler wrote the words for "Alabama," the state song.

- Alabama comprises 67 counties.

- Mobile's RSA Battle House Tower is the state's tallest structure.

- Alabama has 53 miles of coastline and 240 species of commercially harvested freshwater fish, marine fish, and shellfish.

Alabama is a place where the waitresses (not servers, please) may call you darlin'. But don't take it personally—they call everybody that. As for food, many of us agree with a quote by Linda Vice, who represents Alabama's Black Belt in the state's southwestern section: "We can cook like Grandma did, or we can cook fancy. We draw from a number of food traditions. Food is one of our religions, and we worship at every shrine we pass!"

For travel information, maps, and brochures, stop by one of the eight Alabama Welcome Centers; call (334) 242-4169 or visit Alabama.travel. To preview the state parks, log onto alapark.com. You can make reservations at any Alabama state park by dialing (800) 252-7275. So pack your bags, head for the unforgettable Heart of Dixie, anticipate some surprises, and watch out for falling stars.

Fast Facts about Alabama

CLIMATE OVERVIEW

Alabama's climate falls in the temperate range, becoming mostly subtropical near the Gulf Coast. Spring's first flowers appear early, often in February. By April, average statewide temperatures reach the 60s. Summer days often fall in the hot and humid category. Fall brings changing foliage and refreshing cooler weather. Snow is such a rarity in most parts of the state that when the weather person predicts it, everyone gets excited and makes a mad dash to the grocery stores for bread and milk—even if they're curbing their carbs and are lactose intolerant.

FAMOUS ALABAMIANS

Some famous Alabamians include Condoleezza Rice, Helen Keller, Harper Lee, Winston Groom, Fannie Flagg, Lionel Richie, Channing Tatum, Hank Williams Sr. and Jr., Rosa Parks, Kenny Stabler, Hank Aaron, Willie Mays, and Octavia Spencer.

NEWSPAPERS

The state's major newspapers include the *Huntsville Times,* the *Birmingham News,* the *Montgomery Advertiser,* and the *Mobile Press Register.* Since printed papers started in the state around 1806, according to Bill Keller, former executive director of the Alabama Press Association, Alabamians have demonstrated a long-standing appreciation for newspapers. Every county in Alabama produces a newspaper.

Space Capital

Traveling through this area of Alabama, with its wooded glens, rugged mountain vistas, and sparkling lakes, is almost like moving through a calendar of splendid landscapes. Keep your camera handy because you'll discover some spectacular scenery.

Entering at the state's northern border, you'll drive through the rolling Tennessee Valley to reach *Huntsville,* a handy hub whether you're heading east or west to explore north Alabama's numerous attractions.

The birthplace of America's space program, Huntsville also served as an early capital of Alabama and later grew into a cotton mill town. After Dr. Wernher von Braun and his crew of German scientists arrived in the 1950s to pioneer the space program at Redstone Arsenal, Huntsville traded its title as World Watercress Capital for World Space Capital. The decade from 1950 to 1960 saw the population in Rocket City, USA, mushroom from 15,000 to 72,000. Even today, ongoing road construction cannot keep pace with the burgeoning population and traffic.

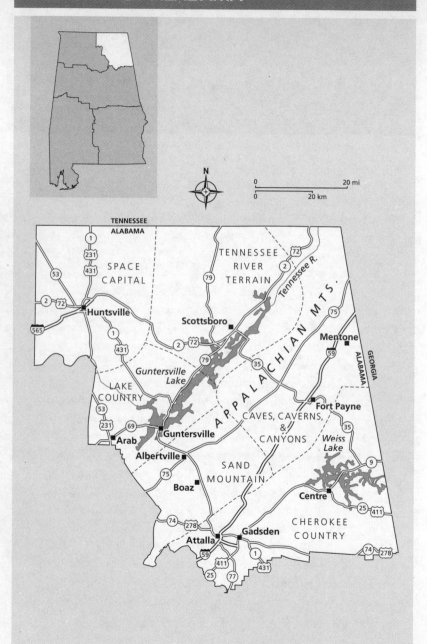

TENNESSEE
ALABAMA

SPACE
CAPITAL

TENNESSEE
RIVER
TERRAIN

Huntsville

Scottsboro

Tennessee R.

Mentone

ALABAMA

GEORGIA

Guntersville
Lake

LAKE
COUNTRY

APPALACHIAN MTS.

Fort Payne

CAVES, CAVERNS,
&
CANYONS

Arab

Guntersville

Weiss
Lake

Albertville

SAND
MOUNTAIN

Boaz

Centre

CHEROKEE
COUNTRY

Attalla

Gadsden

N

0   20 mi
0   20 km

As for the green scene, Huntsvillians recognize the importance of protecting local and global environments and preserving natural resources. In *The Green Guides,* Huntsville recently placed ninth in the nation's top cities for environmental excellence.

If you want to pretend you're in Venice, you can take a gondola ride at **Bridge Street Centre** in the heart of Huntsville's Cummings Research Park. Or enjoy a brisk walk or leisurely stroll through this European-style plaza that features upscale shops, restaurants, and lodging. Only a stone's throw away (depending on how far you can hurl) from the city's famed Space & Rocket Center, the complex features entertainment from multiple movies and a full-size carousel to a 10-acre lake with pedal boats and gondolas. Pavement performers entertain on evenings and weekends. Visit bridgestreet huntsville.com.

A good place to start a local tour is the **Huntsville Depot Transportation Museum** (256-564-8100) at 320 Church Street. Take time to tour the authentically restored depot, a big yellow building where a robotic telegrapher, stationmaster, and engineer welcome visitors and describe railroad life in 1912. During the Civil War the depot served as a prison, and upstairs you'll see some interesting graffiti such as a rather

Watercress Capital of the World

Huntsville acquired the title "Watercress Capital of the World" because in earlier days it produced and shipped a large volume of watercress throughout the eastern half of the country. A member of the mustard family, watercress thrives in limestone springwater and once grew prolifically in the Tennessee Valley's many limestone springs.

Huntsville's old *Russell Erskine Hotel* was noted for its watercress salad, and several local cookbooks feature this specialty, sometimes known simply as "cress." The *Huntsville Heritage Cookbook* contains a section devoted to watercress including the Frozen Cheese and Cress Salad, a tasty recipe, once served at a White House state banquet. Long a local favorite, this book is again in print, thanks to the Huntsville Junior League. Look for it at gift shops and bookstores throughout Huntsville, and while browsing, pick up a copy of the Junior League's award-winning *Sweet Home Alabama,* a handsome volume featuring "Food for Family and Friends from the Heart of the South."

unflattering drawing of Union officer Major Strout and an inscription that reads HAPPY NEW YEARS TO ALL IN THE YEAR OF OUR LORD 1864. The depot's hours are 9 a.m. to 4 p.m. Tuesday through Saturday. Closed January. Admission: adults $12; seniors and children $10; toddlers $5. Visit earlyworks .com/Huntsville-depot-museum.

As you drive around the area, check out the *Von Braun Civic Center* at 700 Monroe Street. This large multipurpose complex may well be hosting a concert, sporting event, or play you'd like to take in while in town.

Continue your self-driving tour through Huntsville's *Historic Twicken-ham District* with more than 65 antebellum houses and churches. Architectural styles represented include federal, Greek revival, Italianate, Palladian, Gothic revival, and others. For a fine example of federal architecture, tour the *Weeden House Museum* (256-536-7718; weedenhousemuseum.com) at 300 Gates Avenue. Built in 1819, the home contains period antiques and features the work of Huntsville artist and poet Maria Howard Weeden, who lived here until her death in 1905. Her impressive body of work includes book illustrations, whimsical drawings, fascinating character studies, and portraits. Hours are 10:30 a.m. to 3 p.m. Thursday through Saturday, with group tours available on weekends by appointment. Admission: adults $5; seniors $4; children (ages 5 and up) $3.

On the square in downtown Huntsville, stop by *Harrison Brothers Hardware Store* (256-536-3631 or 866-533-3631; harrisonbrothershardware .com), located at 124 South Side Square. Here you can purchase marbles by the scoop, old-fashioned stick candy, cast-iron cookware, vintage mix-and-match silverplate flatware, and other merchandise that speaks of yesteryear. The store also features regional and locally handcrafted gifts. Historic Huntsville Foundation volunteers ring up sales on a 1907 cash register. The interior, with pot-bellied stove, ceiling fans, rolling ladders, barrels, tools, and antique safe, looks much as it did in 1879 when the store opened for business a few blocks away before moving to its permanent home on the square. Hours are 9 a.m. to 5 p.m. weekdays and 10 a.m. to 4 p.m. Saturday.

Don't miss *Alabama Constitution Village* (256-564-8100; earlyworks .com/alabama-constitution-village) just around the corner at 109 Gates Avenue. Entering at Franklin Street and Gates Avenue takes you back to 1819, when delegates met here to draft Alabama's first constitution. Afterward, on a tour of the complex, you'll see costumed guides going about

BEST ATTRACTIONS IN NORTHEAST ALABAMA

Alabama Constitution Village,
Huntsville

Buck's Pocket State Park,
Grove Oak

Burritt on the Mountain,
Huntsville

Cathedral Caverns,
Grant

DeSoto State Park,
Fort Payne

EarlyWorks,
Huntsville

Huntsville Museum of Art,
Huntsville

Lake Guntersville State Park,
Guntersville

Little River Canyon National Preserve,
Fort Payne

Noccalula Falls and Park,
Gadsden

Sequoyah Caverns & Ellis Homestead,
Valley Head

Town of Mentone

US Space & Rocket Center,
Huntsville

their seasonal business of preserving summer's fruits or making candles at hog-killing time.

Stop by the gift shop, with such unique items as "ugly jugs," once used as containers for harmful substances. Hours are 9 a.m. to 4 p.m. Monday through Saturday. Hours are adjusted in November and December because of Santa's Village, which is open 5 to 9 p.m. The village is closed January and February and on major holidays. Admission: adults $12; seniors and youth $10; toddlers $5.

Kids—both young and old—love traveling back in time to the 19th century and exploring *EarlyWorks Children's History Museum,* a hands-on history museum (256-564-8100) at 404 Madison Street, where new adventures await around every corner. Special exhibits include an amazing 16-foot-tall tale-telling tree, giant size musical instruments, and a 46-foot keelboat. Youngsters can dress up in vintage clothing and practice tasks that children in the "olden days" performed, and toddlers can milk a "pretend" cow and gather garden vegetables. Except for major holidays, hours run from 9 a.m. to 4 p.m. Tuesday through Saturday. Admission. Special prices are available for combination tours of EarlyWorks with the historic Huntsville Depot and Alabama Constitution Village. Metered parking is available throughout the downtown area with handicapped parking on the Gates Avenue side. Learn more about this hands-on facility at earlyworks.com. Admission: adults $12; seniors and youth $10; toddlers (ages 1 to 3) $5.

Spend some time browsing through the interesting mix of boutiques, galleries, and antiques shops in Huntsville's historic Five Points area. Then treat yourself to a spot of tea or lovely lunch at **Emma's Tea Room** (256-489-5850), which occupies an early 20th-century home at 401 Pratt Avenue Northeast. Painted a buttery yellow, the house beckons with a wide front porch and hanging ferns. Former college English instructor Rebekah Klein named the business for her daughter, then seven years old. Emma still helps out from time to time.

Step inside and you'll see the perfect setting for a girls' get-together (although my husband also enjoys lunch here). With a menu of delectable possibilities enhanced by table settings of glistening china and silver, the tearoom lives up to its slogan—refreshingly elegant. Choose from an assortment of teas and a variety of salads, sandwiches, soups, and quiches. Emma's ever-popular chicken salad with dried cranberries, onion, celery, walnuts, and bleu cheese is served on mixed greens. The menu also features daily specials plus a dessert of the day, which may be a seasonal fruit creation, bread pudding, coconut cake, or something chocolate.

A spiral staircase leads to the second-floor private dining room, which is used for events like card clubs, book clubs, private wedding and baby showers, and business meetings. Emma's also offers catering, cooking classes, tea tastings, etiquette classes, live music, and much more.

Emma's Tea Room is open from 10:30 a.m. until 2 p.m. Monday through Saturday with reservations suggested for lunch. Moderate. Also, you may book an elegant afternoon tea party (minimum of four) on Friday and Saturday between 3:30 and 5:30 p.m. Visit emmastearoom.com.

Don't miss **Monte Sano Mountain,** which offers sweeping views of Huntsville and the surrounding Tennessee River valley. **Burritt on the Mountain,** a living-history museum (256-536-2882), at 3101 Burritt Drive, just off Monte Sano Boulevard, features 167 wooded acres with walking trails and picnicking facilities. At this living-history site, you'll find a black-smith shop, smokehouse, church, barnyard with live animals, and some log houses depicting rural life between 1850 and 1900. An X-shaped house, built in 1937 by Dr. William Henry Burritt, serves as the park's focal point. Both a physician and gifted inventor who held 20 patents during his life, Burritt combined classical and Art Deco elements when he designed this unusual home.

Inside you'll see archaeological and restoration exhibits, clothing, toys, and displays on Huntsville's history. One room features the paintings of local artists. Special events include Spring Farm Days, International Heritage Festival, fall festivals, and Candlelight Christmas. Admission prices are slightly higher for special events. The museum is open Tuesday through Saturday from 10 a.m. to 4 p.m. and Sunday noon to 4 p.m. November through March. Summer hours are Tuesday through Saturday 9 a.m. to 5 p.m. and Sunday noon to 5 p.m. Admission: adults $10; seniors $9; children (ages 3–18) $8. Visit burrittonthemountain.com.

Dogwood Manor (256-859-3946) at 707 Chase Road makes a lovely base for exploring the Huntsville area. Valerie and Patrick Jones own this restored federal-style home, set on a sweeping lawn with century-old trees. The home's builder once operated a thriving nursery here and shipped his plants all over the country. Patrick, an attorney, shares history about the home and the Chase community with interested guests.

The couple reserves four charming rooms—appropriately named Dogwood, Magnolia, Azalea, and Rose—for overnight visitors and serves afternoon tea on request. The Devon Cottage offers two bedrooms, full kitchen, dining area, patio, garage, and much more. Valerie, a school counselor, prepares gourmet breakfasts, complemented by her own homemade breads and muffins. She often makes apple French toast, crumpets, and English scones. Moderate rates. Visit Dogwood Manor's website at dogwoodmanor bandb.com.

Across from Dogwood Manor's driveway stands the *North Alabama Railroad Museum* (256-851-6276) at 694 Chase Road. The restored green-and-yellow Chase Depot houses a waiting room, freight room, and agent office filled with exhibits. Home of the Mercury and Chase Railroad and the country's smallest union station, the facility now features a walk-through passenger train and more than 30 pieces of major railroading stock. The museum

A Tribute to Everybody's Favorite Aunt

For more than half a century, Eunice Merrell served what many considered the best country ham and homemade biscuits in the world. Former governor Fob James declared her biscuits "the best in Alabama," and his proclamation made them the official state biscuit.

Although Eunice (better known to her customers as "Aunt" Eunice) described her diner as "just a little greasy spoon," the fame of her homemade biscuits made the *Congressional Record* in a tribute introduced by US Senator Howell Heflin, who represented Alabama.

At *Eunice's Country Kitchen,* you often had to wait a bit for a table or share one with someone else. Some people even kept their own favorite brand of jelly or preserves in Eunice's refrigerator, retrieving it when the hot biscuits arrived, but most folks dipped into the honey or Sand Mountain sorghum on every table.

In this small cafe that did a booming business with no advertising, it was customary to warm up your neighbors' coffee if you got up to pour yourself a refill. In fact, when prospective candidates for office visited (this was a popular stop on political campaigns), Aunt Eunice expected them to follow protocol and wait on her customers; otherwise, they did not deserve the office to which they aspired — and she told them so.

Look for an authentically replicated Eunice's Country Kitchen at the Historic Huntsville Depot. You'll see the cafe's famous "Liars' Table," with its suspended wooden sign reserving it for politicians and preachers. (During a meal, Eunice sometimes presented customers with an official "Liar's License," permitting them to prevaricate "at any time or place without notice.") Other memorabilia include favorite quotes and an extensive collection of autographed photos from governors, congressmen, actors, astronauts, sports figures, and even a president.

Aunt Eunice, we miss you.

can be visited from 9 a.m. to 4 p.m. daily, and a staff member is available each Wednesday and Saturday from 8:30 a.m. to 2 p.m. The facility offers guided tours and excursion train rides. Children enjoy watching for the concrete animals staged along the track. In addition to regular trips, a Peter Cottontail Express, Pumpkin' Pickin' Train, and Santa Trail Special are also scheduled. Call for more information on schedules, fares, and reservations, or visit the website at northalabamarailroadmuseum.com for current happenings.

Tennessee River Terrain

From Huntsville take US 72 east to **Scottsboro**, home of **First Monday**, one of the South's oldest and largest "trade days." This outdoor market might feature anything from cast-iron skillets, church pews, and butter churns to gingham-checked sunbonnets and pocketknives—all displayed around the Jackson County Courthouse Square. Lasting from morning till dark, the event dates to the mid-1800s, when people met at the courthouse square on the day Circuit Court opened to visit as well as to trade horses, mules, and other livestock. The merry mix of folks who still come to browse, banter, and barter carry on a Southern tradition, and many have honed their trading techniques to a high level of skill. Although this event takes place on the first Monday of every month (plus the Saturday and Sunday preceding it), the Fourth of July and Labor Day weekends typically prove most popular.

alabamatrivia

During its territorial and statehood days, Alabama had five capitals.

If you miss Scottsboro's First Monday, you can console yourself by dipping into a chocolate milk shake, ice-cream soda, or banana split at **Payne's** (256-574-2140), located at 101 East Laurel on the town square's north side. This eatery occupies the site of a former drugstore dating from 1869. The interior, complete with old-fashioned soda fountain, features a black-and-white color scheme with red accents. You can perch on a bar stool, order a fountain Coke that's mixed on the spot and served in a traditional Coca-Cola glass, and munch on a hot dog with red slaw straight from the original drugstore menu. Other options include Payne's popular chicken salad and a variety of sandwiches. Hours are 10 a.m. to 4 p.m. Monday through Saturday. To learn about the area's history, visit the **Scottsboro-Jackson Heritage Center** (256-259-2122; sjhc.us), located at 208 South Houston Street. This neoclassical–style structure, built in 1881, houses some interesting exhibits, including Native American artifacts found on land later flooded by the Tennessee Valley Authority (TVA) and rare photographic displays depicting the early days of Skyline, a unique community north of Scottsboro.

Behind the big house stands the small 1868 Jackson County Courthouse. Nearby, a pioneer village called Sage Town features a collection of authentic log structures that includes a cabin, schoolhouse, barn, and blacksmith shop, all filled with vintage items.

The museum offers a wealth of genealogical materials, says Judi Weaver, who promotes archaeological awareness in her role as director. The facility focuses on the area's history from the Paleo-Indian era through the 1930s. Special events include heritage festivals and art exhibitions. Hours are 11 a.m. to 4 p.m. Monday through Friday, or by appointment. A modest admission is charged.

If, after a plane trip, you've ever discovered yourself divorced from your bags and wondered about their final destination, it's entirely possible that your lost luggage wound up at *Scottsboro's Unclaimed Baggage Center* (256-259-1525), located at 509 West Willow Street (although your bags may have traveled instead to nearby Unclaimed Baggage in Boaz). At this unique outlet you can find such items as cameras, caviar, clothing, hammocks, hair dryers, jewelry, scuba gear, and ski equipment. The ever-changing merchandise from around the world also features baby strollers, books, briefcases, luggage, personal electronic devices, and high-tech equipment. Over one million items pass through the store annually with about 60 percent being clothing.

"We have to stay on top of technology to know what's coming in here," says a company executive. The diverse inventory of lost, found, and unclaimed items comes from various airlines to be sorted and offered for sale at reduced rates—20 to 80 percent or more off retail prices. In this shopping mecca, which now covers more than a city block, you can enjoy a mug of brewed Starbucks coffee or some Dippin Dots at the facility's in-house cafe, called Cups Expresso Cafe.

Business boomed here—even before Oprah spread the word on her TV show. The parking lot gets especially crowded on weekends, and car tags reveal shoppers from many states. Recent visitors also came from Ontario, Bavaria, New Zealand, South America, France, and England. Closed on Sunday, hours are 9 a.m. to 6 p.m. Monday through Friday and 8 a.m. to 6 p.m. Saturday. The website is unclaimedbaggage.com.

After sightseeing in the Scottsboro area, you can easily head south on State Route 79 toward Guntersville to take in some Marshall County attractions, or you can continue your loop northeast to Stevenson. *Goose Pond Colony* (256-259-2884 or 800-268-2884), a peninsula surrounded by the Tennessee River, is located 5 miles south of Scottsboro on State Route 79 at 417 Ed Hembree Drive and offers vacation cottages, picnic facilities, camping sites, swimming pool, marina and launching ramp, golf course, and nature/walking trail. Popular with both geese and golfers, the golf course is noted for its beauty and design. Named by *Golf Digest* as one of "The Places to Play," Goose Pond's course also made the top five in a previous PGA opinion poll ranking courses in the Dixie section. For more information visit goosepond.org.

The Docks (256-574-3071), a restaurant on the grounds behind the swimming pool, offers a variety of seafood including Cajun fare. You can dine on the deck with a fine view of the water. Some diners arrive by boat and tie up at the property's private pier. The restaurant is open from 5 to 9 p.m. Tuesday through Thursday and 5 to 10 p.m. Friday and Saturday. Live entertainment is featured on Thursday, Friday, and Saturday. Prices range from moderate to expensive.

Before leaving this area, you may want to call the Scottsboro/Jackson County Chamber of Commerce (800-259-5508; jacksoncountychamber.com) or stop by the headquarters at 407 East Willow Street to pick up brochures on various local and area attractions.

Although you might find the tiny town of Pisgah on your road map, you won't find **Gorham's Bluff** (256-451-VIEW [8439])—yet. This traditional neighborhood community (inspired by Florida's Seaside) offers travelers some stunning scenery, especially from the Overlook Pavilion, and accommodations at The Lodge. The property commands sweeping bluffside views of the Tennessee River. *Travel and Leisure* magazine chose Gorham's Bluff for inclusion in "The 30 Great US Inns," and *Southern Living* magazine voted the property "Most Romantic Spot in Alabama."

This lovely site remained undeveloped until Clara and Bill McGriff (a CPA still remembered by locals as a basketball star) started exploring their daughter Dawn's idea of creating a brand-new, arts-oriented Appalachian town—a walking town with a strong sense of community where residents stop for front-porch chats. With each new home and resident, the McGriffs watch the family vision being translated to reality.

"There is a peace that pervades this place," says Clara, a former English teacher. "We feel it, and guests feel it." The Lodge on Gorham's Bluff gives guests ample opportunity to sample this serenity and beauty.

Spacious suites, individually decorated by Clara (who also creates the beautiful floral arrangements), double-sided fireplaces, and whirlpool tubs make accommodations even more inviting. Gorham's Bluff also offers rental cottages.

Hiking, biking, birding, rocking, reflecting, reading, and listening to classical music all rank as popular pastimes here. Dawn frequently schedules special events such as concerts, the Alabama Ballet's summer residency, and storytelling.

Sometime during your stay, slip up to the observation deck for a panoramic overview. Many visitors want to linger at Gorham's Bluff forever. A quote from the guest book reads: "Forward our mail. We are not leaving."

Meals (enhanced by the property's own fresh herbs) feature traditional Appalachian food—served with flair. Dinners are served with candlelight and white tablecloths as a pianist plays old and new favorites by request on Friday and Saturday nights. By reservation only, the lodge's 30-seat dining room offers dinner for guests and the public nightly at 7 p.m. Dress is casual. From Pisgah, located on Jackson County Road 58, signs point the way to Gorham's Bluff. Call for hours and specific directions or write the staff at 101 Gorham Drive/Gorham's Bluff, Pisgah 35765. Lodge rates range from moderate to deluxe. Make reservations for an evening or a weekend. You just may decide to become one of the town's new residents. For more background or a map, visit gorhamsbluff.com or e-mail reservations@gorhamsbluff.com.

To reach the *Stevenson Railroad Depot Museum* (256-437-3012), take US 72 and travel northwest. Near Stevenson turn at State Route 117 to go downtown. At 207 West Main Street, you'll see the museum positioned between two railroad tracks. Look carefully before crossing the tracks because the Iron Horse still whizzes by. This railroad junction played a strategic role during the Civil War, and the museum director showed me an assortment of uniform buttons, coins, and other military items brought in by a resident who had dug them up nearby. The Stevenson Depot also contains displays of Native American artifacts, period costumes, early farm tools, and railroading history information.

Each June the annual Stevenson Depot Days celebration commemorates the city's past with a variety of family activities that might include an ice-cream social, spelling bee, pioneer breakfast, wagon ride to the nearby Civil

TOP ANNUAL EVENTS IN NORTHEAST ALABAMA

Siege of Bridgeport
Bridgeport, fourth weekend of March
(256) 437-8873 or (256) 495-3614
siegeatbridgeport.com

Art on the Lake
Guntersville, third weekend of April
(256) 571-7597 or (256) 558-4331
artonthelake-guntersville.com

Panoply Arts Festival
Big Spring International Park, Huntsville
last full weekend of April
(256) 519-2787
artshuntsville.org

Riverfest
Gadsden, June
(256) 543-3472
gadsdenriverfest.com

Stevenson Depot Days
Stevenson, first full week of June
(256) 437-3012
stevensondepotdays.com

World's Longest Yard Sale
Gadsden, Alabama, to West Unity,
Ohio
First Thursday through Sunday in
August
(800) 327-3945
127sale.com

St. William's Seafood Festival
Guntersville, early September (Labor
Day weekend)
(256) 582-4245
stwilliamchurch.com

Depot Days Festival
Hartselle, September
(256) 773-4370 or (800) 294-0692
hartsellechamber.org

Harvest Festival
Boaz, early October
(256) 593-8154
boazchamberofcommerce.com

Heritage Festival
Attalla, October
(256) 543-3472
attallacity.org

Mentone Fall Colorfest
Mentone, third weekend of October
(256) 634-0704
mentonealabama.org

Christmas at the Falls
Noccalula Falls, Gadsden
Thanksgiving through December
(256) 543-7412

Galaxy of Lights
Huntsville/Madison County Botanical
Garden
Thanksgiving through New Year's Eve
(256) 830-4447
hsvbg.org

War fort, square dancing, tour of homes, parade, old-fashioned street dance, and fireworks. The museum is open Monday through Friday from 8 a.m. to 3:30 p.m. April through November. Closed weekends. Admission is free.

From Stevenson return to US 72 and continue to *Bridgeport,* in Alabama's northeastern corner.

Caves, Caverns, & Canyons

While exploring this region in June 1540, Spaniard Hernando de Soto and his crew chose this area for their entry into what is now Alabama. You might like to take a driving tour of Bridgeport, once called Jonesville but renamed in the 1850s for the railroad bridge that spans the Tennessee River.

Drive through Kilpatrick Row Residential District and up bluff-based Battery Hill, the site of several Civil War battles, to see the lovely historic homes of Victorian vintage with turrets, fishscale shingles, and wraparound porches.

Russell Cave National Monument (256-495-2672), about 8 miles west of Bridgeport, is located at 3729 Jackson County Road 98. Long before de Soto's visit, the large limestone cave served as an archaic hotel for Native Americans traveling through the area about 9,000 years ago.

The visitor center, in addition to housing a museum that displays weapons, tools, pottery, and other artifacts found in the cave, also offers several audiovisual presentations. After browsing through the museum, you can walk about 250 yards to the cave's big opening at the base of craggy bluffs. A ranger-led tour takes you to the cave, where you can learn about how the occupants fed, clothed, and protected themselves.

One of the century's most significant archaeological finds, the relic-filled cave remained pretty much a secret until 1953 when some members of the Tennessee Archaeological Society discovered the history-rich shelter and alerted Smithsonian Institution officials, who collaborated with the National Geographic Society to conduct extensive excavations here. The National Park Service carried out more excavations in 1962. Their joint research revealed Russell Cave to be one of the longest, most complete, and well-preserved archaeological records in the eastern US. Radioactive carbon from early campfires placed human arrival between 6500 and 6145 BC. Remains of animal bones, tools, weapons, and pottery all helped archaeologists fit

Exploring Cathedral Caverns

Both Native Americans and Confederate soldiers used these caverns as a refuge, and Disney used them as a movie setting for *Tom and Huck*. Ensconced in Marshall County's northeastern corner near the town of Grant, Cathedral Caverns (256-728-8193) opened as a state park in August 2000.

You don't have to assume a crouching position to enter because the opening to these caverns measures 125 feet wide by 25 feet high. Meandering along the lighted walkway takes you past Goliath, a massive stalagmite that appears to be a floor-to-ceiling column, and what are believed to be the world's largest stalagmite forest and frozen waterfall. Besides stalagmites and stalactites, other cave features include drapery, soda straws (capillary tubes), all the common types of shields, and "just about any formation you can expect to find in a cave," said a guide.

The deeper you go into the cave's interior, the more wondrous the surroundings. Before the grand finale, you'll enter a magnificent chamber that soars to a height of 120 feet and presumably contains the largest flowstone wall in any commercial cave. Then, to top that off, the Cathedral Room features a staggering number of fanciful, stalagmitic formations. Beyond the portion open to the public lies a magnificent crystal room with stunning calcite configurations (or so they say).

Former owner Jay Gurley, who died in 1996, dedicated much of his life and fortune to making the caverns accessible so others might share their wonder. His active involvement in developing the park spanned the period from 1952 until 1974 when he sold the property. Although the caverns were open from time to time after Gurley's tenure, they closed in 1986, and the state bought the site in 1987. Inside the cave, a plaque acknowledges Gurley's contribution and serves as a monument, as does the Jay Gurley Memorial Bridge that transports visitors across Mystery River.

The river is aptly named because you can't see where the stream comes from or where it goes. Normally placid, the river can reach a depth of 40 feet during flooding conditions when the swirling water becomes chocolate-colored.

Bring a jacket (the temperature hovers at 57 to 60 degrees Fahrenheit) and jogging shoes. The 1.5-mile round-trip takes about an hour and 15 minutes. Future plans for this 461-acre park include additional hiking trails and camping facilities. Hours change seasonally. Call or check the schedule at alapark.com and follow the link to Cathedral Caverns. The park is open seven days a week from 9 a.m. to 5 p.m. Admission.

together portions of this ancient jigsaw puzzle. The evidence implies seasonal occupation, suggesting that various groups of early people wintered in Russell Cave, then moved on to hunt and live off the land during warm-weather months.

Be sure to ask a ranger about a living-history demonstration. I found it fascinating to watch a piece of flint fashioned into an arrowhead in about four minutes with the same simple tools early Native Americans used.

Except for Thanksgiving, Christmas, and New Year's Day, you can visit Russell Cave from 8 a.m. to 4:30 p.m. seven days a week, and there's no admission charge. For more information, write to park personnel at 3729 County Road 98, Bridgeport 35740. Explore the cave on the Internet by clicking on nps.gov/ruca.

One block off State Route 117 in the center of **Valley Head** stands **Winston Place** (256-635-6381 or 888-494-6786), a white-columned antebellum mansion owned by Leslie and Jim Bunch. Located 2 miles from Mentone, the property features a panoramic view of Lookout Mountain. Two levels of encircling porches with ferns, white wicker rocking chairs, and a nanny swing invite guests to relax and savor the setting. Built by William Overton Winston from Virginia, the circa-1831 home boasts a rich history. During the Civil War, Union officers occupied the home, and 30,000 soldiers camped on its grounds before leaving to fight at Chickamauga. Leslie, who shares anecdotes about her family home and its fascinating background, has amassed a collection of books and articles detailing Winston Place's role in history.

alabamatrivia

In Valley Head's "triangle," you can delve into the mystery of a vanished village at the Ruins of Battelle. For more background on this supposedly haunted site, click on tourdekalb.com.

Previously selected for inclusion in *National Geographic's Small Town Getaways,* Winston Place contains lovely period antiques and lends itself well to entertaining, just as its builder intended. Original outbuildings include servants' quarters, a slanted-wall corncrib, and a smokehouse with hand-painted murals depicting the area's history.

While immersing yourself in the home's ambience, take time to see the tucked-away media room with Jim's football awards—trophies, plaques, and photos. A former Alabama football All-American (whose mastery of the game took him to three Sugar Bowls and a Liberty Bowl), Jim played under legendary coach Bear Bryant.

The couple offers six elegant suites for guests and a full breakfast, served in the dining room. Rates range from moderate to deluxe. Visit the property at virtualcities.com/al/winstonplace.htm or search Winston Place on the Internet.

From Valley Head it's a short but scenic drive up to *Mentone,* a charming hamlet perched on the brow of Lookout Mountain at the intersection of State Route 117 and DeKalb County Route 89. Once a fashionable summer resort town that flourished through the Gay Nineties, Mentone attracted visitors from all over the country with its cool mountain temperatures, especially appealing in the days before air-conditioning.

Shops, rustic and quaint, line the single main street, but the large, rambling *Mentone Springs Hotel* (6114 State Route 117; 256-634-4040) remains the town's focal point. The three-story structure with turrets, dormers, porches, and steep-sloped roof captured my imagination the first time I saw it three decades ago. Open for bed-and-breakfast guests, the building also houses *Mentone Springs Restaurant.* Rates are moderate. Go to mentone springs.com for more information.

The name Mentone translates into "musical mountain spring," appropriate because the hotel's grounds once boasted two springs—Mineral Springs and Beauty Springs—which were reputed to possess "strengthening and curative properties." The hotel's early guests enjoyed nature walks, croquet, billiards, boating, and other genteel pursuits.

Although you can't join a picnicking party with a basket lunch packed by the hotel and you won't be summoned to meals by a dinner bell, you can explore the town's shops. Some of them close or limit their hours in winter, so it's best to check ahead. Also, you might inquire about the dates of upcoming festivals because Mentone stages special events throughout the year.

The downtown *Moonlight Bistro Restaurant* (6080 State Route 117; 256-634-4560), originally a Native American trading post, serves sandwiches, salads, plate lunches, and dinner entrees including seafood, pasta, and hand-cut beef filets, as well as specials. Try the fried green tomatoes with aioli sauce. The eatery, where you'll find a cozy fire when temperatures drop, is open Wednesday through Sunday. Call ahead for hours. Prices range from economical to moderate.

Take a break at **The Wildflower Cafe** (256-634-0066), located at 60078 Alabama State Road 117. The eatery offers espresso, cappuccino, and other specialty coffees and a variety of food choices from soups, sandwiches, and vegetarian dishes to gourmet pizzas and a casual gourmet dinner on weekends. Hours are 9 a.m. to 2 p.m. seven days a week. Ask about the musical nights every Friday through Sunday. Standard to moderate.

Take time to browse for hand-blended herbal teas, gourmet coffees, and hand-blended bath and body products in the complex. Hours vary.

Across the road from the old hotel is **St. Joseph's on the Mountain.** Be sure to notice the log structure, dating to 1826, that serves as the central portion of this unusual church. North of the church on the mountain's brow, you'll find Eagle's Nest, a massive rock formation overlooking Valley Head.

After exploring the village, take a drive along the area's meandering roads. You'll see strategically placed destination markers nailed to trees and posts at junctions—these are quite helpful because the mountain terrain can prove confusing to newcomers.

Tucked away at 651 County Road 644 stands **Raven Haven** (256-634-4310), a bed-and-breakfast perched atop Lookout Mountain. Owners Eleanor and Tony Teverino welcome travelers to share their 10 acres of nature and theme rooms: Queen Anne, Nautical, Casablanca, and Prairie Room—each with private bath.

"Two things that drew us here were the beauty of the place and the people," said Eleanor, who was born in Northern Ireland. "When I came to Mentone, it was very much like going back home." The Teverinos hosted recent guests from Ireland, who compared some of Mentone's narrow boulder-flanked curves with "driving on the roads right back at home."

Eleanor whisks warm and wonderful pastries from her oven and prepares a delightful breakfast daily, complete with homemade jams. Served buffet style, the menu always features a main dish, fruit, and vegetable to get your day off to a good healthy start. From Scotch eggs to fried green tomatoes to sticky buns, each morning's choices offer plenty of variety. A copy of *The Raven Haven Cookbook* makes a great souvenir. Afterward, you can trek through the woods and admire the wildflowers along the property's ¼-mile walking trail. Standard rates. For more information on this hideaway, pay a visit to ravenhavenbandb.info.

While driving through the area, you'll pass a number of summer camps for youngsters. In fact boyhood days spent at one such camp called Cloudmont inspired local landowner Jack Jones to pursue his unlikely dream of creating a ski resort in Alabama. After buying Cloudmont in 1947, he started developing the property as a resort and opened "the southernmost ski resort in the country" in 1970. *Cloudmont Ski and Golf Resort* (256-634-4344), about 3 miles from Mentone on DeKalb County Road 89, is marked by a large roadside sign on the left. To reach the information center, take a left onto County Road 614 for a half mile or so. Besides skiing (and, yes, Mother Nature does get help from snow machines), this unique family enterprise offers golfing, hiking, fishing, and swimming for guests. Jack's son Gary and his instructors have taught thousands of people to ski. Winter season at Cloudmont usually begins around mid-December and extends through March 15. It's a good idea to call ahead and check on slope conditions. Better yet, log onto cloudmont.com for lodging packages, schedules, rates, and information on current activities,

alabama*trivia*

Alabama ranks 12th in the nation for attracting retirees, and 8th in the nation for attracting military retirees.

which include golfing, horseback riding, and more at both Cloudmont and *Shady Grove Dude Ranch.* You can write the resort at PO Box 435, Mentone 35984.

While in this area, don't miss the *Sallie Howard Memorial Chapel,* on County Road 165 located 6.7 miles from downtown Mentone and adjacent to DeSoto State Park. A 20-foot-tall boulder serves as the rear wall of the small church, and stones from Little River form the pulpit. Visitors often attend worship services held here each Sunday at 10 a.m.

To more fully explore this area's magnificent terrain, consider headquartering at *DeSoto State Park* (256-845-5380 or 800-568-8840; alapark .com/desotoresort) on County Road 89, about 7 miles from Mentone. You'll find almost 5,000 acres of breathtaking beauty and glimpses of unspoiled nature at every turn. The gorgeous scenery around here makes it hard to concentrate on driving, but if you don't, you might bash into one of the big weathered boulders that partially jut into the road.

The park extends about 40 miles along Little River, a unique waterway that runs its complete course on top of a mountain. Resort facilities include a stone lodge with large restaurant, chalets, cabins, nature trails, playgrounds, a store, and picnic areas. Miles of hiking trails, bordered by Queen Anne's lace, blackberry vines, honeysuckle, and black-eyed Susans, beckon you to explore the terrain. The park's wheelchair-accessible boardwalk attracts families and features a covered pavilion and waterfall view. Don't miss spectacular **DeSoto Falls** (about 7 miles northeast of the park's information center), where water rushes over a dam to crash more than 100 feet before continuing its journey.

About 10 miles away in the park's southern section, you'll find the beginning of **Little River Canyon National Preserve,** the largest and one of the deepest chasms east of the Mississippi River. Stretching about 16 miles, the canyon drops to depths of some 700 feet. Skirting the western rim, a canyon road offers breathtaking views of rugged bluffs, waterfalls, and the rushing river.

Start your local exploration here at **Little River Canyon Center,** a great place to learn about the canyon's incredible geography as well as other area attractions. Located on State Route 35 just a few hundred yards from the bridge across Little River Falls, this $7 million facility represents a major commitment to environmental sustainability.

Here, you can step out to the large rear deck for a sweeping view of the area, check out the multimedia exhibits about Little River Canyon, and stretch your legs on one of the short hiking trails. If buildings can multitask, this one gets an A+. More than a full-scale visitor center, the lodge-type facility is home base for Jacksonville State University's Little River Canyon Field School, an instrumental force in environmental education in northeast Alabama. Also, it serves as National Park Service ranger headquarters for Little River Canyon National Preserve.

Many recycled materials went into the construction of this interesting structure that relies on geothermal energy for heating and cooling. "It's probably the greenest building in the state," said Pete Conroy, Canyon Center director, who oversees JSU's Environmental Policy and Information Center and Field Schools. For more information on the Canyon Center, call (256) 845-3548.

Don't miss *Fort Payne,* the stomping ground of award-collecting country music group Alabama and home to the redbrick *Fort Payne Opera House* at 510 North Gault Avenue. The building, which dates to 1889, has served as a vaudeville playhouse, a theater for silent movies, and an upholstery shop. The opera house is listed on the National Register of Historic Places and the National Register of Nineteenth-Century Theatres in America. Restored in 1969 the opera house now opens for special events and performances. Tours can be arranged by appointment. Call (256) 845-6888.

The building on the opera house's north side is home to the *DeKalb County Hosiery Museum* and the *Richard C. Hunt Reception Hall.* The hall's interesting mural, entitled *Harvest at Fort Payne,* dates back to the Great Depression when President Franklin D. Roosevelt initiated the Work Projects Administration (WPA) to aid the unemployed. Harwood Steiger, an out-of-work artist from New York, received a commission to paint murals for Southern post offices, and this is one of his creations. Before its placement here, the mural was housed in the old post office building and later the DeKalb County Courthouse. Visitors to the hosiery museum can see early mill machinery and other exhibits as well as a video providing background on the industry that played a major role in the area's history and economy. For more information contact the DeKalb County Tourist Association at (256) 845-3957.

Nearby, the Fort Payne Depot at 105 Fifth Street Northeast houses the *Fort Payne Depot Museum* (256-845-5714; fortpaynedepotmuseum.com). Completed in 1891, the handsome Romanesque depot of pink sandstone served as a passenger station until 1970. The museum's permanent collection includes artwork, early farm equipment, pottery, glassware, and a restored caboose containing railroad memorabilia. You'll also see beaded moccasins, Iroquois baskets made of birch bark trimmed with porcupine quills, and Mayan and pre-Columbian artifacts dating from AD 400 to 800. An area resident willed to the museum her Cherokee, Hopi, Pueblo, Apache, and Seminole artifacts. Be sure to notice the collection of dioramas that were once part of a traveling medicine show and an unusual bed that belonged to local resident Granny Dollar, whose lifetime spanned more than a century. The museum is open 10 a.m. to 3 p.m. Wednesday through Friday. Sunday

Visit Tigers for Tomorrow at Untamed Mountain

For a walk on the wild side, head to Untamed Mountain, home of more than 160 animals ranging from the barnyard variety to exotic big cats. Located in the state's northeastern corner about 8 miles from Collinsville, this rescue preserve now serves as home base for Tigers for Tomorrow (TFT).

When you arrive, say hello to Tootles and Zack (the camel and zebra greeters), who will be on hand to welcome you. Then head to the barnyard contact area and meet the sheep, llamas, emus, pigs, goats, and other creatures. Kids will love their encounters with these animals, and so will you.

Nearby, you'll see the carnivore compound, where more than 40 big cats, wolves, and bears roam about 18 acres in the sanctuary. Timber wolves Bear and Lakota may howl a hello to you. Handlers and keepers provide visitors with spontaneous interactions and give talks throughout the day. "This is the closest you will get to the big cats in a natural setting," said Susan Steffens, TFT president.

And how did this area become a habitat for tigers, lions, leopards, cougars, and other exotic animals, you ask? After Hurricanes Frances and Jeanne battered their South Florida home, Benny the leopard and Tinkerbell the Bengal tiger along with other cohorts made the move north to this 140-acre refuge. Here, they joined 25 other animal residents at the former Bluegrass Farm Sanctuary. The two operations later merged to become Tigers for Tomorrow at Untamed Mountain. Many of these exotic animals were rescued from animal attractions or came from individuals who could not provide proper care for them.

When you visit TFT, consider packing a picnic to enjoy in the pavilion, and don't forget to bring bottled water. Also, slather yourself in sunscreen and wear closed-toe shoes or hiking boots—no sandals or flip-flops—because this adventure calls for lots of walking over hilly terrain with limited shade. When the weather heats up, the big cats become languid and prefer napping to prowling. So for the best viewing during hot months, plan your arrival early. No photos or cell phones are allowed. Photos are only allowed on private guided tours. A two-hour private tour costs $25 per person for a minimum of four people.

The park (256-524-4150) opens for public walk-abouts from 9 a.m. to 4 p.m. Saturday and Sunday. Private tours, group tours, and school field trips are available by reservation. Hours are seasonal, so before you strike out, check tigersfortomorrow.org for current operating times, admission prices, and directions. You'll find Untamed Mountain at 708 County Road 345 in Dekalb County, just minutes from I-59. Watch for the signs. Also, check out the link to TFT's guardian angel program and consider adopting the care of an animal for one year. Admission: adults (ages 12 and up) $12; children (ages 3 to 11) $6.

hours are 2 to 4 p.m. Admission: adults (ages 19 and up) $3; students (ages 7 to 18) $1; children (ages 6 and under) free.

Before leaving the "Sock Capital of the World," stop by **Big Mill Antique Mall** (256-845-3380) and browse among yesteryear's treasures. Located at 151 Eighth Street Northeast, this 1889 structure, once home to Fort Payne's first hosiery mill, now houses antiques, collectibles, reproductions, a deli, and a bakery. Mall hours are 10 a.m. to 4 p.m. Monday through Saturday.

While traveling through **Collinsville,** you might want to consider spending some time at **Trade Day,** an event that draws some 30,000 or so bargain hunters and browsers every Saturday. Spread over 65 acres near Collinsville on US 11 South, this weekly occasion has had a country carnival flavor since it first cranked up in 1950. Vendors start setting up their wares at the crack of dawn and stay until early afternoon. Sightseers can munch on snacks such as boiled peanuts and corn dogs while surveying displays of wares from antiques and crafts to fresh vegetables and houseplants. Swans, ducks, rabbits, geese, goats, peacocks, hunting dogs, game cocks, and other animals often find new owners here. Parking costs $1, but admission is free. Overnight camper parking with electrical hookup is $6 per night. For more information call (256) 524-2127 or (866) 262-2127.

Cherokee Country

From Collinsville it's just a short jaunt to **Leesburg** and **The Secret Bed & Breakfast Lodge** (256-523-3825). Located at 2356 Highway 68 West on a mountaintop overlooking Weiss Lake, the lodge boasts a view that won't stop. Innkeepers Charlie and Kris Thomas own this property perched on the eastern brow of Lookout Mountain.

The view, the sunsets and sunrises, and the deer make The Secret a special place. Breakfast is served on a 10-foot-wide round table topped by a lazy Susan. Four guest rooms are located on the second floor above the Main Lodge: Tranquility, Serenity, Remembrance, and Enchantment. The Lodge also offers a lovely rooftop pool and suspended deck. Four cottages also are available for guests—the Treehouse with a tree trunk and ceiling of greenery; the 1850s Jail House with a wooden life-size gunslinger named Shakes; the Sugar Shack, a layered stone cottage; and the Nautical Cottage with its lighthouse motif. Movie buffs will find a video library containing more than 400 titles. Moderate to deluxe rates. Visit The Secret Bed & Breakfast Lodge via the Web at secretbedandbreakfastlodge.com.

Cherokee County, home of *Weiss Lake,* offers beautiful scenery. Add a chunk of Little River Canyon to this 30,200-acre lake bordered by 447 miles of shoreline, and you've got plenty of recreational options. Famous for its fine fishing, the Crappie Capital of the World also offers ample opportunities for catching bass and catfish. The water attracts large populations of wintering birds such as seagulls, wild ducks, and cranes.

While exploring Cherokee County's many scenic spots, don't overlook *Cornwall Furnace Park,* about 3 miles east of Cedar Bluff. To reach the park, take State Route 9 east and turn left onto Cherokee County Route 92. Then make another left onto a gravel road and follow the signs. A flight of steps leads down a steep bank (covered by lilies in spring) to the picturesque stone stack that stands about 5 feet tall—all that remains of a structure built to supply crude iron to be transformed into Confederate arms. General Sherman's forces destroyed the furnace works during the Civil War.

The well-kept grounds offer attractive picnicking facilities and a short nature trail. The park, which opens at daylight and closes at sundown, can be visited year-round. Running water is available, but there are no bathroom facilities. Admission is free.

Afterward take State Route 9 to *Centre,* about 6 miles away. Next to the courthouse stands the *Cherokee County Historical Museum* (256-927-7835), located at 101 East Main Street. This museum, formerly a department store, houses historical objects and memorabilia that characterize the area's past. You'll see a Pennsylvania Amish town buggy. Other exhibits include Bob Hope's first typewriter, Grand Ole Opry memorabilia, wagons, housewares, antique telephones, Civil War relics, early appliances, Native American artifacts, a printing press, a telephone switchboard, a doll collection, and a bale of cotton. The basement contains a blacksmith shop as well as old farm equipment such as plows, mowing machines, cotton planters, and tractors. The museum has a collection in excess of 15,000 items. Admission: adults $3; senior citizens and children (ages 7 to 18) $2; children (under age 7) free. The museum is open from 9 a.m. to 4 p.m. Tuesday through Friday. For more information visit museumatcentre.com.

Continue toward *Gadsden,* situated in Lookout Mountain's foothills. *Turkeytown,* named for Chief Little Turkey during the late 1700s, is a tiny community on the Coosa River's banks near Gadsden that once served as the capital of the Cherokee nation.

Although long known as one of the state's leading industrial centers with abundant deposits of iron, manganese, coal, and limestone, Gadsden is gaining recognition for its rich Cherokee legacy. The Turkeytown Association of the Cherokee, a nonprofit organization, works to preserve and promote the region's Native American heritage.

Downtown at Gadsden's Broad Street entrance to the Coosa River Bridge stands the statue of Emma Sansom, who, at age 16, helped Confederate troops find a place to ford Black Creek after Union forces crossed and burned the local bridge.

While in Gadsden, stop by the **Mary G. Hardin Center for Cultural Arts** (256-543-2787) on the corner of Fifth and Broad Streets at 501 Broad Street. The complex, with

alabamatrivia

Alabama ranks among the top 10 states with conditions most favorable for starting a small business.

a bold gold-and-black exterior in a Mondrian-like design, offers plays, concerts, lectures, classes, and art exhibits. To see the current art shows, take the escalator to the second floor. Before returning downstairs, be sure to notice the model railroad layout depicting Gadsden during the 1940s and 1950s with trains traveling past miniature reproductions of more than 100 historical structures, including the Gulf States Steel complex. The complex also houses the Courtyard Cafe. Admission: adults $6; children $5. Call for information on current exhibits or visit the website at culturalarts.org. Open Monday through Thursday 10 a.m. to 6 p.m.; Friday and Saturday 10 a.m. to 8 p.m.; Sunday 1 to 5 p.m.

Adjacent to the Center for Cultural Arts, the historic Kyle Building now houses the **Imagination Place Children's Museum** (256-543-2787). Youngsters can play in a life-size tree house or a kid-size city complete with Grandma's House, a bank, grocery store, doctor's office, fire station, and other interesting sites. Hours are Monday through Saturday 10 a.m. to 5 p.m.; and 1 to 5 p.m. Sunday. Admission is free for kids 2 and under. Admission: adults $6 and children $5 (ages 2 to 12). An adult must accompany children at all times. Imagination Place is closed the first Monday of every month for cleaning.

At *Noccalula Falls and Park* (256-549-4663), situated on Lookout Mountain Parkway (and easily reached from I-59), the bronze statue of a legendary Cherokee princess stands ready to leap to her destiny in a rushing stream 90 feet below. Legend says Noccalula loved a brave of her own tribe and chose to die rather than marry the wealthier suitor selected by her father.

Explore the park's botanical gardens, especially attractive in spring with masses of azaleas in bloom. You can either walk through the park or take a mini-train ride to see the Pioneer Homestead, a village of authentic log structures including a barn, blacksmith shop, gristmill, school, and cabins moved here from various sites in Appalachia. Also here you'll find the restored Gilliland-Reese Covered Bridge and a miniature golf course.

Nearby are campgrounds, hiking trails, picnic tables, play areas, and a pool. The park closes from November through mid-March. Hours vary so check to be sure when the park is open. Admission: adults $6; seniors $4; children (ages 4 to 12) $3; children (age 3 and under) free. Admission includes unlimited train rides. The campground number is (256) 543-7412.

If you're in the area on a weekend, you may want to schedule a jaunt to *Mountain Top Flea Market,* which is open every Sunday from 5 a.m. to about 3 p.m. or 4 p.m. year-round. You'll find this all-day market with some 1,500 dealers about 6 miles west of Attalla at 11301 US 278. For more information call (800) 535-2286 or (205) 589-2706 or visit the website at lesdeal.com.

Attalla, home of the world's first hydroelectric generator and birthplace of Alabama Power, lures antiques shoppers. Clustered in the downtown area are more than a dozen shops. *Emma Kate's Cottage Antique Mall & More* (256-504-7810) at 309 Fifth Avenue houses several shops inside the 1869 building. The mall is open Monday through Saturday from 10 a.m. to p.m. Call ahead before traveling because dealers keep their own hours, and these vary from shop to shop.

To reach Boaz, located on Sand Mountain, take US 431 north from Attalla.

Sand Mountain

A foothill of the Appalachians, Sand Mountain covers an area 25 miles wide by 75 miles long. Atop this plateau, you'll find Boaz Plaza Outlet Center. At one time, Boaz was ranked among America's top outlet centers in its day and you can still find plenty of bargains here.

Approximately 30,000 people descend on **Boaz,** population 9,653, for the annual Harvest Festival held the first full weekend in October. The weekend celebration features an antique car show, musical entertainment, an Indian powwow, and some 200 booths brimming with handcrafted items ranging from birdhouses, cornshuck dolls, and crazy quilts to paintings, leather items, and furniture. Music runs the gamut from bluegrass, country, and gospel to jazz. For more information on the outlets or the festival, contact the Boaz Chamber of Commerce, 100 E. Bartlett St., Boaz 35957; call (256) 593-8154; or visit the website at boazchamberofcommerce.com.

Strange as It Sounds

Buck's Pocket State Park (256-659-2000), a secluded expanse of rugged nature that spills into three counties—DeKalb, Jackson, and Marshall—is rich in botanical beauty and local lore. Covering more than 2,000 acres of craggy canyon scenery on the western side of Sand Mountain, the park is located near Grove Oak.

For a magnificent overview of the entire canyon, head first to Point Rock, the park's highest area and a wonderful place for picnicking and hiking. According to local legend, early Native Americans took advantage of the area's geography to help them acquire their food supply by driving deer over the edge at Point Rock right into the "pocket." Both spring, with its plentiful supply of wildflowers, and fall make great times to visit.

To reach the headquarters and campground, you'll descend from Point Rock about 800 feet via a curving road to the canyon's base. The bottom line on the park's wooden sign says: HAVEN FOR DEFEATED POLITICIANS. Buck's Pocket acquired its reputation as a refuge for election losers after "Big Jim" Folsom, a former Alabama governor, lost a senate bid and announced his intention to go to Buck's Pocket, get his thoughts together, and "lick his wounds." He invited other defeated candidates to join him at this favorite retreat.

In addition to trails for hiking and rocks for climbing, recreation options include swimming and fishing at South Sauty Creek. Also, nearby Morgan's Cove offers a fishing pier and boat launching ramps. Rappelers and rock climbers should first stop by headquarters for a permit, good for a year. Write to Buck's Pocket at 393 County Road 174, Grove Oak 35975. For reservations call (800) ALA–PARK. Visit the website at alapark.com/buckspocket. Open daily 7 a.m. until sundown.

After exploring Boaz, continue north on US 431 toward Albertville, watching for the WINERY sign. To reach *Jules J. Berta Vineyards* (256-891-5115) at 1409 Darden Avenue, turn right and drive a short distance until you see a white fence on the left with vines growing beyond. Stop by to meet owners Jules Berta and his wife, Becky, learn about the challenges of growing grapes in Alabama, and sample a vintage or two in the tasting room.

"We have one-acre tracts of Chardonnay, Merlot, Cabernet Franc, and Sylvaner with small tracts of Blaufrankisch, Petit Syrah, Riesling, and Aurore grapes," said Jules. Vineyards cover five of the farm's 22 acres. The Bertas also import muscadines from local farmers.

Jules's parents (his father was a Freedom Fighter in Hungary's 1956 Revolution) immigrated to America in 1959. His father's career as a materials engineer later brought him to Alabama, where he planted his first vines in 1987. "Those first plantings, a combination of vinifera and French-American hybrid grapes, evolved from a hobby into an obsession," said Jules, who joined his father in this venture in 1993, having previously served in the Gulf War and Special Forces with the Navy. Jules continued to develop the vineyard after his father's death in 2005. Although still in the experimental stage, the vines are doing well, and the family is committed to making quality wines. Future plans call for adding varietals more suitable to the state's climate. Despite the challenges of sandy soil and hot, humid weather, Jules finds it gratifying to carry on his father's "impossible dream—grape growing in Alabama." You can visit the grapes between 10 a.m. and 7 p.m. Monday through Saturday. Check out jules jbertavineyards.com for a wine list and more information.

alabamatrivia

Boaz, population 9,653, was named for a biblical character in the Book of Ruth.

Afterward continue about 5 miles north to *Albertville,* the "Heart of Sand Mountain." Albertville's former Freedom Festival, chosen many times by the Southeast Tourism Society as one of July's Top Twenty Events, has evolved into an event called *Taste of Freedom BBQ Cookoff,* which draws a large crowd in late June.

For a look at some of the city's lovely historic homes, drive along East Main Street off US 431. At the street's end stands the 1891 *Albertville Depot,* which is listed on the National Register of Historic Places. The depot now houses a senior citizens center.

Albertville acquired its title as "Fire Hydrant Capital of the World" because the local Mueller Company turns liquefied steel into dome-topped fire hydrants and ships them to countries near and far. In front of the chamber of commerce building, you'll see a special nickel-plated version that marks Mueller's one-millionth locally manufactured fire hydrant.

At 113 Sand Mountain Drive, you'll find *Whitten's* (256-878-3901), a clothing store that features upscale town and country fashions for women and men. Hours are 9 a.m. to 5 p.m. Monday through Saturday. The shop closes on Thursday afternoon.

When visiting a new place, some travelers like to search out a restaurant where the locals eat. Here it's *The Food Basket* (256-878-1261), located just off US 431 at 715 Sampson Circle. The Daniel family has been feeding folks in Albertville since 1959.

Noted for its country ham and homemade biscuits, the restaurant draws a big breakfast crowd. Lunch specialties include Sand Mountain fried chicken and home-style fresh vegetables. Economical to moderate. Hours are 5:30 a.m. to 2:30 p.m. seven days a week for breakfast and lunch.

Take time to drive along some of Marshall County's rural roads. Along the way you'll notice fertile rolling farmland and chicken houses. Broilers, eggs, and turkeys produced on the state's individual farms add up to a billion-dollar poultry industry. In broiler production, Alabama ranks second in the nation.

When your taste buds crave Cajun cuisine and you can't make it to Louisiana, then stop by *Papa Dubi's Cajun Kitchen* (256-894-7878) on the Albertville-Guntersville line. Located at 3931 Brasher's Chapel Road, the eatery offers seafood gumbo, jambalaya, red beans and rice with sausage, Creole dishes, po'boys, and more.

While living in Germantown, Tennessee, Dan and Lisa Younghouse hit the road to celebrate their 25th wedding anniversary. After visiting the Shrine of the Most Blessed Sacrament of Our Lady of the Angels Monastery near Hanceville, they toured the surrounding area—never dreaming they would soon become Alabama residents. But that's exactly what happened when they fell in love with the area's beauty while staying at Lake Guntersville State Park Lodge.

Their restaurant takes its name from Lisa's grandfather, a Cajun descendant, who lived in Gulfport, Mississippi, and the recipes—including the one for tasty gumbo—came from her grandmother, Nanny Dubi. Parents of seven, the couple and various family members have some restaurant experience, but starting their own eatery represented a leap of faith. However, the locals kept them so busy they had to expand soon after opening. The kids pitch in to help with this family venture. Hours are 11 a.m. to 8:30 p.m. Monday through Thursday, 11 a.m. to 9 p.m. Friday and Saturday. Economical to moderate.

Lake Country

The lodge at *Lake Guntersville State Park* (256-571-5440 or 800-548-4553) makes a handsome base while exploring this area. Perched atop Taylor Mountain with views nothing short of stunning, the lodge sits just off State Route 227 at 1155 Lodge Drive. Simply seeing the sunset from the sweeping rear deck overlooking Lake Guntersville makes the trip worth it.

The lodge's 13 suites and 99 hotel rooms contain refrigerators, microwave ovens, large TVs, DVD players, pillow-top mattresses, and more. (Be sure to request a bluffside view.) Other park accommodations include cabins and chalets. Moderate to deluxe. The lodge's Pinecrest Dining Room serves breakfast, lunch, and dinner.

Nature lovers will enjoy seeing the wildlife and exploring 36 miles of color-coded hiking trails with varying degrees of difficulty. The park's pastimes also include tennis, fishing, canoeing, golf, sailing, and water skiing. Fishing boats and pontoons can be rented during spring, summer, and fall.

The park features several miles of scenic drives, a helipad, and camping facilities. Campsites range from primitive to fully equipped with utility hookups, tables, grills, bathhouses, hot showers, and play areas. You'll also find a camp store and nature center. For more information about the park and special packages like Eagle Awareness weekends, see alapark.com/lakeguntersville.

Continue to nearby Guntersville Lake, a Tennessee Valley Authority (TVA) creation, where sailboats and fishing vessels dot shining expanses of open water. "The most striking thing about Guntersville," says local newspaper editor Sam Harvey, "is that it's a country town with a lake all around it. Of the five approaches to Guntersville, four take you across water." With 69,100 acres of water, **Guntersville** bills itself as a vacationer's paradise. Truly a haven for water-sports enthusiasts, the area offers boating, swimming, skiing, and fishing. The Bass Anglers Sportsman Society calls Lake Guntersville "one of the finest sport fishing lakes in America," and the Alabama Bassmasters stage invitational tournaments here. *Field & Stream* magazine placed Guntersville in America's top 10 fishing towns. And *Where to Retire* magazine recently ranked the town one of the country's top choices for retirees, citing a variety of reasons including its heart, the lake.

Drive through the downtown area and stop by Lake Guntersville Chamber of Commerce and Welcome Center (256-582-3612; lakeguntersville.org), which is in a house with a beckoning front porch at 200 Gunter Avenue near the big river bridge. Here you can pick up brochures on area attractions and inquire about current happenings. For instance, the local theater group The Whole Backstage mounts a mix of productions throughout the year, so check on possible performances during your visit. For more information about The Whole Backstage, call (256) 582-7469 or visit the website at wholebackstage.com.

Atop a hill, **Lake Guntersville Bed and Breakfast** (256-505-0133) at 2204 Scott Street offers suites with private entrances and more lovely water views from its two levels of wraparound porches. While living in Fairfield, Connecticut, former Guntersville resident Carol Dravis dreamed of returning. She got to do just that when an unexpected opportunity came along to purchase the handsome circa-1910 white brick home.

Carol picks up guests who arrive by boat and airplane and serves a bountiful breakfast—on the veranda when weather permits. A full gourmet-style breakfast might feature her special European pancakes, beautiful and puffy with various toppings, or a sausage-and-cheese strata. Accompaniments include breakfast breads and a special mixture of fruit juices called Morning Sunshine. Based on individual interests, Carol recommends local activities and provides directions to nearby walking trails and other scenic spots. In the foyer you'll see a small gift shop with works by local artists and writers.

Carol offers several special-occasion packages such as birding, pamper yourself (with one-hour massages), Valentine, anniversary, birthday, theater, etc. One guest wrote, "How wonderful to have found such a thoughtful,

Encounters with Eagles

Sipping hot apple cider or coffee, listening to Appalachian music, and basking in a fireplace's glow set the tone for eagle-watching adventures at Lake Guntersville State Park. Each year from the second weekend in January through the first weekend in February, birders can band together for stimulating interpretive programs, live birds, and guided field trips.

"As if seeing the eagles were not worth it, the educational programs are fantastic," said a previous participant from Boston. The weekend gathering starts on Friday evening with a social hour at the park's lodge. Attendees meet each other and get an overview of the scheduled birding activities. Everyone is encouraged to get a good night's sleep because the first eagle sighting takes place Saturday at dawn's early light. (And don't forget your goose down jacket.)

"There's just something about eagles," said former state park naturalist Linda Reynolds. "I see the birds every winter day, and I still get goose bumps." Eagles from the Great Lakes area start trickling in during October, but most arrive in November to make the park's wooded terrain and lake their winter resort until their exodus in February.

As the stars disappear in dawn's silvery light, watchers scrutinize the sky over a valley lacking summer's lush foliage but still beautiful in its starkness. The greenery of pines softens interlacing barren tree branches. With all eyes searching the sky, the waiting group listens intently for that first whispered announcement: "There goes one!" Watchers continue to study the horizon with their scopes, which range from binoculars to serious tripod versions. During an hour's watch, you might see a dozen or so bald eagles soar from their roosts and spiral toward the nearby lake.

After the birds depart, the group also heads to the lake for a chance to see the eagles dip down to the water, extend their talons, and grasp fish—their favorite breakfast. From the vantage point of a nearby bank, it's thrilling to see the great birds at close range. "Morning is feeding time, and afternoons are for play," said a staffer helping with Eagle Awareness programs. "Then it's home to the roost at dusk."

The group also gathers at twilight to watch the eagles return for the evening. Before retiring, the birds preen and strike regal poses as if compelled to perform

talented hostess! Your charming B&B has been a true lagniappe [a lower Alabama expression meaning something extra special], and we've discovered again the great delight of porch-sitting. Thank you for a lovely and delicious visit." Visit Lake Guntersville B&B's website atlakeguntersvillebed andbreakfast.com. Standard to moderate rates.

for the audience training binoculars in their direction. Some watchers set up telescopes, inviting others to enjoy the view. You might find yourself sharing a scope with a pharmacist, truck driver, teacher, dentist, computer programmer, retiree, or student.

The group's mix confirms that you don't have to be an ornithologist to get excited by encounters with eagles. "We've noticed that everyone loves eagles even if they're not bird enthusiasts," Reynolds said. "I don't know if it's a spiritual thing or because the eagle is our national symbol. Historically, eagles symbolize that which is uplifting and inspirational."

After the morning sighting, you can head to the lodge for a bountiful breakfast. Later, you may want to take a daytime field trip with one of the designated guides. Depending on your individual interest, you can choose a park tour, a visit to the Nature Center located near the campground, an outing to the water bird refuge, or opt for more eagle viewing at other observation points. Eagle watchers come not only from Alabama, but also from Tennessee, Georgia, North and South Carolina, Florida, Mississippi, Louisiana, and beyond, and repeaters make up about a third of each group.

Each weekend features a different program. At the birding seminar, which stars live raptors, you might see eagles, hawks, owls, falcons, and other previously injured birds that recovered with the help of individual volunteers and such groups as the Southeastern Raptor Rehabilitation Center and the Alabama Wildlife Rescue Service. The agenda also includes programs on various birds of prey and their mating, nesting, migration, and feeding habits.

In addition to bald eagles, many species of birds populate the area. This lovely wild region is also home to deer, weasels, raccoons, opossums, muskrats, beavers, bobcats, cougars, and foxes. Some of the park's hiking trails follow paths once traveled by the Cherokee and the area's early settlers through forests of red cedar, ash, maple, hickory, sumac, redbud, oak, black walnut, poplar, sweet gum, and pine. Most of the land has been left in its natural state, and hiking allows you to study firsthand the local flora and fauna. For more information on Eagle Awareness weekends and other special packages at the park, visit alapark.com/lake guntersville or call (256) 571-5440.

At ***Kala's Cottage*** (256-582-5580), 217 Gunter Avenue, you can anticipate a warm welcome, great gift ideas, and a large selection of fine wines. Kala and JoAnne, who know their wines, will help you select the perfect vintage for that special occasion or simply to sip while enjoying a lakeside visit to Guntersville. (And speaking of spirits, ask them about Charlie.)

Ham Cups a Breakfast Treat at Lake Guntersville B&B

One of the favorite breakfast treats at the Lake Guntersville Bed and Breakfast is a quick and delicious recipe known as Ham Cups. Innkeeper Carol Dravis is happy to share the recipe.

GG's Green Eggs & Ham Cups
Created by Gay Martin for *Lake Guntersville Bed & Breakfast Cookbook*

6 very thin slices of deli-style ham

1 cup loosely packed fresh spinach leaves cut in slivers

1 cup cottage cheese

2 tablespoons melted butter

3 eggs

Pinch of salt

1 tablespoon flour

Line six (1-cup) muffin tins with ham slices. Top with slivered spinach divided equally among cups. Mix remaining ingredients and pour on spinach. Bake at 350°F about 25 minutes or until toothpick inserted in center of cup comes out clean.

Yields 6 cups

Browse through rooms crowded with art, antiques, home accessories, jewelry, and gourmet foods. Choose some personalized gifts and maybe pick up a package of those sugarcoated rose petals from France to drop in your cup of tea.

From art classes and demonstrations to costume parties and even meeting and greeting a baby tiger, you never know what surprises await here. Hang out with the locals at Friday wine tastings ($10 per person) from 5:30 to 7:30 p.m. and get some sightseeing tips. The shop opens at 10-ish in the morning Tuesday through Saturday; and closing time is 5 p.m. Tuesday through Saturday. Visit kalascottage.com.

Continue to nearby ***Fant's Department Store*** (256-582-3845) at 355 Gunter Avenue. The rambling structure offers a bargain basement and plenty of treasures. Your sightseeing excursion may take you past the ***Guntersville Museum*** (256-571-7597) at 1215 Rayburn Avenue. Built under the Works Progress Act (WPA), this handsome structure of rough limestone and mortar dates to 1936 and houses an art gallery, archives, and intriguing collections. Guntersville's past comes alive here with exhibits from Native American artifacts to sepia pictorial views of the Tennessee Valley Authority's dam construction and lake creation. Guntersville is named for John Gunter, great-grandfather of famed humorist and social commentator Will Rogers. Rogers is an honorary son of the city. The museum also hosts traveling exhibits. Hours are 10 a.m. to 4 p.m. Tuesday through Friday and

Angels in Arab

One spring day, a friend and I drove to Guntersville for an art exhibit and lunch. Walking into a local restaurant, we saw two angels, dressed in flowing white tunics with gold accessories—which included halos. One of the angel-women wore gold combat boots.

We soon found out the ***B-Team Angels,*** Paula Joslin and Kay Jennings, came from nearby Arab. They were "on a quest to earn their wings by spreading happiness." Wafting a wand in our direction, the angels then glided outside, where traffic screeched to a halt.

A year later I met the B-Team Angels and learned their league had grown and their happiness ministry had expanded. Each month, for example, they surprise a local resident with an Earth Angel award, honoring people who bring happiness to others, often without recognition. On Valentine's Day the angelic band entertains at area nursing homes, churches, conferences, and retreats. They charge nothing for their programs of songs, skits, puppet shows, and birthday parties.

"We feel that sharing love with others is what life's all about," writes Kay, in her introduction to *The B-Team Angels' Quest,* a book filled with Paula's whimsical photo-collages featuring 700 Arab residents. (A professional artist, Paula works in all mediums and has won numerous awards in juried shows.) Proceeds from the book sales help defray costs incurred for this ministry—gifts, certificates, photography, costumes, transportation, etc. Also, the group has published a cookbook called *Angel Food,* featuring some heavenly recipes.

So if you see an angel flitting about Arab, you know why: She's out to brighten someone's day—maybe yours. If you need to speak to a B-Team Angel or order a cookbook, call (256) 586-8463.

Strange as It Sounds

If a boat outing fits into your travel schedule, try to catch the evening exodus of bats from *Hambrick Cave.* Some 350,000 American gray bats, a protected species, consider this cave home from late April to mid-October (although the females migrate the first of August). You'll probably join a bevy of other boaters, clustered around the water-level cave mouth at the base of a bluff, all waiting for the sunset performance as a cloud of bats swoops overhead on its nocturnal foraging flight. Going downriver toward Guntersville Dam, look for a cave (marked by a small overhead sign) on your right. Flashlights are prohibited. (For more information on this and other area bat caves, call the *Wheeler National Wildlife Refuge* at 256-353-7243 or visit fws.gov/wheeler.)

1 to 4 p.m. on Saturday and Sunday. Admission is free. See guntersville museum.org.

Other local events include a series of summer evening lakeside concerts on Tuesdays, and the MOVA Arts Festival featuring a songwriter competition. The latter, a fall event presented by the Mountain Valley Arts Council, also features a juried art exhibit, children's activities, and lots of food and drink. For more information or to see a current art exhibit, stop by the Mountain Valley Arts Council (MVAC) office at 300 Gunter Avenue, or call (256) 571-7199. For an updated schedule, see mountainvalleyartscouncil.org.

Guntersville's popular two-day *Art on the Lake Show* draws crowds on the third weekend in April. The show features more than 120 artists and craftsmen, plus food vendors, outdoor games and rides, and a bake sale. The show promotes the arts while providing scholarship programs for local high school graduates. Held along beautiful Lake Guntersville, the show takes place rain or shine from 9 a.m. to 5 p.m. Admission is $2 for ages 3 and older. Visit the website for more information, artonthelake -guntersville.com.

On the Saturday before Labor Day, *St. William's Seafood Festival* features more than 5,000 pounds of fresh shrimp, oysters, crab, flounder, and other fish imported from coastal waters. Parish members prepare the seafood, which includes making about 400 gallons of gumbo. The festival is held at St. William's Catholic Church (929 Gunter Avenue; 256-582-4245; stwilliamchurch.com/seafood_festival).

If you prefer the privacy of a vacation rental, check out *Guntersville Getaway* (256-582-3013 or 256-571-5888) on Buck Island near Gunter's Landing and the Yacht Club. Only five minutes from downtown Guntersville and one mile from the public boat launch, this waterfront home at 280 Morrow Drive comes with private pier and many amenities.

The house, which offers three bedrooms and can accommodate nine, is ideal for families or a group of fishing buddies. Enjoy the lake view, natural wooded setting, and wildlife. Say hello to the great blue heron who seems to have a proprietary interest in the place, as do the turtles sunning on a log in the lake out back. (We counted 10 napping turtles with a duck serving as sentinel.) Devise your own easygoing schedule and relax in the backyard hammock with a good book. Grill your catch or a steak on the rear patio and dine outside. Owner Lyndall Hamlett has decorated the place with whimsical touches and provides information on local restaurants and attractions. Amenities include free Wi-Fi, good cell-phone reception, cable TV, TVs in the living room and each bedroom, and a washer and dryer. Moderate to deluxe. See guntersvillegetaway.com.

For some good old-fashioned fun and a mess of "poke salat," take State Route 69 to *Arab* during the first weekend in May. When the Arab Liars' Club (the self-appointed title for a group of local men who meet daily for coffee at L Rancho Cafe) came up with the idea for the *Poke Salat Festival,* they probably did not expect it to become an annual affair with everything from street dances and craft shows to beauty contests and drama productions.

In downtown Arab, notice the weather-beaten Farmer's Exchange, a local landmark that now houses a garden center. Also, you may wish to explore the city's dozen or so antiques shops.

At the southern edge of town on Arad Thompson Road, you'll find the inviting Arab City Park with the Shoal Creek Trail, ball fields, a pool, and modern, well-equipped playground. The park is also home to several historical structures including the Hunt School, Rice Church, Elvin Light Museum, and Smith's Country Store. Look for a statue of town founder Tuttle Thompson in Tuttle Thompson Park at the corner of Highway 89 and Main Street. Tuttle named the town in honor of his son, Arad Thompson, but the post office mistakenly changed the spelling to Arab. So it has remained. Afterward head toward Huntsville to launch an exploration of Alabama's northwestern region.

Places to Stay in Northeast Alabama

ALBERTVILLE

Microtel Inn & Suites
220 Alabama Hwy. 75
North
(256) 894-4000 or (800)
771-7171

Quality Inn
315 Martling Rd.
(256) 891-2600 or
(800) 526-3766

ATTALLA

Days Inn of Attalla
801 Cleveland Ave.
(256) 538-7861 or
(800) DAYSINN

BOAZ

Key West Inn
10535 State Rte. 168
(256) 593-0800 or
(800) 833-0555

FORT PAYNE

DeSoto State Park
7104 Desoto Pkwy.
(256) 845-5380 or
(800) 568-8840
alapark.com/desotoresort

GADSDEN

Gadsden Inn & Suites
200 Albert Rains Blvd.
(256) 543-7240 or
(800) 637-5678
gadsdeninnandsuites.com

Hampton Inn
129 River Rd.
(256) 546-2337 or
(800) HAMPTON

GUNTERSVILLE

Guntersville Getaway
280 Morrow Dr.
(256) 582-3013 or
(855) 499-0001
guntersvillegetaway.com

**Hampton Inn of Lake
Guntersville**
14451 US 431
(256) 582-4176

**Holiday Inn Lake
Guntersville**
2140 Gunter Ave.
(256) 582-2220 or
(800) 439-4745

**Lake Guntersville Bed
and Breakfast**
2204 Scott St.
(256) 505-0133
lakeguntersvillebed
andbreakfast.com

**Lake Guntersville State
Park Lodge**
1155 Lodge Dr.
(256) 571-5440 or
(800) 548-4553
alapark.com/
lakeguntersville

HUNTSVILLE

**Bevill Conference Center
and Hotel**
550 Sparkman Dr.
(256) 721-9428 or
(888) 721-9428
uah.edu/bevill-center

Courtyard by Marriott
4804 University Dr.
(256) 837-1400 or
(800) 321-2211

Dogwood Manor
707 Chase Rd.
(256) 859-3946
dogwoodmanorbandb
.com

Hampton Inn
4815 University Dr.
(256) 830-9400 or
(800) HAMPTON

Huntsville Marriott
5 Tranquility Base
(256) 830-2222 or
(888) 299-5174

The Westin Huntsville
6800 Governor's West
Northwest
(256) 428-2000 or
(866) 716-8808

LEESBURG

**The Secret Bed &
Breakfast Lodge**
2356 State Rte. 68 West
(256) 523-3825
secretbedandbreakfast
lodge.com

FOR MORE INFORMATION ABOUT NORTHEAST ALABAMA

Alabama Mountain Lakes Tourist Association
402 Sherman St.
PO Box 2537
Mooresville 35649
(800) 648-5381
northalabama.org
info@northalabama.org
This organization covers 16 north Alabama counties that are home to some 100 attractions in a 100-mile radius.

DeKalb County Tourist Association
1503 Glenn Blvd. SW
PO Box 681165
Fort Payne 35968
(256) 845-3957 or (888) 805-4740
discoverlookoutmountain.com
info@lookoutmountain.com

Greater Gadsden Area Tourism
90 Walnut St.
PO Box 8269
Gadsden 35901
(256) 549-0351 or (888) 565-0411
greatergadsden.com

Greater Jackson County Chamber of Commerce
407 E. Willow St.
PO Box 973
Scottsboro 35768
(256) 259-5500 or (800) 259-5508
jacksoncountychamber.com
chamber@scottsboro.org

Huntsville/Madison County Convention & Visitors Bureau
500 Church St.
Huntsville 35801
(256) 551-2230 or (800) 843-0468
huntsville.org
info@huntsville.org

Marshall County Convention & Visitors Bureau
200 Gunter Ave.
PO Box 711
Guntersville 35976
(256) 582-7015 or (800) 582-6282
marshallcountycvb.com

MENTONE

Crystal Lake Lodge
3291 County Rd. 165
(256) 634-8209
angelfire.com/al4/
crystallakelodge

Mentone Springs Hotel
6114 State Rte. 117
(256) 634-4040
mentonesprings.com

Mountain Laurel Inn Bed & Breakfast
624 Rd. 948
(256) 634-4673 or
(800) 889-4244
mountain-laurel-inn.com

Raven Haven
651 County Rd. 644
(256) 634-4310
ravenhavenbandb.info

PISGAH

The Lodge at Gorham's Bluff
101 Gorham Dr.
Gorham's Bluff
(256) 451-2787
gorhamsbluff.com

MAINSTREAM ATTRACTIONS WORTH SEEING IN NORTHEAST ALABAMA

Alabama Fan Club & Museum
101 Glen Blvd.
Fort Payne
(256) 845-1646 or (800) 557-8223
This museum showcases the band's musical achievements, which are many: The group has garnered numerous awards, gold albums, and plaques for such releases as "My Home's in Alabama," "Mountain Music," and "Fallin' Again." Fans can purchase souvenirs ranging from T-shirts and jackets to photographs and mugs—and of course albums. The museum features individual sections on band members Randy Owen, Teddy Gentry, Jeff Cook, and Mark Herndon. For a little background and a Web tour, visit thealabamaband.com.

Huntsville Museum of Art
300 Church St. South
Huntsville
(256) 535-4350 or (800) 786-9095
Save time for browsing through the $7.5 million home of the Huntsville Museum of Art. This beautiful building stands in Big Spring International Park, the heart of the city, and offers a wide range of exhibitions, art classes, and educational programs. You'll see an outstanding permanent collection with works by Picasso, Matisse, Toulouse-Lautrec, Goya, and other renowned artists as well as exhibits on loan from major institutions. The Pane e Vino Cafe on the Plaza Level offers pizza, pasta, and sandwiches. Admire student artwork in the Children's Community Gallery, sign up for an art class at the museum academy, and shop for treasures at the Museum Store, opened in 2009. Visit hsvmuseum.org.

US Space & Rocket Center
Huntsville
(256) 837-3400 or (800) 637-7223
rocketcenter.com
At One Tranquility Base on Huntsville's western side, you may feel like a character out of a science fiction movie as you wander through a world of rockets, spaceships, shuttles, nose cones, and lunar landing vehicles. Other interesting exhibits include a moon rock, Apollo 16's command module, the overpowering *Saturn V* moon rocket, history of the space shuttle with artifacts, and an SR-/1 Blackbird reconnaissance plane. Don't miss the featured film presentation at the Spacedome Theater, or, for a unique adventure, sign up for Space Camp. You'll find Space Camp dates, rates, registration information, and everything else you need to know for blasting off at spacecamp.com.

SCOTTSBORO

Goose Pond Colony
417 Ed Hembree Dr.
(256) 259-2884 or
(800) 268-2884
goosepond.org

Quality Inn
208 Micah Way
US 72
(256) 574-6666

VALLEY HEAD

Winston Place
353 Railroad Ave.
(256) 635-6381 or
(888) 4-WINSTON

Places to Eat in Northeast Alabama

ALBERTVILLE

Asia Garden Restaurant
210 State Rte. 75 North
(256) 891-1616

Catfish Cabin
8524 US 431 North
(256) 878-8170

The Food Basket
715 Sampson Circle
(256) 878-1261

Giovanni's Pizza Italian Restaurant
711 Miller St.
(256) 878-7881

Papa Dubi's Cajun Kitchen
3931 Brasher's Chapel Rd.
(256) 894-7878

Sebastien's on Main
102 Main St.
(256) 660-1222
sebastiens.com

ARAB

Fonseca Factory
1082 N. Brindlee Mountain Pkwy.
(256) 931-7687

Son's House of Barbecue
2425 N. Brindle Mountain Pkwy.
(256) 931-7667

BOAZ

Grumpy's
8679 Hwy. 168
(256) 593-0599

CENTRE

Tony's Steak Barn
804 Alexis Rd.
(256) 927-2844

GADSDEN

The Choice
531 Broad St.
(256) 546-9055

Courtyard Cafe
501 Broad St.
(256) 547-1066

Top O' the River
1606 Rainbow Dr.
(256) 547-9817
topotheriverrestaurant.com

GRANT

Mi Mi's Cafe
12 Third St.
(256) 728-7483
mimiscafe.com

GUNTERSVILLE

El Camino Real
14274 US 431
(256) 571-9089

Top O' the River
7004 Val Monte Dr.
(256) 582-4567
topotheriverrestaurant.com

Wintzell's Oyster House
14455 US 431
(256) 582-5600
wintzellsoysterhouse.com

HUNTSVILLE

Cafe Berlin
964 Airport Rd.
(256) 880-9920
cafeberlinhsv.com

Cantina Laredo
330 The Bridge St.
6872 Old Madison Pike
(256) 327-8580
cantinalaredo.com

Landry's Seafood House
5101 Governor's House Dr.
(256) 864-0000
landrysseafood.com

Ol' Heidelberg
6125 University Dr.
(256) 922-0556
olheidelberg.com

Surin of Thailand
975 Airport Rd.
(256) 213-9866
surinofthailand.com

MADISON

Main St. Cafe
101 Main St.
(256) 461-8096
mainstreetcafe-madison
.com

MENTONE

Log Cabin Restaurant and Deli
6080 State Rte. 117
(256) 634-4560

The Wildflower Cafe
83 Cutter Ave.
(256) 634-0066
mentonewildflower.com

PISGAH

The Lodge at Gorham's Bluff
101 Gorham Dr.
(256) 451-2787
gorhamsbluff.com

SARDIS CITY

Garcia's Grill & Cantina
13026 US 431
(256) 840-5694

SCOTTSBORO

McCutchen's Magnolia House
303 East Willow St.
(256) 259-3077

Carlile's Restaurant
2011 E. Willow St.
(256) 574-5629
carliles.net

The Docks
Goose Pond Colony
417 Ed Hembree Dr.
(256) 574-3071
goosepond.org/
dine-the-docks

Liberty Restaurant
907 E. Willow St.
(256) 574-3455

Payne's
101 E. Laurel St.
(256) 574-2140

Triple R Bar-B-Q
2940 Veterans Dr.
(256) 574-1620
triplerbbq.com

STEVENSON

Friday's
507 Second St.
(256) 437-8201

NORTHWEST ALABAMA

Tennessee Valley

Mooresville, just east of I-65 at exit 2 on I-565 between Huntsville and Decatur, makes a good place to start a tour of Alabama's northwest region. For information on local and area attractions, call the North Alabama Tourism Association's office at (800) 648-5381.

To best see Mooresville, a town that dates to 1818 (it's one year older than the state itself), plan to take a walking tour. Not only does everybody know everybody in this community of some 20 families, everybody knows everybody's dog. Don't be surprised if the local canines choose to accompany you on your stroll through town. Listed on the National Register of Historic Places, this charming village occupies an area of one-quarter square mile and can easily be covered in half an hour. Cedar trees and wild hydrangeas make lovely accents as you wend your way through the town. Strolling along streets lined by picket fences and fine old shade trees, you'll see a variety of vintage structures including lovely old federal-style homes.

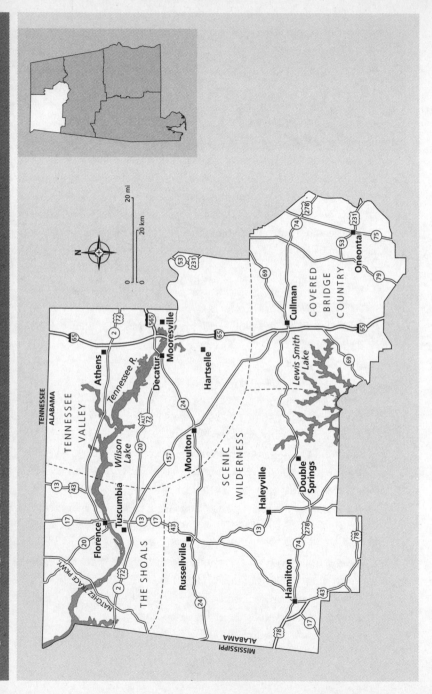

On Lauderdale Street you'll pass a brick church that dates to 1839 and contains its original pews. Although regular worship services no longer take place here, the historic structure is sometimes used for weddings and meetings. Notice the herringbone pattern of the brick walkway in front of the church. Mooresville's former postmistress, Barbara Coker, using many of her lunch hours, excavated through grass and layers of dirt to expose the original brickwork.

Be sure to stop by the tiny post office on the corner of Lauderdale and High Streets. Built around 1840, this small weathered poplar building, with tin roof, pegged joints, and square-head nails, contains the town's 48 original post boxes (first installed at the nearby Stagecoach Inn and Tavern).

The Stagecoach Inn, built sometime before 1825, once sold "supper for two bits." Across the street from the inn stands a small cottage, an example of Downing Gothic architecture. Dating to about 1890, the home was built and owned by Uncle Zack Simmons, a black carpenter, and his wife, Aunt Mandy. Former Mooresville mayor Kathleen Lovvorn says that Aunt Mandy, famous for her jellies and pickles, often handed out homemade treats to the village youngsters.

Turning Back the Clock to Mark Twain's Time

If you saw the Disney production *Tom and Huck*, you visited the well-preserved village of Mooresville via video. Jonathan Taylor Thomas (of TV's *Home Improvement* fame) and Brad Renfro (*The Client*) starred in this remake of a Mark Twain classic.

"The moment I saw Mooresville, I knew this was the perfect setting for Tom Sawyer," said the film's production manager, Ross Fanger, after searching for a town that fit the 1876 era of Mark Twain's novel.

For the movie, Mooresville's paved streets became dirt-covered lanes, and a Hollywood facade of 19th-century stores sprang up. Film crews shot some scenes along the Tennessee River and inside *Cathedral Caverns,* a state park in Marshall County. The caverns served as a backdrop for the novel's account of Tom and his girlfriend Becky Thatcher's lost-in-a-cave adventure.

If you missed the movie, don't despair—the film is available on DVD, and you can still visit Mooresville.

Mooresville Walking Tours

Village residents often lead walking tours for groups, large and small. Contact Susan Goldby, who can gear the tour focus to the group's common interest—architectural, gardening, or historical. Tours take about one and a half hours and the cost is $5 per person. All proceeds benefit the Historical Preservation Fund, used for preservation of Mooreville's town-owned structures and trees. For more information, e-mail sgoldby@earthlink.net and include "Walking Tour" in the subject line or call (256) 353-3628.

The *Hurn-Thach-Boozer-McNiell House,* built around 1825 and located near the end of Market Street, once housed a tailor shop, where Andrew Johnson, who later became president, studied drafting and construction techniques under the supervision of Joseph Sloss (who specialized in making Prince Albert coats for gentlemen).

After departing Mooresville you may want to travel north to *Athens,* Limestone County's seat. Start your local tour by visiting the downtown courthouse square with its surrounding stores and stately old churches. Founded in 1818, Athens barely missed being the state's oldest incorporated town. (Nearby Mooresville won the race by only three days.) To see some of the town's antebellum and Victorian homes—many are identified by historic markers—drive along Beaty, Pryor, Jefferson, and Clinton Streets.

You may want to stop by the *Houston Memorial Library and Museum* (256-233-8770). Located at 101 North Houston Street, this house dates to 1835 and served as the home of George S. Houston (a former Alabama governor and US senator) from 1845 to 1879. Exhibits include family portraits, period furniture, Native American artifacts, Civil War relics, and various items relating to local history. Hours are 10 a.m. to 5 p.m. Monday through Friday and 9 a.m. to noon Saturday.

For a toe-tapping good time, plan to take in the *Tennessee Valley Old Time Fiddlers Convention* held at Athens State University each October. Visitors converge on campus for two days of outdoor competitions featuring harmonica, banjo, fiddle, mandolin, dulcimer, and guitar playing and buck dancing sessions. For more information about the fiddlers, call (256) 233-8141 or visit athens.edu/fiddlers.

The Greater Limestone County Chamber of Commerce office at 101 South Beaty Street (256-232-2600; tourathens.com) stocks brochures the visitor will find helpful. Pick up the *Beaty Historic District Walking Tour* guide to explore this area. Listed on the National Register, this historic district was named for Robert Beaty, cofounder of Athens. Although some of the district's homes date back before the Civil War, most were built during the early 1900s.

Beaty Street takes you to Athens State University, Alabama's oldest institution of higher learning. While on this street, be sure to notice the Beaty-Mason House built in 1826, now the college president's home. Located at 302 North Beaty Street, the lovely 1840s Greek revival *Founder's Hall* houses school offices, a library, and a chapel. This building's original portion escaped being burned by the Yankees when a letter allegedly written by President Lincoln appeared in the nick of time. On the second floor, the Altar of the New Testament features fine woodcarvings in tulip poplar. Founder's Hall may be visited Monday through Friday from 8 a.m. to 4:30 p.m. Admission is free. For more information, call (256) 233-8215.

Before leaving Athens, plan to tour the *Donnell House.* Completed in 1851, the T-shaped home contains some period furnishings and is located at 601 South Clinton Street on the Middle School campus. A chinked log cabin kitchen with working fireplace stands nearby. The home is open from 1 to 3 p.m. on Friday, or by appointment. For more information call (256)

Traveling the Antebellum Trail

Greater Limestone County boasts a rich legacy of antebellum and late-19th- and early-20th-century architecture. Near the neighboring industrial and technological centers of Decatur and Huntsville, you'll find an area of contrasting culture—think past, present, and future tenses if you will. The trail begins in Athens and ends in Mooresville. The trail delineates a driving tour with a number of antebellum structures, which translates to the time period between 1812 and 1861. You'll drive past 24 homes, three churches, a college, two working cotton plantations, a post office, and stagecoach inn and tavern. Call the Greater Limestone County Chamber of Commerce at (256) 232-2600 or (800) 648-5381, click on the website at tourathens.com, or visit at 101 South Beaty Street in Athens for more information.

232-0743 or contact Jacque Reeves at (256) 536-5737 or visit donnellhouse .org. Modest admission.

Reeves also offers several walking tours including the Maple Hill Cemetery Walk, which visits the graves of five Alabama governors, Revolutionary War and Civil War soldiers, the first Secretary of War for the Confederacy, and the family of actress Tallulah Bankhead. Tours are tailored to fit your needs and cost a modest fee.

After exploring Athens, head south to **Decatur** for another dose of history along with wildlife. Founded on the banks of the Tennessee River and originally called Rhodes Ferry, Decatur acquired its current name in 1820. At that time Congress and President James Monroe decided to honor Commodore Stephen Decatur by naming a town after him. A daring naval hero who commanded a three-ship squadron during the War of 1812, Decatur once proposed the following toast: "Our country: In her intercourse with foreign nations may she always be in the right; but our country, right or wrong."

alabamatrivia

America's first wave pool was built in 1970 at Point Mallard Park in Decatur.

You can see mallards along with blue buntings, herons, owls, woodpeckers, bald eagles, and other birds on exhibit at **Cook's Natural Science Museum** (256-350-9347; cookspest .com/education/museum), located at 412 13th Street Southeast. Hands-on exhibits and changing displays present the world of nature—from insects and seashells to reptiles and rocks. The privately owned museum features displays of iridescent butterflies and a mounted, life-size black bear dripping with honey. Hours are 9 a.m. to noon and 1 to 5 p.m. Monday through Saturday and 2 to 5 p.m. Sunday. Admission is free. A new Cook Museum of Natural Science is being developed in downtown Decatur and is scheduled to open in late 2015.

Nearby at 1715 Sixth Avenue Southeast, the folks who work at **Big Bob Gibson's** (256-350-6969) say they cook "the best barbecue in town." A Decatur tradition since 1925, the restaurant serves real hickory-smoked pit-barbecued pork, beef, and chicken. Barbecued potatoes (baked and topped with meat) also prove popular menu items. You can grab a bite here or get an order to go. Hours are "can to can't" (9 a.m. to 8:30 p.m.) seven days a week, excluding Easter, Thanksgiving, Christmas, and New Year's Day. Economical prices. The restaurant is so popular, it has another Decatur location at 2520 Danville Road Southwest (256-350-0404; bigbobgibson.com). Oh, yes, and be sure to pick up a bottle of barbecue sauce here—they make several varieties.

Stop by the Decatur-Morgan County Convention and Visitors Bureau at 719 Sixth Avenue Southeast for a pamphlet called *A Walking Tour of Historic Decatur,* which notes many of the city's late-19th-century homes that can be seen in the Old Decatur and New Albany historic districts. Call (256) 350-2028 or (256) 232-5449 or visit decaturcvb.org for more information on local attractions.

Head to the city's northern section to tour the handsome *Old State Bank* (256-350-5060), established during Andrew Jackson's presidency. Located at 925 Bank Street Northeast, Alabama's oldest surviving bank building now serves as a museum. Upstairs you'll see the head cashier's spacious living quarters, furnished in the 1830s style.

During the Civil War this classic-style structure served as a hospital for both Union and Confederate soldiers. The bank's thick vault possibly became a shielded surgery chamber during the heat of battle. Outside, the large limestone columns still retain traces of Civil War graffiti along with

BEST ATTRACTIONS IN NORTHWEST ALABAMA

Alabama Music Hall of Fame,
Tuscumbia

Ave Maria Grotto,
Cullman

Bankhead National Forest,
Double Springs

Blount County Covered Bridges,
Oneonta

Dismals Canyon,
Phil Campbell

Indian Mound and Museum,
Florence

Ivy Green,
Tuscumbia

Natural Bridge,
Natural Bridge

The Shrine of the Most Blessed Sacrament of Our Lady of the Angels Monastery,
Hanceville

battle scars from musket fire. The bank was among Decatur's few buildings to survive the Civil War. Bank tours are free, and the building is open Monday through Friday from 9:30 a.m. to noon and 1 to 4:30 p.m., or by appointment. To sample a good mix of shops featuring antiques, clothing, toys, and gifts, take a stroll down Bank Street.

Nearby, at 207 Church Street Northeast, you can view some great traveling exhibits and work by regional artists at **Carnegie Visual Arts Center** (256-341-0562). One of millionaire philanthropist Andrew Carnegie's projects, the building dates to 1904 and served as Decatur's library until 1973. Hours run from 10 a.m. to 5 p.m. Tuesday through Friday and 10 a.m. to 2 p.m. on Saturday. Check out carnegiearts.com for current offerings and exhibits.

When hunger pangs hit, head to **Simp McGhee's** (256-353-6284; simpmcghees.com), at 725 Bank Street Northwest. Named for a colorful early-20th-century riverboat captain, this pub-style eatery offers Simp's stuffed Gulf flounder as well as many pasta, poultry, and beef entrees. The upstairs section, Miss Kate's Place, takes its name from a famous former madam, who ran a turn-of-the-20th-century bordello nearby. Dinner hours are Monday through Thursday from 5 to 9 p.m., Friday and Saturday from 5 to 9:30 p.m.

Standing in Decatur's New Albany downtown area at 115 Johnston Street Southeast, you'll see the **Old Cotaco Opera House** (334-887-3007). Often called the Old Masonic Building, the big brick structure dates to 1890. Although you won't see a touring vaudeville act here today, you'll find the complex offers other enticing treats. For instance, hungry travelers can visit **Curry's on Johnston Street** (256-350-6715; currysrestaurant.com), located on the building's lower level at 115½ Johnston Street, for lunch or pick-up items. The eatery serves homemade soups, sandwiches, casseroles, fresh bread, and desserts. Moderate rates. Hours are 8 a.m. to 5 p.m. Monday through Friday and 11 a.m. to 2 p.m. Saturday.

To visit one of *The 100 Best Small Towns in America* (selected by Norman Crampton for his nationwide guide), head south for **Hartselle,** now a mecca for antiques shoppers. (For a list of the other 99 towns, you'll have to buy the book.) Hartselle boasts the largest number of contiguous buildings on the Historic Register in Alabama.

Make your first stop the historic **Depot Building** at 110 S. Railroad Street, which houses the Hartselle Area Chamber of Commerce (256-773-4370 or

800-294-0692; hartsellechamber.org). On one wall you'll see a Works Progress Administration (WPA) mural painted in 1937 that illustrates the major role cotton played in the area's early economy. While here collect a map and guide to local shops. Open by 10 a.m., most shops close on Wednesday and Sunday. Also, some shops close on Monday.

Afterward stroll to *The Freight House* (256-773-4600; freighthouse catering.com), located at 200 Railroad Street in a former freight building. You can occasionally hear a passing train. Try the lasagna or daily specials. The restaurant also features a lunch express weekdays from 11 a.m. to 2 p.m. A tasty brunch on Saturday and Sunday from 11 a.m. to 2 p.m. offers create-your-own omelet and waffle stations. Open Monday and Tuesday 11 a.m. to 2 p.m., Thursday through Saturday 11 a.m. to 8 p.m., and Sunday 11 a.m. to 2 p.m. Standard to moderate.

Browsing along Main Street, you'll see *Ragtime Antiques* at 112 West Main Street (256-773-2188) and other specialty shops, with an array of everything from bric-a-brac and potpourri to primitive antiques and quilts. At *Slate Gallery,* you'll find work by local artists at the shop at 333 West Main Street (256-778-1211; slategalleryandframing.com).

After leaving Hartselle, follow State Route 36 west, watching for the *Oakville* turn and signs directing you to *Jesse Owens Memorial Park* (256-974-3636) at 7019 County Road 203. The park's focal point is an 8-foot, one-ton bronze statue of Owens, who won four gold medals in the 1936 Olympics. Branko Medenica, a native of Germany who now lives in Birmingham, sculpted the piece, which depicts Owens running and incorporates the familiar Olympic rings. Mounted on a 6-foot granite base, the statue was unveiled in a 1996 ceremony attended by members of the athlete's family when the Olympic torch passed through Oakville en route to Atlanta's games.

alabamatrivia

Alabama symbols include: the yellowhammer, the state bird; the camellia, the state flower; and the Southern pine, the state tree.

The park also offers a visitor center, museum, softball field, basketball court, walking trail, picnic pavilions, and replicas of the 1936 Olympic torch and Owens's modest home. Owens, who was born in Oakville and spent his early life here, once said, "It behooves a man with God-given ability to

stand 10 feet tall. You never know how many youngsters may be watching."
The park is open during daylight hours, and admission is free. The museum
is open from 10 a.m. to 4 p.m. Monday through Saturday and from 1 to 4
p.m. Sunday. Free admission to the museum. Check out jesseowensmemorial
park.com.

Before leaving the vicinity, take time to visit the **Oakville Indian
Mounds,** a park and museum (256-905-2499) at 1219 County Road 187.
Located 8 miles southeast of Moulton just off State Route 157, the complex
features a massive 2,000-year-old Woodland Indian Mound, a Copena Indian
burial mound, and a museum modeled after a seven-sided Cherokee Council
House. The museum contains a 12-foot wooden statue of Sequoyah plus
thousands of artifacts—some dating back to 10,000 BC. Generally, hours are
8 a.m. to 4 p.m. Monday through Friday, 1 to 4 p.m. Saturday, and noon to
4 p.m. Sunday. Admission is free.

Afterward continue your journey toward **Moulton.** Try to hit Moulton
at mealtime so you can sample the terrific lemon-pepper grilled catfish fil-
let at **Western Sirloin Steak House** (256-974-7191), with a huge grain-bin
entrance and tin walls. Located at 11383 State Route 157 (behind Foodland),
the restaurant also features charbroiled chicken breast and rib-eye steak at
economical to moderate rates. Open daily from 11 a.m. to 9 p.m.

Continue west on State Route 20 to **Courtland,** named to the National
Register of Historic Places for its 1818 development of the early town plan.
Local architectural styles span almost two centuries. For a brochure on
Courtland, which details a driving tour of the historical district, stop by
Town Hall.

After exploring Courtland, continue to **Doublehead Resort & Lodge**
(800-685-9267; doublehead.com) for some relaxation and outdoor recreation.
Located at 145 County Road 314 near Town Creek, the complex underscores
a Native American theme from its name to its design and furnishings. A split-
rail fence defines pastures, and wooden poles frame the metal entrance gate
with its "Welcome Friends" greeting in Cherokee characters.

The property takes its name from Doublehead, a Cherokee chief who
once lived on this land. The management wants to sustain a Native American
awareness as it continues to develop this distinctive resort. The main lodge
features a 5,000-square-foot deck overlooking Wilson Lake. Hammered
metal designs of free-floating feathers and an upward-pointing arrowhead

TOP ANNUAL EVENTS IN NORTHWEST ALABAMA

Bloomin' Festival at St. Bernard
Cullman, early April
(256) 739-6682 ext. 7133 or (800)
722-0999
bloominfestival.com

North Alabama Birding Festival
Wheeler Wildlife Refuge
Highway 67 East
Decatur, May
decaturcvb.org
(256) 350-2028 or (800) 232-5449

Alabama Jubilee Hot-Air Balloon Classic
Point Mallard Park, Decatur
Memorial Day weekend
(256) 350-2028 or (800) 232-5449
alabamajubilee.net

Helen Keller Festival
Tuscumbia, late June
(256) 383-4066 or (888) 329-2124
helenkellerfestival.com

The Spirit of America Festival
Point Mallard Park, Decatur, July 3–4
(256) 350-2028 or (800) 232-5449
spiritofamericafestival.com

W. C. Handy Festival
Florence, late July to early August
(256) 766-7642
wchandymusicfestival.org

September Skirmish
Point Mallard Park, Decatur
Labor Day weekend
(256) 350-2028 or (800) 524-6181

Oktoberfest
Cullman, early October
(256) 739-1258 or (800) 533-1258
cullmanoktoberfest.com

Southern Wildlife Festival
Decatur, October
(255) 350-2028 or (800) 524-6181
decaturcvb.org

Alabama Renaissance Faire
Florence, fourth weekend of October
(256) 740-4141 or (888) 356-8687
alarenfaire.org

Covered Bridge Festival
Oneonta, fourth weekend of October
(205) 274-2153
blountoneontachamber.org

frame the double hand-carved front doors. A locally found Cherokee medallion inspired the lodge's unique chandelier.

Nestled among the trees are 38 split-level cedar log cabins, each with three bedrooms, two baths, and a completely equipped kitchen. Other features include a wood-burning fireplace, satellite TV, and washer and dryer. (After all, Doublehead's appreciation for creature comforts is well documented.) Beds are constructed from rustic cedar posts, and Indian wall hangings echo the motif. Each cabin comes with a beckoning hammock, grill, picnic table, and private pier. Recreational activities range from fishing, boating, and hunting to horseback riding. Golfers will want to inquire about special packages with land and water shuttles to the nearby Robert Trent Jones championship golf courses, *Fighting Joe* and *The Schoolmaster,* at the Shoals. Other amenities include two tennis courts, a basketball court, and a 2.5-mile walking/nature trail. The facility offers rentals for Jet Skis, pontoons, canoes, other watercraft, a sporting clays course (shooting range), and a private 1,100-acre hunting preserve. Deluxe rates.

Afterward head west toward Tuscumbia.

The Shoals

You will be transported back in time when you arrive in *Tuscumbia.* At 301 South Dickson Street stands *The Log Cabin Stagecoach Stop at Cold Water,* an authentic structure from the pioneer period. The Stagecoach Stop is open by appointment and on special occasions. Call (256) 383-0783 for more information or check out visittuscumbiaal.com. Continue to Commercial Row, located on the north side of West Fifth Street between Water and Main Streets. This block of seven bordering brick buildings, dating to the 1830s, represents local antebellum commercial architecture. During the 1880s, Capt. Arthur Keller (Helen Keller's father) published his newspaper, the *North Alabamian,* here in the corner building.

While exploring downtown, step inside the restored *Palace Drugstore* for a bit of nostalgia and maybe a milk shake at the 1950s soda fountain. Also, you'll want to see Spring Park's 51-jet fountain with water surging to heights of more than 150 feet. On weekend evenings, you can take in a special show, choreographed to lights and the music of Alabama's nationally known artists with a focus on those who recorded in Muscle Shoals. The large fountain serves as a memorial to Princess Im-Mi-Ah-Key, wife of Chickasaw Chief Tuscumbia, for whom the town is named. For more information, call (256) 386-5670 or visit tuscumbiarailway.com.

Nearby at 300 West North Commons stands *Ivy Green,* the birthplace of Helen Keller. After her graduation from Radcliffe College, Miss Keller worked tirelessly on behalf of those with disabilities by lecturing, writing articles and books (some of which have been translated into more than 50 languages), and appealing to legislative bodies to improve conditions for those with impaired sight and hearing. Because she conquered her own disabilities and gained an international reputation for inspiring other persons with disabilities to live richer lives, she became known as America's "First Lady of Courage."

Of Ivy Green Miss Keller wrote, "The Keller homestead . . . was called 'Ivy Green' because the house and surrounding trees and fences were covered with beautiful English Ivy." On the grounds you'll also see English boxwood, magnolia, mimosa, roses, and honeysuckle. The family home contains many original furnishings, photographs, letters, awards, books, and Miss Keller's braille typewriter.

Summer visitors can watch a miracle reenacted at a performance of William Gibson's drama *The Miracle Worker* staged on Ivy Green's grounds and directed by Darren Butler. The play culminates with a vivid portrayal of the poignant incident at the water pump when teacher Anne Sullivan helped the blind and deaf child break through her black void into "a wonderful world with all its sunlight and beauty."

Except for major holidays, Ivy Green is open year-round. The home can be toured Monday through Saturday from 8:30 a.m. to 4 p.m. Admission: adults $6, seniors $5, and students (ages 5 to 18) $3. For more information on Ivy Green, the play, or the annual *Helen Keller Festival* (scheduled for a weekend in late June each year), call (256) 383-4066. Visit helenkellerbirth place.org for more background information.

About 3.5 miles south of Tuscumbia, you'll find another interesting home, *Belle Mont* (256-637-8513) at 1569 Cook Lane. Constructed between 1828 and 1832, the U-shaped brick structure suggests the influence of Thomas Jefferson. Dr. Alexander William Mitchell, who moved here from Virginia, built this home, now considered the state's finest example of Jefferson Palladian architecture. Partially furnished, most of the home's pieces date to the period between 1840 and 1860. Owned by the Alabama Historical Commission, Belle Mont is open Thursday through Saturday from 9 a.m. to 4 p.m., Sunday 1 to 5 p.m. Admission: adults $4, seniors citizens $3, children (ages 6 to 18) $2. Check out this property and other historic sites at preserveala.org.

At some point during your visit, you may want to learn more about this area, called *the Shoals.* Looping through north Alabama, the Tennessee River comes into its own here in the state's northwest corner. At one time navigators found the Muscle Shoals rapids too formidable to negotiate, but the Tennessee Valley Authority (TVA) solved this problem with a series of strategically placed dams. The jagged rocks that created perilous swirling currents and wrecked boats now lie "buried" far below the water's surface.

To get a good idea of the river's impact on the region, you can visit the TVA Reservation at Muscle Shoals to see *Wilson Dam.* With its north end in Lauderdale County and its south end in Lawrence County, the dam stretches almost a mile and serves as a bridge for State Route 101. Named for President Woodrow Wilson, the dam was initiated during World War I to supply power for making munitions. Today, visitors enjoy camping, boating, and fishing at Wilson Reservoir. The site features a network of hiking and walking trails. While on a trek, enjoy the nature area's ideal habitat for lovely ferns. Look for the walking fern, rarely seen in Alabama but a favorite natural inhabitant of the Wilson Dam area. For more information, visit tva .gov/sites/Wilson.

Afterward follow Veteran's Drive to downtown *Florence,* which features a number of interesting attractions such as the *Indian Mound and Museum* at 1028 South Court Street near the river. The ancient mound looms to a height of 42 feet, the largest of several in the Tennessee Valley. Near the mound, called *Wawmanona* by Native Americans, stands a museum containing displays of tools, ornaments, pottery, fluted points, and other artifacts along with exhibits on the Mississippian culture's mysterious mound builders. Admission: adults $2, students 50 cents. Except for major holidays, the site is open Tuesday through Saturday from 10 a.m. to 4 p.m. For more information call (256) 760-6427.

Nearby, at 601 Riverview Drive, you'll find the *Frank Lloyd Wright's Rosenbaum Museum* (256-740-8899). Conceived by Wright in 1939 and completed in 1940, the home so reflected Wright's iconoclastic approach to organic domestic architecture that Stanley and Mildred Rosenbaum could not find a local contractor to take on this project. Along with his final plans, Wright sent an apprentice to supervise the construction of this Usonian house, now on the National Register of Historic Places.

Designed for a two-acre site overlooking the Tennessee River, the house uses large areas of glass to take advantage of the view and innovative radiant heating because of the proximity of Tennessee Valley Authority's low-cost electricity. "Mr. Wright wanted to use all natural materials," Mrs.

Strange as It Sounds

South of Russellville and west of Phil Campbell (that's the town's name) lies a unique attraction known locally as the Dismals. Located at 901 County Road 8, *Dismals Canyon* once served as a ceremonial ground for Native Americans and a hiding place for outlaws. In addition to caves, waterfalls, craggy rock formations, rainbows, and unusual vegetation, the canyon contains phosphorescent creatures called "dismalites" that glow in the dark. By signing up for a guided night tour, offered Friday and Saturday (the time depends on the degree of darkness), you can actually see the rare dismalites. According to a research scientist from Auburn University, these little glow worms only can be found here in this canyon, New Zealand, or China.

Geologists speculate that a prehistoric earthquake produced the place's chaotic geography with its many natural grottoes and bridges. This eerie but intriguing site also features both a natural arboretum and winding staircase.

After hiking through this place primeval, you may decide to take advantage of other activities—canoeing down Bear Creek, biking a 4-mile mountain trail, or swimming in Dismals Creek. For overnight visitors the site offers lodges (with fireplaces), a country store, and camping facilities. To wet your whistle, take a walk back in time to the Soda Fountain and Grill inside the Country Store. Open every day, the soda fountain offers old-fashioned milk shakes, malts, sundaes, and sodas. Open only on Saturday, the grill features Slug Burgers, corn bread salad, and much more. For more information call (205) 993-4559. Pay a virtual visit via dismalscanyon.com.

Rosenbaum said, "no paint or plaster—only cypress wood, brick, glass, and concrete." After the couple's four sons arrived, Wright designed an addition—its clean lines flow naturally (and imperceptibly) from the original structure. The home is open for tours Tuesday through Saturday from 10 a.m. to 4 p.m. and Sunday from 1 to 4 p.m. Admission: adults $8, senior citizens and students $5. Visit wrightinalabama.com for more information.

To see the birthplace of the "Father of the Blues," head for 620 West College Street, where you'll find the *W. C. Handy Home and Museum* (256-760-6434), fronted by a fence of split rails. The hand-hewn log cabin, birthplace of William Christopher Handy, contains furnishings representative of the period around 1873. The adjoining museum features Handy's legendary trumpet and the piano on which he composed "St. Louis Blues." Handy also wrote more than 150 other musical compositions, including such standards as "Memphis Blues" and "Beale Street Blues." You'll see handwritten sheet music, photographs, correspondence, awards, and other items pertaining to Handy's life and legacy. An addition houses Handy's extensive book collection and serves as a resource center for black history and culture. The museum is open Tuesday through Saturday from 10 a.m. to 4 p.m. Admission: adults $2, students 50 cents.

For a week of swinging jazz, plan to visit Florence from late July to early August and take in the *W. C. Handy Music Festival*. Special events include parades, jam sessions, the "DaDooRunRun" for joggers, a picnic-jazz evening on the Tennessee River's banks, the colorful "Street Strut" led by the Grand Oobeedoo, and a concert with celebrated musicians.

The Handy Festival evolved from a chance meeting in the Muscle Shoals Airport when two men struck up what turned out to be more than a casual conversation. Local veterinarian David Mussleman happened to ask Willie Ruff, a Yale music professor, about the horn he carried. This led to a discussion about native son W. C. Handy and his tremendous musical contribution—and subsequently to the annual festival held in Handy's honor. For more information call the festival office at (256) 766-7642 or visit wchandyfestival.org.

While exploring Florence, you'll pass Wilson Park on the corner of Tuscaloosa Street and Wood Avenue. This setting serves as a backdrop for a number of local festivities, such as the *Alabama Renaissance Faire* (256-740-4141 or 888-356-8687; alarenfaire.org). In fact, if you visit the park during this October gala, you can enjoy diversions ranging from derring-do with sword and shield to music, dance, and drama as residents bring to life some of the color, action, and excitement of the Renaissance period.

Beside the park you'll see the *Kennedy-Douglass Center for the Arts* at 217 East Tuscaloosa Street (256-760-6379). This 1918 Georgian-style mansion and adjacent structures serve as a performing arts center. Stop by to view the current art exhibit and visit the gift shop.

At 316 North Court Street, you'll find *Trowbridge's* (256-764-1503), which offers sandwiches, soups, chili, ice cream, and Oh My Gosh—a brownie piled high with vanilla ice cream and topped with hot caramel, whipped cream, and a cherry. The dessert gets its name from what most people say when they see it.

A mirrored soda fountain lists ice-cream flavors and drink choices. Third-generation owner Don Trowbridge credits the eatery's longevity to keeping the menu simple. Don's grandfather built Trowbridge's Creamery in 1918, and local farmers brought their milk and cream in to be processed. The family occupied the second floor over the ice-cream shop, and the dairy stood behind. The founder's original recipe for Orange-Pineapple Ice Cream, now shipped from New Orleans, remains a favorite with today's patrons.

A large painting on the rear wall depicts Trowbridge's interior from previous years—with almost no changes. Posters publicizing past local festivals pay tribute to Helen Keller and W. C. Handy, "Father of the Blues." Framed photos depict early Florence scenes and the construction of Wilson Dam, which originated as a World War I project to supply power for making munitions. Hours run from 9 a.m. to 5:30 p.m. Monday through Saturday. Economical rates.

A short distance away at 203 Hermitage Drive stands *Pope's Tavern* (256-760-6439), now a history-filled museum. Originally built as a stage-coach stopover and tavern, the attractive structure of white-painted bricks dates to 1811. Travelers on the Natchez Trace stopped here, and so did

Tee Time at the Shoals

The Robert Trent Jones Golf Trail continues to lure golfers from near and far with an unbeatable combination of great golf and value. In the Shoals, you can tee off at two 18-hole championship RTJ courses and dip into a little history, too. Named for Civil War Gen. Joseph Wheeler, the Fighting Joe has earned high marks for new courses from golfing publications and attracts near overflow crowds. The Schoolmaster pays tribute to President Woodrow Wilson, "the schoolmaster" of politics, who was instrumental in getting the Wilson Dam built here. To play either or both of these courses situated between the Wheeler and Wilson Dams on the Tennessee River, call (256) 446-5111. Visit rtjgolf.com or pchresorts.com for more information on the Trail's offerings.

For the record, Florence makes a great starting point if you want to research the new RTJ Spa Trail. Golf widows (and everyone else, too) will appreciate the opportunity to de-stress at this world-class spa. Just look for the soaring tower and head for *Marriott Shoals Hotel & Spa* at 10 Hightower Place (256-246-3600; marriott.com). You'll emerge feeling like you made an eagle.

Andrew Jackson when he passed through in 1814 on his way to fight the British at the Battle of New Orleans. During the Civil War the inn served as a hospital where wounded Confederate and Union soldiers lay side by side to receive medical treatment from local doctors and the townswomen.

Inside the tavern you'll see period furnishings, kitchen utensils, tools, firearms, Civil War uniforms, photos, letters, and pioneer artifacts. Be sure to notice the worn silk Stars and Bars. This flag, hand-stitched by local ladies, traveled to Virginia with the Lauderdale Volunteers (one of northwestern Alabama's first Confederate military units) when they left to fight in the first Battle of Manassas. Before you leave, notice the Florence Light Running Wagon, made in a local factory that at one time was the world's second-largest wagon-building operation. Admission: adults $2, students 50 cents. Except for major holidays, hours are 10 a.m. to 4 p.m. Tuesday through Saturday.

Scenic Wilderness

Leaving the Shoals, you might enjoy taking the **Natchez Trace Parkway.** A portion of the historic Trace cuts across this corner of Alabama through Lauderdale and Colbert Counties. Once a pioneer footpath, this route took travelers from Natchez, Mississippi, to Nashville, Tennessee. To intercept the Trace, which offers plenty of scenic stops, picnic spots, and nature trails, head northwest on State Route 20. For more information, visit nps.gov/natr.

Heading south to **Winfield** takes you to another fascinating attraction, **Natural Bridge** (205-486-5330). Located on US 278 about a mile west of the intersection of State Routes 5 and 13, this double-span, 60-foot-high sandstone bridge, thousands of years in the making, looms majestically in its pristine setting. Surrounding this impressive formation, presumably the longest natural bridge east of the Rockies, you'll see massive moss-covered boulders and lush vegetation. Local flora includes ferns, bigleaf magnolias, mountain laurel, and oakleaf hydrangeas. Inviting nature paths and picnic areas make this a pleasant place for an outing. Admission: adults $3.50, children (ages 6 to 12) $2.50, children (age 5 and under) free. Except for Thanksgiving and Christmas days, the facility is open daily year-round from 8 a.m. till sunset.

Continuing east through Winston County, you'll find the town of **Double Springs,** located in the **William B. Bankhead National Forest.** This huge

Meet Jerry Brown, Ninth-Generation Potter

While exploring this region of scenic wilderness, consider a visit to **Brown's Pottery** (205-921-9483 or 800-341-4919), located at 1414 County Road 81, 3 miles south of Hamilton. Here, Jerry Brown carries on a family tradition of pottery making that spans nine generations. In 1992 Jerry and his wife, Sandra, made a trip to Washington, DC, where he received a National Heritage Fellowship Award, presented by President and Mrs. Bush. Jerry's work is exhibited in galleries across the country as well as the Smithsonian, where he has been invited several times to demonstrate pottery making. The traditional Southern folk potter has captured numerous awards at shows and festivals, and his work is sought by collectors. "Folk pottery increases in value," said Jerry, who signs and dates his pieces. In a "Quest for America's Best," QVC shopping network featured his work on national television. For this show Jerry filled an order for 1,500 pitchers, which sold out in two minutes.

One of the nation's few practicing traditional potters, Jerry remembers "playing around on the potter's wheel before I was old enough to start school." He performs his magic by combining water with local clay, which "looks almost blue. The South is known for its good clay," he added. Using a backhoe to dig the clay from a 150-year-old-pit, Jerry then turns the process over to his four-legged assistant, Blue, who does the mixing by walking circles around a mule powered clay grinder. Jerry designed and built the brick oval kiln, in which he fires his work at temperatures that exceed 3,000 degrees Fahrenheit.

The pottery's showroom features blue-speckled pitchers, bowls, churns, candleholders, crocks, mugs, pie plates, bluebird houses, and more. Face jugs, Jerry's specialty, were historically used to hold harmful substances. Sometimes called ugly jugs, the vessels feature faces that don't win beauty contests but do earn awards and are coveted by collectors. The jugs sell for prices ranging from $30 to $200 and vary in size up to the largest, a five-gallon container. Jerry's newest additions include bacon cookers, egg separators (with faces), and mule mugs. (And yes, the mule's tail serves as the handle.)

Before leaving the pottery, I purchased several gifts. The crocks do double duty, Jerry pointed out, demonstrating how to use the container's lip to sharpen a knife. Even now as I write, I am drinking coffee from a thick mug with a blue, feathered design. (Ask Jerry to tell you the story of how a mishap with flying chicken feathers inspired one of his popular patterns.)

To view the pottery-making process as it was done in the olden days or to buy unique gifts (for yourself and others), head to Hamilton, near the Mississippi border. The Pottery's hours run from 9 a.m. to 5 p.m. Monday through Saturday, Sunday by appointment only.

On the Coon Dog Trail

Way off the beaten path in northwest Alabama, the *Key Underwood Coon Dog Memorial Graveyard* projects a sense of serenity—at least for 364 days of the year. But that changes each Labor Day when this site, located beyond Tuscumbia and near tiny Cherokee, attracts a throng of visitors for a rollicking celebration.

Festivities include an afternoon of live bluegrass music, buck dancing, and a liars' contest. "And they can really tell some whoppers," said one visitor. If it's an election year, political hopefuls often show up for this occasion.

Now a park, the site features markers and tombstones for more than 185 coon dogs—with each grave decorated on Labor Day. The graveyard's origin dates to the death of Troop, a famous coonhound owned by Key Underwood. On September 4, 1937, Underwood and some friends buried his faithful coon dog in this wooded area, where they often congregated to compare dogs, spin yarns, and launch their hunts. On an average day, the surroundings look pretty much like they did way back when Troop picked up the scent of a coon here.

"When I buried Troop, I had no intention of establishing a coon dog cemetery," Underwood said. "I merely wanted to do something special for a special coon dog." Other hunters started doing the same when their favorite coon dogs died. Take time to walk around and read the names and tributes. Hunter's Famous Amos, a hound named Ralston Purina's Dog of the Year in 1984, is buried here as well as several World Champion coon dogs. Others honored include Preacher, Old Blue, Queen, Patches, Smoky, Barney, Bean Blossom Bomma, Bluetick, Old Roy, Strait Talk'n Tex, and Night Ranger.

Some headstones contain only names and dates. On others, the owners memorialize their dogs with such tributes as "A joy to hunt with" and "He wasn't the best, but he was the best I ever had." Black Ranger, who died in 1976, "was good as the best and better than the rest." Monuments range from those made of wood and sheet metal to field stones and marble.

forest (named for the distinguished political family of actress Tallulah Bankhead) spreads over most of Winston County and north into Lawrence County.

In front of the Winston County Courthouse at Double Springs stands *Dual Destiny,* the statue of a Civil War soldier flanked by billowing Confederate and Union flags. Contrary to common assumption, many Alabamians remained staunch Unionists during the Civil War, and "the Free State of Winston" represented such a contingent. After Alabama's secession (which

Only bona fide coon dogs can qualify for burial in this unique cemetery, and three requirements must be met: First, the owner needs to claim his pet is an authentic coon dog and present proper credentials. Then a witness, who has observed the animal tree a coon in the past, must declare the deceased is indeed a coon dog. Finally, a member of the local coon hunters' organization must be allowed to view the coonhound and verify it as such.

"It is good to see a place like this exists. I bet there are a hundred stories to go along with each gravestone," reads an entry in the Coon Dog Cemetery guestbook on the Web. (Yes, it's true. You can visit the Coon Dog Memorial Graveyard at coondogcemetery.com for photos and comments or call 256-412-5970.)

Another reader observes, "The younger generation of today will never know just how great the sport is because of the expansion of the cities into rural America and a sport that is slowly dying."

Apparently, many moviegoers from across the country learned of the cemetery's existence while watching *Sweet Home Alabama*. Using their literary license, however, the producers placed the Coon Dog Graveyard in south Alabama.

Labor Day visitors can dig into some finger-licking Southern barbeque—free for those who belong to the Tennessee Valley Coon Hunters Association, and membership applications are available on the spot. Otherwise, attendees can purchase barbecue plates. Soft drinks and bottled water along with T-shirts and caps featuring the Coon Dog Graveyard logo are for sale for this occasion, but don't forget your lawn chair. Admission is free. Coon hunters will want to put this event on their list, and maybe you will, too—especially if you're running for office.

For a brochure, call (256) 383-0783 or (800) 344-0783 and check out colbert countytourism.org for more information on other attractions in Colbert County. To reach the Coon Dog Graveyard, head 7 miles west of Tuscumbia on US 72 and turn left on Alabama Highway 247. Then travel 12.8 miles and turn right. Continue 5 miles, following signs to this attraction. The site is open year-round during daylight hours.

passed by a narrow vote), these hill-country people, led by local teacher Christopher Sheats, took the position that if a state could secede from the Union, then a county could secede from a state.

While visiting the Free State of Winston, take time to explore some of the surrounding **Sipsey Wilderness.** With 25,988 acres, Sipsey provides plenty of off-the-beaten-path territory, including 20 miles of hiking trails.

Afterward take US 278 east and head toward Cullman.

Covered Bridge Country

To see Alabama's largest covered truss bridge, continue east from Winston County on US 278. Watch for the left turn to **Clarkson Covered Bridge** (sometimes called the Legg Bridge), located a short distance north of the highway on Cullman County Road 11. The bridge, situated in a picturesque park setting, stretches 270 feet across Crooked Creek. Supported by four large stone piers, this "town-truss" structure features latticed timbers, clapboard siding, and a roof of cedar shingles. The bridge, restored in 1975, dates to 1904.

Once the site of a Civil War battle, the surrounding area offers picnic grounds and woodland hiking trails. During our visit my husband and I met a man who showed us a gum tree with a carving—a message left for him by a fellow Cherokee some 35 years earlier. The park is open year-round, and there's no admission charge.

Continuing east on US 278 takes you to **Cullman,** a city that dates to 1873 when Col. John G. Cullmann bought a large tract of land and established a colony for German immigrants here. A reproduction of the founder's Bavarian-style home (which burned in 1912) now serves as the **Cullman County Museum** (256-739-1258 or 800-533-1258), located at 211 Second Avenue Northeast. The museum's eight rooms, each with a theme, preserve some of the city's German heritage and the area's history. You'll see a 7-foot wooden sculpture of a Native American warrior, china, jewelry, vintage clothing, fainting couches, early tools, and other local items. Admission: adults $5, senior citizens $4, children (under age 12) $3. Hours run from 8 a.m. to 4 p.m. Monday through Friday. Sunday hours are 1:30 to 4:30 p.m. Visit cullmancountymuseum.com for more information.

For a good meal, stop by **The All Steak** (256-734-4322; theallsteak restaurant.com), located just a few blocks away on 323 Third Avenue Southwest. Contrary to its name, the restaurant serves a wide variety of entrees, including seafood and poultry. In addition to its beef specialties, the eatery is famous for homemade breads and desserts, especially the orange rolls, as well as its vegetable lunches. Prices are moderate. Hours are 10:30 a.m. to 10 p.m. Tuesday through Friday and 7:30 a.m. to 10 p.m. on Saturday. Sunday's schedule is 7:30 a.m. to 3 p.m.

Sample a bit of Cullman's heritage by stepping into **A Touch of German** (256-739-4592) at 218 First Avenue Southeast. Here, you'll be greeted by owner Peggy Grobe plus a flock of chirping birds popping out of their cuckoo clock homes to remind you that time is passing much too fast to browse through all the city's great shops.

Peggy stocks European and American collectibles such as handcrafted nutcrackers, music boxes, German and European Christmas ornaments, Steiff stuffed bears, table linens, laces, tapestries, Dutch blue delftware, Bavarian steins, scrumptious chocolate, Russian nested dolls, Reuge music boxes, and more. Hours run Monday through Saturday from 10 a.m. to 5 p.m.

Continue a few steps farther to *The Duchess Bakery* and pick up some doughnuts. This family-owned business at 222 First Avenue Southeast opened in 1939.

At *Southern Accents* (256-734-0684 or 877-737-0554), you'll find an array of architectural antiques—everything from carved mantels, leaded-glass windows, statuary, and stately columns to chandeliers, hitching posts, molding, staircases, and claw-foot bathtubs. Housed in historic quarters at 308 Second Avenue Southeast, the inventory draws clients from across the US. Owner Garlan Gudger Jr. searches the globe for treasures from the past. His father, Dr. Garlan Gudger, started the business in 1969 when he began rescuing architectural objects from local buildings slated to be demolished. Gudger offers an antique floor salvaging and cutting service plus door and window framing, which makes today's carpenters happy.

A sign near the entrance reads: YOUR HUSBAND CALLED . . . HE SAID TO BUY ANYTHING YOU WANT. (I especially admired a Victorian cherry parlor mantel, wearing a SOLD sign and soon to be shipped to New York.) Hours run Tuesday through Friday 9 a.m. to 5 p.m., Saturday 10 a.m. to 4 p.m. Take a look at sa1969.com and order anything you want.

"We will serve no swine before its time," promise Ron Dunn and Gary Wiggins, first cousins who operate *Johnny's Bar-B-Q* (256-734-8539; johnnysbarbq.com), a family business at 1404 Fourth Street Southwest that opened in the early 1950s. Here, you can opt for a barbecue sandwich or a plate with all the fixings: coleslaw, beans, and potato salad. Other popular items include smoked chicken with white barbecue sauce, catfish, or barbecue-topped baked

alabamatrivia

Cullman, known as the City of Churches, has more than 200 churches within its city limits.

potatoes. "Closed on Sunday for church and closed on Monday for rest," the restaurant's hours run Tuesday through Saturday from 10 a.m. to 9 p.m. Economical rates.

Afterward continue to 1600 Saint Bernard Drive Southeast, off US 278, on the town's east side. At *Ave Maria Grotto* (256-734-4110), on the grounds of a Benedictine monastery, visitors can take a Lilliputian world tour in a unique garden filled with more than 150 miniature reproductions of famous landmarks. Brother Joseph Zoettl, a Bavarian who arrived at St. Bernard Abbey in 1892, constructed these reduced versions of various buildings. At age 80 the gifted monk completed his final work, the Lourdes Basilica. His architectural miniatures also include the Hanging Gardens of Babylon, ancient Jerusalem, Rome's Pantheon, and St. Peter's Basilica.

Using ingenuity and an unlikely assortment of materials, from playing marbles and fishing floats to cold-cream jars and even a discarded bird cage (for the dome of St. Peter's), along with the more standard cement, limestone, and marble, Brother Joe fashioned a small world that continues to delight travelers. Check it out at avemariagrotto.com. Except for Christmas and New Year's Days, the grotto can be visited daily from 9 a.m. to 5 p.m. October through March, and to 6 p.m. April through September. Admission: adults $7, children (ages 6 to 12) $4.50.

alabamatrivia

Cullman acquired the title "Die Deutsche Kolonie von Nord Alabama" because the town's founder, Col. John G. Cullmann, who came from Frankweiler, Germany, attracted approximately 10,000 German settlers to north Alabama.

In south Cullman County near Hanceville, you can make a personal pilgrimage to *The Shrine of the Most Blessed Sacrament of Our Lady of the Angels Monastery.* To reach the shrine, take State Route 91 through Hanceville, watching for signs that lead to County Road 747 and then to County Road 548. A long, white-fenced approach winds through a portion of the site's 380 acres of rolling farmland. More than three years in construction, the shrine opened in December 1999, and has become a major mecca for visitors. Home to the Poor Clare Nuns of Perpetual Adoration, the building of this facility was dear to the heart of Mother Angelica, founder of the Eternal Word Television Network (EWTN).

The shrine's Romanesque–Gothic style of architecture echoes Franciscan churches and monasteries of 13th-century Assisi. To reach the shrine, you'll cross an expansive colonaded piazza. As you approach, notice the T-shaped cross. The original top portion was struck by lightning, leaving the form of a Tau cross, the symbol that St. Francis used in signing his letters.

From inlaid Italian-marble floors and stately columns to vaulted ceiling, the awe-inspiring interior leaves no detail to chance. Made of carved cedar, the main altar is covered in gold leaf. The stained-glass windows were created in Munich, Germany, and the stonework embellishments were crafted by artisans in Spain. Other features include mosaics fashioned by Italian artisans using a four-century-old method of hand-chiseling and fitting.

Castle San Miguel stands below the piazza and houses a great hall, conference facilities, and a gift shop; hours are Monday through Saturday from 8 a.m. to 4:45 p.m. The shrine is open to the public from 6 a.m. to 6 p.m. on Sunday and until 9:30 p.m. Monday through Saturday. The nuns' Conventual Mass takes place at 7 a.m. daily. To learn more about the circumstances that led to the erection of this magnificent structure in the hills of Alabama, you can attend one of the brothers' commentaries, generally scheduled at 9 a.m. daily, depending on the crowd. For more information call (256) 352-6267 or visit olamshrine.com, where you will find a map and specific directions.

For a relaxing base on crystal blue waters, head to Crane Hill and **Smith Lake Bed & Breakfast** (256-747-6057). Located at 994 County Road 4230 and situated on the Rock Creek branch of the finger-shaped Lewis Smith Lake (the nation's third cleanest), the property promises all the amenities laced with warm hospitality and gorgeous natural surroundings, plus water recreation.

Owners Alexandra (better known as Alex) and Jim Cox offer two suites, the Loft and the Dock, and a vintage Airstream trailer. Both suites have balconies overlooking the lake—wonderful spots for sipping your morning coffee. Jim's job as a civil engineer took the couple to countries all over the world, including Germany, Israel, Saudi Arabia, and Japan. During the decade they lived in Japan, Alex taught cooking classes and conversational English to Japanese ladies and started thinking about a B&B of her own when she returned to the States. Now, that's a reality, and guests can enjoy this inviting getaway filled with antiques and fine Asian art.

Breakfast here starts with a fresh fruit medley and might feature quiche or stuffed French toast. Alex offers information on area restaurants, but some guests enjoy grilling their own dinner while watching a sunset. Perfect for couples or families, the suites can accommodate four comfortably, and the owners welcome kids. When weather permits, Jim takes guests out on his pontoon boat and also provides a double kayak and bikes for their use. The couple will send you to interesting spots nearby, perhaps to an artist's studio in Crane Hill or a year-round trout fishery in Jasper or to nearby Bankhead National Forest with its miles of hiking and biking trails. Visit smithlake bandb.com and check out the views. Moderate rates.

Continue east on US 278 until it intersects US 231, then turn south to see the **Blount County Covered Bridges.** Known as the Covered Bridge Capital of Alabama, this area features three covered bridges, all still in daily use and marked by road signs on nearby highways. If you're on a tight schedule, choose the Horton Mill Covered Bridge, probably the most picturesque of the bunch. Located about 5 miles north of Oneonta on State Route 75, the latticed structure looms some 70 feet above the Warrior River's Calvert Prong—higher above water than any other covered bridge in the US. Adjacent to the highway there's a parking area with nearby picnic facilities and nature trails, making this a relaxing place to take a driving break.

Continuing your exploration, you'll find the county's shortest covered bridge southeast of Rosa. The 95-foot-long, tin-topped Easley Covered Bridge stands about a half-mile off Blount County Road 33 and spans Dub Branch.

Northwest of Cleveland, 1 mile off State Route 79, Swann Bridge appears rather suddenly as you're rounding a curve. The three-span bridge extends 324 feet over the Locust Fork of the Black Warrior River. You can park in a turn-off lane on the bridge's opposite side to explore the nearby terrain, where Queen Anne's lace, ferns, mountain laurel, wild hydrangeas, and muscadine vines grow. You might hear a mockingbird's serenade in the background.

Each October on the fourth weekend, the **Oneonta** area stages an annual **Covered Bridge Festival** featuring bridge tours, arts and crafts exhibits, and other festivities. For additional information on the festival, award-winning Palisades Park, or other area attractions, call the Blount County/Oneonta Chamber of Commerce at (205) 274-2153.

Before leaving Blount County, head to *The Benedikt Restaurant* (205-274-0230; thebenediktrestaurant.com), located at 4125 Blount County Road 27, about 8 miles southeast of Oneonta on Straight Mountain. Some folks just stumble on the restaurant by accident while taking a scenic drive; others make a deliberate effort, traveling regularly from Birmingham and surrounding areas to eat here. The restaurant's Sunday meal is served "buffeteria" style.

On her menu, Ruth Benedikt writes, "Ladies and Gentlemen, we are 12th generation Charlestonians: Scotch, Irish and German. Our recipes belong to our mother, aunts, grandmother and all who came before them." Sister "Ms. Joice" has prepared family recipes for the public for three decades and considers herself "among the last of the scratch cooks in the restaurant business."

Choices might include German pot roast, golden fried chicken, or ham steak along with side dishes of real mashed potatoes, mixed broccoli-cauliflower with cheese sauce, sweet tomato relish, fresh creamed corn, purple hull peas, and fried green tomatoes in season. In addition to regular menu items, on Friday night a catfish bar features this specialty prepared seven different ways. A barbecue bar supplements the Saturday night menu.

The eatery is open Friday and Saturday from 8:30 a.m. to 8:30 p.m. and Sunday from 8:30 a.m. to 3:30 p.m. Call the Benedikts for Sunday reservations. Rates are economical to moderate.

Across the road at *Capps Cove* (205-625-6045 or 800-583-4750), you'll find a country getaway with a mountain on one side and a river on the other. Located at 4126 Blount County Road 27, the complex offers two cabins and much, much more. Owners Sybil and Cason Capps, native Alabamians who lived in several states over 15 years before moving back to Alabama from St. Louis when Cason retired from a broadcasting career.

"We think we're unique," Sybil says, "a country village with a barn, wedding chapel, and two old-style country cabins." Guests can enjoy a continental breakfast basket. Moderate rates. Visit the property at cappscove.com.

Continue to the state's central section. Nearby Ashville, easily reached by taking US 231 south, makes an interesting stop.

Places to Stay in Northwest Alabama

ATHENS

Country Hearth Inn
1500 US 72 East
(256) 232-1520 or
(888) 443-2784

CRANE HILL

Smith Lake Bed & Breakfast
994 County Rd. 4230
(256) 747-6057
smithlakebandb.com

CULLMAN

Hampton Inn
6100 State Rte. 157
(256) 739-4444 or
(800) 426-7866

DECATUR

Comfort Inn & Suites
2212 Danville Rd.
(256) 355-1999 or
(800) 424-6423

Courtyard by Marriott
1209 Courtyard Circle
(256) 355-4446 or (800) 321-2211

Garden Plaza Hotel & Suites
1101 Sixth Ave. NE
(256) 355-3150 or
(800) 553-3150
hidecaturalabama.com

Hampton Inn
2041 Beltline Rd.
(256) 355-5888 or
(800) 426-7866

FLORENCE

Marriott Shoals Hotel & Spa
800 Cox Creek Parkway South
(256) 246-3600 or
(800) 593-6450

ONEONTA

Capps Cove
4126 County Rd. 27
(205) 625-6045 or
(800) 583-4750
cappscove.com

ROGERSVILLE

Joe Wheeler State Park Lodge
4401 McLean Dr.
(256) 247-5461 or
(800) 544-5639 or
(800) 252-7275

TOWN CREEK

Doublehead Resort & Lodge
145 County Rd. 314
(800) 685-9267
doublehead.com

TUSCUMBIA

The ColdWater Inn
712 US 72
(256) 383-6844
coldwater-inn.com

Key West Inn
1800 US 72 West
(256) 383-0700 or
(800) 833-0555

WINFIELD

Hampton Inn & Suites
505 S. Court St.
(256) 767-8282

Places to Eat in Northwest Alabama

CULLMAN

The All Steak
323 Third Ave. SW
(256) 734-4322
theallsteakrestaurant.com

Johnny's Bar-B-Q
1404 Fourth St. SW
(256) 734-8539
johnnysbarbq.com

Rumors Deli
105 First Ave. NE
Suite 100
(256) 737-0911
rumorsdeli.com

DECATUR

Big Bob Gibson Bar-B-Q
1715 Sixth Ave. SE
(256) 350-6969
bigbobgibson.com

Cafe 113
113 Grant St.
(256) 351-1400
cafe113.com

FOR MORE INFORMATION ABOUT NORTHWEST ALABAMA

Alabama Mountain Lakes Tourist Association
402 Sherman St. SE
Decatur 35602
(256) 350-3500 or (800) 648-5381
northalabama.org
This organization covers 16 north Alabama counties that are home to some 100 attractions in a 100-mile radius.

Colbert County Tourism & Convention Bureau
719 Hwy. 72 West
PO Box 740425
Tuscumbia 35674
(256) 383-0783
colbertcountytourism.org

Cullman Area Chamber of Commerce
301 Second Ave. SW
Cullman 35055
(256) 734-0454 or (800) 313-5114
cullmanchamber.org
info@cullmanchamber.org

Decatur/Morgan County Convention & Visitors Bureau
719 Sixth Ave. SE
PO Box 2349
Decatur 35601
(256) 350-2028 or (800) 232-5449
decaturcvb.org
info@decaturcvb.org

Florence/Lauderdale Tourism
One Hightower Place
Florence 35630
(256) 740-4141 or (888) 356-8687
flo-tour.org
visitflorenceal.com

Curry's on Johnston Street
115 Johnston St. SE
(256) 350-6715
currysrestaurant.com

Simp McGhee's
725 Bank St. NE
(256) 353 6284
simpmcghees.com

Simply Delicious
2215 Danville Rd., SW
(256) 355-7564
wearesimplydelicious.com

DOUBLE SPRINGS

Sapore Grill
26641 Hwy. 195
(205) 489-1172
saporegrill.com

FLORENCE

Ricatoni's Italian Grill
107 North Court St.
(256) 718-1002
ricatonivalentino.com

Trowbridge's
316 North Court St.
(256) 764-1503

The 360 Grill
One Hightower Place
(256) 246-3660

HALEYVILLE

Cazadores
1918 21st St.
(205) 486-2108

MAINSTREAM ATTRACTIONS WORTH SEEING IN NORTHWEST ALABAMA

Alabama Music Hall of Fame
617 US 72 West
Tuscumbia
(256) 381-4417 or (800) 239-2643
You can immerse yourself in the state's musical heritage at this facility, which features exhibits, audiovisual galleries, and memorabilia related to musicians either from Alabama or associated with the state. Artists represented include Hank Williams, Elvis Presley, Emmylou Harris, the Temptations, and many others. For a little music and a Web tour of the museum, click on alamhof .org.

Point Mallard Park
2901 Point Mallard Cir.
Decatur
(256) 341-4900
Named for nearby Wheeler National Wildlife Refuge's wintering ducks, this park for all seasons offers aquatic fun in the summer and year-round golfing on a championship course. You may even see Capt. Mike Mallard, a human-size mascot in nautical attire, wandering about. Not only does the 750-acre complex contain a wave pool, an Olympic-size diving pool, water slides, sand beach, and "Squirt Factory," you'll also find a 173-acre campground, hiking and biking trails, and picnicking facilities here. For more information, visit pointmallardpark.com.

HARTSELLE

The Freight House
200 Railroad St. SW
(256) 773-4600
freighthousecatering.com

Las Vias Mexican Grill
711 Nance Ford Rd. SW
(256) 751-1402
lasviasmexicangrill.com

MOULTON

Western Sirloin Steak House
11383 State Rte. 157
(256) 974-7191

Muscle Shoals

New Orleans Transfer
1682 South Wilson Dam Rd.
(256) 386-0656

ONEONTA

The Benedikt Restaurant
4125 Blount County County Rd. 27
(205) 274-0230
thebenediktrestaurant .com

SHEFFIELD

George's Steak Pit
1206 Jackson Hwy.
(256) 381-1531
georgessteakpit.com

TUSCUMBIA

Claunch Cafe
400 South Main St.
(in Spring Park)
(256) 386-0222

CENTRAL ALABAMA

Ridges, Springs, & Valleys

Alabama's midsection presents a pleasing pastoral land-scape, a panorama of ridges, springs, and valleys. Heading south, the Birmingham area serves as a convenient base from which to branch out into the state's central region. From here, too, you can easily sweep down into Alabama's southeastern section to explore the historic *Chattahoochee Trace* (877-766-2443; chattahoocheetrace.com) as well as the state capital area.

Start your area exploration with a trip to downtown *Ashville,* home of one of St. Clair County's two courthouses (the other is in Pell City). This neoclassical revival structure, an enlargement of an earlier courthouse, dates from the early 1840s.

A charming southern town, Ashville offers many historic structures. Start off at the circa-1852 *Inzer House* at 229 Fifth Street, a striking structure now reincarnated as a Civil War museum, the John W. Inzer Museum (205-338-2412). A number of black cast-iron Confederate crosses dot the grounds of nearby *Ashville Cemetery.*

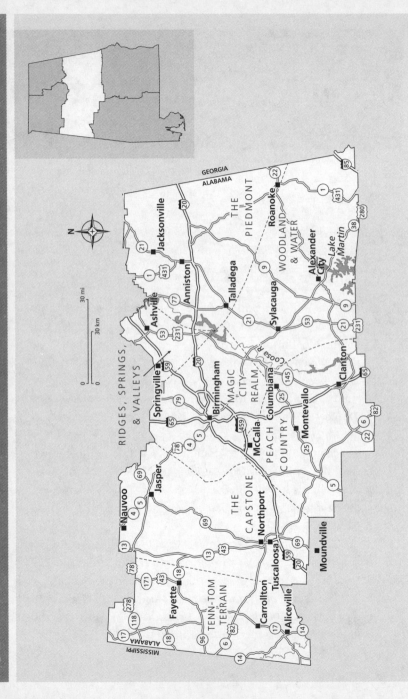

GEORGIA
ALABAMA

THE PIEDMONT

WOODLAND & WATER

Jacksonville

Anniston

Talladega

Sylacauga

Roanoke

Alexander City

Lake Martin

Ashville

Springville

Birmingham

MAGIC CITY REALM

McCalla

Columbiana

Montevallo

Clanton

PEACH COUNTRY

RIDGES, SPRINGS, & VALLEYS

Coosa R

Nauvoo

Jasper

THE CAPSTONE

Northport

Tuscaloosa

Moundville

Fayette

Carrollton

Aliceville

TENN-TOM TERRAIN

MISSISSIPPI
ALABAMA

N

30 mi

30 km

BEST ATTRACTIONS IN CENTRAL ALABAMA

Aliceville Museum, Aliceville	**McWane Science Center,** Birmingham
The American Village, Montevallo	**Moundville Archaeological Park,** Moundville
Anniston Museum of Natural History, Anniston	**Paul W. Bryant Museum,** Tuscaloosa
Birmingham Civil Rights Institute, Birmingham	**Tannehill Historical State Park,** McCalla
DeSoto Caverns Park, Childersburg	**The Westervelt Warner Museum of American Art,** Tuscaloosa
International Motorsports Hall of Fame, Talladega	

To learn more about local history, drive out to see the *John Looney House,* one of Alabama's oldest two-story log dogtrot structures. (The term "dogtrot" refers to a central hallway connecting two rooms also known as "pens." Although covered, this passage was left open and often proved a popular napping place for the family canines, hence its name.) Located a little over 4 miles southeast of Ashville on St. Clair County Road 24, this rare example of pioneer architecture dating to about 1820 may be visited on weekends. Current hours are Saturday and Sunday from 9 a.m. to 4 p.m. during June through August. Modest admission. For more information, call (205) 629-6897.

While in Ashville, stop by the *Ashville House Quilt Shop* (35 Third St.; 205-594-7046; ashvillehousequiltshop.com), with its wonderful display of quilts, fabrics, notions and other items. The shop also offers quilting lessons. For a tasty snack, visit *The Two Sisters Homestyle Cafe* (36438 Hwy 231; 205-594-5777). The cafe is known for its fried chicken, roast beef, and chicken salad, which often sells out.

From Ashville take State Route 23 south until you reach US 11 leading to *Springville,* a town that takes its name from several area springs. First called Big Springs and settled about 1817, the town became Springville with the post office's establishment in 1834; the entire downtown district is on the National Historic Register.

Take time to explore some of this state historic district's nostalgic shops. Nearby *Homestead Hollow* (205-467-3681, homesteadhollow.com), a 55-acre pioneer homestead with a blacksmith shop, log cabin, barn, and gristmill, serves as a quaint backdrop for art-and-craft festivals throughout the year. During such events, visitors may sample sorghum and apple cider made on the premises.

The Piedmont

Located in the Appalachian foothills, Calhoun County occupies a portion of the state's Piedmont region. Start your tour in *Anniston,* an attractive, arts-oriented city that named William Shakespeare its citizen of the year in 1984—before the Alabama Shakespeare Festival left its birthplace here and moved to Montgomery.

"It's your world. Explore it!" urges the staff at the *Anniston Museum of Natural History* (256-237-6766; annistonmuseum.org), located a couple of miles from downtown at 800 Museum Drive. Some adventures promised by the museum's slogan include treks through jungles, deserts, and savannahs at this handsome facility surrounded by 187 acres on Anniston's northern outskirts. Entering the museum's Lagarde African Hall, you'll see a rogue elephant keeping vigil beside a towering baobab tree (the world's largest replica of an "upside-down" tree). Preserved specimens of more than a hundred creatures inhabit this African complex, most collected by Annistonian John B. Lagarde, a big-game hunter who donated his award-winning assemblage to the museum.

From antelope to zebras, all animals appear in the most realistic habitats possible. And through it all visitors see the versatility with which nature's creatures adapt to their world. Every effort has been made to achieve the effect of authenticity; for example, light in the bamboo forest filters through a type of Venetian blind to create a network of slanted rays.

Spacious corridors wind from the African depths to the Ornithology Hall with its impressive array of more than 600 specimens of North American birds, many now either extinct or on the endangered species list. Naturalist

Strange as It Sounds

Deadly beauty and intrigue await at the *Berman Museum* (256-237-6261) in Anniston's LaGarde Park. Here you'll find an arsenal of rare weapons collected from all over the world by a former secret agent. Suits of armor that now stand still once clanked as knights did battle. Beheading axes and swords from ancient China and Japan hang in silence—not divulging their roles in past dastardly deeds.

A stunning royal Persian scimitar set with 1,295 rose-cut diamonds, 60 carats of rubies, and an exquisite 40-carat emerald in a three-pound gold handle mesmerizes sightseers here just as it once did Russian audiences during the reign of Catherine the Great. Other rare items include a Greek helmet dating to 300 BC. Jefferson Davis's traveling pistols, Adolf Hitler's silver tea service, and Napoleon Bonaparte's ivory comb and brush set. Also displayed is a saber used in the dramatic "Charge of the Light Brigade." The collection contains 88 guns from the American West, Fraser's famous *End of the Trail* sculpture, and bronzes by Frederic Remington, Charles Russell, and Karl Kauba.

Army colonel Farley Lee Berman worked in counterintelligence, and he and his wife, Germaine (a Parisian with a comparable position in French Intelligence), met during World War II. Afterward they traveled the world on a decades-long quest for historical weapons and art.

Personnel from several metropolitan museums approached Berman about acquiring his collection, but he chose to donate it to the city of Anniston, saying he knew "the people of Alabama would enjoy it." Located at 840 Museum Drive next to the Museum of Natural History, the Berman Museum's hours run from 10 a.m. to 5 p.m. Monday through Saturday, and 1 to 5 p.m. Sunday from June through August; Tuesday through Saturday from 10 a.m. to 5 p.m. and Sunday from 1 to 5 p.m. from September through May. Admission: adults $5, senior citizens $4.50, children (ages 4 to 17) $4, and children (age 3 and under) free.

William Werner assembled this priceless bird collection more than a century ago, and several diorama groupings include nests (some with eggs) built by the birds themselves. The museum boasts one of the world's finest models of a pteranadon, a prehistoric flying reptile with a 30-foot wingspan. In Dynamic Earth Hall, which features a life-size model of an albertosaurus, you can explore an Alabama cave complete with waterfall, stalactites, and stalagmites. The museum's newest hall, "Alabama: Sand to Cedars," features a walk through the state from seashore to mountains. NatureSpace encourages children to explore beyond backyard boundaries with a unique exhibit of natural resources.

Accredited by the American Association of Museums and a Smithsonian affiliate, the Anniston facility has received national recognition for its innovative participatory exhibits. The museum also offers rotating art exhibits, a fine gift shop, picnicking facilities, and several nature trails, including the recently added Bird of Prey Trail. The museum is open Tuesday through Saturday from 10 a.m. to 5 p.m. (plus Monday during summer) and Sunday from 1 to 5 p.m. Admission: adults $6, senior citizens $5.50, children (ages 4 to 17) $3, children (age 3 and under) free.

Don't miss the historic Episcopal **Church of St. Michael and All Angels** (256-237-4011) at 800 Museum Drive on West 18th Street at Cobb Avenue. With an exterior of Alabama stone, this 1888 Norman-Gothic structure features a magnificent marble altar backed by an alabaster *reredos* (ornamental screen). Bavarian woodworkers carved the church's entire ceiling by hand, and angels on corbels all face the altar at slightly different angles. Admission: adults $6, senior citizens $5.50, children (ages 4 to 17) $5, and children (age 3 and under) free. You can visit year-round between 10 a.m. and 5 p.m. Tuesday through Saturday, and 1 to 5 p.m. Sunday.

Take time to drive through the Tyler Hill Historic District and along tree-lined Quintard Avenue, where you'll see grand Victorian homes. At one such mansion, **The Victoria Inn** (256-236-0503), you can drop in for a fine meal or an overnight stay. Look for a turreted, three-story structure, painted taupe and trimmed in white with a burgundy awning covering a walkway in front, on a hill at 1604 Quintard Avenue. This 1888 home, donated to Jacksonville State University in December 2008, has served as a country inn for two decades. Accommodations include three lovely suites—decorated in period antiques—in the main house, a guest house, and a tasteful addition containing 56 rooms (all with private baths) connected to the inn by covered walkways.

alabamatrivia

Alabama's name comes from a Native American tribe, the Alibamu.

The menu changes seasonally but always includes steak and fresh seafood—and by popular demand, the jumbo lump crab cakes. Appetizers might range from the chef's daily soup creation to fried green tomatoes with

Much Ado in Anniston

For our first anniversary, friends invited my husband and me to visit them in Anniston and take in some plays. At that time summer visitors to Anniston—the birthplace of the Alabama Shakespeare Festival (ASF)—could watch actors "strut and fret their hour upon the stage" in five rotating weekend productions.

Martin L. Platt came from Carnegie Mellon University to direct the community theater and soon started the festival, which attracted throngs each summer. He personally picked the performers, auditioning many of them in New York.

I remember the gorgeous costumes, noted for their quality of workmanship. In a production of *Romeo and Juliet,* for instance, the Capulets were clothed in various shades of bronze and the Montagues in lavender and rose tones, enabling the audience to easily identify members of the feuding families. Gifted ASF Guild members spent countless volunteer hours hand-sewing seed pearls on dress hems or crocheting an army's "chain" mail headgear. Other Guild members found or provided lodging for actors, stuffed envelopes, ushered playgoers, or baked cookies for "meet the cast" parties.

We enjoyed immersing ourselves in the Elizabethan era by attending "Shakespeare Sundays" at the historic Church of St. Michael and All Angels. Filled with pomp and splendor, these services featured the use of a 1559 prayer book and the talents of the festival's company.

We continued to spend each anniversary in Anniston seeing ASF productions until the festival moved to its magnificent home in Montgomery and became a year round theater. Although we still see occasional plays (Montgomery is much farther from our home), we miss those special summers. And on each wedding anniversary, we propose a toast to Shakespeare and all the wonderful times the curtain went up in Anniston.

lime crème fraîche and tasso ham. The Victoria also offers a wide selection of wines. Prices are moderate to expensive.

The Victoria Inn is open to the public for dinner from 5:30 to 9:30 p.m. Tuesday through Saturday. Lunch is served Thursday and Friday from 11 a.m. to 2 p.m. and champagne brunch is featured on Saturday from 10 a.m. to 2 p.m. Guests can enjoy a bountiful breakfast buffet in the main house. Moderate rates. Visit the inn at thevictoria.com.

Sometime during your stay stroll down to the old carriage house on the grounds, now home to an art gallery called **Wren's Nest** (256-238-0710;

larrykmartin.com), which has original works and limited prints by noted wildlife artist Larry K. Martin.

While in the area, head to *Munford* via State Route 21 for a visit to *Talladega National Forest, Cheaha State Park,* and other nearby spots for nature lovers. After basking in the country's serenity, head to nearby *Talladega* and immerse yourself in history. If you take the Jackson Trace Road, you'll follow a wagon route cut by Gen. Andrew Jackson and his Tennessee Volunteers as they marched southward through the Creek Indian nation. For a self-guided driving map of the town's historical sites, head to the Greater Talladega and Lincoln Area Chamber of Commerce office (256-362-9075; talladegachamber.com), just off the courthouse square in the old L&N Depot at 210 East Street. Start with the Silk Stocking District (outlined on your map), a sizable concentration of homes listed on the National Register of Historic Places. Stop by *Heritage Hall Museum* (256-761-1364;

TOP ANNUAL EVENTS IN CENTRAL ALABAMA

Sakura Festival
Tuscaloosa, March
(800) 538-8696

Dogwood Festival
Aliceville, second weekend of April
(205) 373-2820

Operation New Birmingham
Magic City Art Connection
Linn Park, Birmingham, April
(205) 595-6306
magiccityart.com

Dickens Downtown
Northport, first Tuesday in December
(205) 339-7000
cityofnorthport.org

Heritage Week
Tuscaloosa, third week in April
(800) 538-8696

Kentuck Festival of the Arts
Kentuck Park, Northport, mid-October
(205) 758-1257
kentuck.org

Moundville Native American Festival
Moundville Archaeological Park,
October
(205) 371-8732
moundville.ua.edu

**Geico 500 Talladega
Superspeedway**
Talladega, October
(877) GO2DEGA
talladegasuperspeedway.com

Christmas Village Festival
Birmingham-Jefferson Convention
Complex Exhibition Hall, Birmingham
first weekend in November
(205) 836-7178 or (800) 458-8085
christmasvillagefestival.com

heritagchallmuseum.org), a restored 1908 Carnegie Library at 200 South Street East, for a look at its current exhibits. The museum is open Tuesday through Friday from 10 a.m. to 4 p.m. Afterward drive by *Talladega College* at 627 Battle Street West (256-362-0206; talladega.edu), established in 1867, to see Hale Woodruff's striking *Amistad* murals at Savery Library. Other points of interest include the campus chapel and Swayne Hall, the college's first building.

For a delightful history lesson and a fun-filled family adventure, don't miss nearby *DeSoto Caverns Park* (256-378-7252; desotocavernspark .com), 5 miles east of Childersburg at 5181 DeSoto Caverns Parkway. A one-hour tour presents highlights of the cave's role in history and features a spellbinding laser light and sound show in the magnificent onyx chamber, taller than a 12-story building and bigger than a football field.

After the tour children can climb DeSoto's cave wall, wander through a lost trail maze, pan for gemstones, do battle with water balloons, and enjoy a picnic on the grounds. The facility features more than 26 attractions, and you can make arrangements to stay overnight in the cave. The park's hours run from 10 a.m. to 4:30 p.m. Monday through Saturday, and 1 to 4:30 p.m. on Sunday (or to 5:30 p.m. April through October). Admission: cave tours are $20.99 for adults, and $17.99 for children (ages 3 to 11). Other attractions are $5.99 each or $21.99 for five attractions and $33.49 for 10 attractions.

Magic City Realm

Before exploring busy, bustling Birmingham, you can enjoy another back-to-nature experience at *Oak Mountain State Park* (205-620-2524; alapark .com/oakmountain), 15 miles south of Birmingham off I-65 at 877 Findlay Drive in Pelham. This state park offers canoeing, fishing, swimming, golfing, picnicking, horseback riding, and a demonstration farm. Children especially enjoy seeing the geese, peacocks, rabbits, pigs, calves, donkeys, horses, and other animals. The park, most of it in a natural state, occupies almost 10,000 acres. A drive to the top of Double Oak Mountain affords some sweeping views of the park's steep slopes and rugged terrain.

Other features include some 40 miles of hiking trails and four lakes. Don't miss the Treetop Nature Trail, where the Alabama Wildlife Rescue Service houses injured birds of prey. Climbing a boardwalk through woodsy surroundings takes you past large enclosures containing hawks, great horned owls, and other raptors. Call for park information or reservations at Oak Mountain's lakeside cabins or campground. Admission: adults $3, senior citizens and children (ages 6 to 11) $2.

After basking in serenity you can pick up the pace with a jaunt to *Birmingham.* Named for the British industrial city, Birmingham acquired its nickname, Magic City, when soon after its 1871 incorporation it burgeoned into Alabama's major metropolis. No longer a fire-breathing, smoke-spewing dragon, the city projects a much-changed image—from gray smog to crisp skyline and green-bordered boulevards. As a leading medical and technological center, the city boasts an economic base broadened far beyond its mineral resources. The financial impact of the University of Alabama at Birmingham (UAB) Medical Center beefs up the local economy enormously.

As the state's biggest city, Birmingham boasts many choice restaurants. For a memorable dinner with a focus on freshness and simplicity, add *Highlands Bar & Grill* (205-939-1400) at 2011 11th Avenue South to your itinerary. Classically trained chef Frank Stitt's regional Southern creations have been dubbed "New American" cuisine, and his accolades fill walls and books. *Gourmet* magazine awarded Highlands Bar & Grill its number five slot for the "50 Best American Restaurants" in 2001. The James Beard Foundation named Stitt "Best Chef of the Southeast" the same year and nominated him as "Outstanding Chef in America in 2008. *Bon Appétit* listed him as one of the culinary "Legends of the Decade."

alabamatrivia

Birmingham ranks as the state's largest city.

Start with an appetizer of baked grits, and select an entree ranging from beef, duck, and seafood to rabbit and veal. Renowned for its crab cakes, the restaurant also serves such specialties as pan roast quail with corn pudding and grilled leg of lamb with basil aioli and ratatouille. Try the Fudge Farms pork, fresh bacon, and braised shoulder with potatoes and Snow Bend's spring onions. Or savor the pork cheek and lobster with parsnip puree, pickled onions, and natural jus. The popular dessert list includes strawberry shortcake with sweet biscuits from Cullman, Alabama strawberries and mascarpone cream, and a petite strawberry milk shake. Moderate to expensive. Dinner hours are 5:30 to

10 p.m. Tuesday through Saturday. Visit highlandsbarandgrill.com for more background.

If you love to cook, be sure to pick up a copy of *Frank Stitt's Southern Table,* featuring recipes from the Highlands Bar and Grille. If you don't, this handsome book will make you want to learn. In either case, you'll enjoy the stories. Also, look for the companion book, *Frank Stitt's Bottega Favorita: A Southern Chef's Love Affair with Italian Food.*

Nearby, **The Hotel Highland** at Five Points South (205-933-9555) makes a handy base in the heart of this charming area brimming over with restaurants, shops, galleries, and nightspots. Formerly the Pickwick Hotel, this trendy boutique property at 1023 20th Street South wears a chic new look with contemporary furnishings but retains the original marble floors and other touches from its rich past. Bold lighting and vibrant colors, which showcase the hotel's public spaces, are balanced by subdued guestroom interiors. For unwinding after a busy day, there's the hip H Martini Bar in the lobby. The hotel offers an extended continental breakfast with gourmet

All About Art

While in the Birmingham area, stop by **Artists Incorporated** (205-979-8990; artistsincorporated.com) at 3365 Morgan Drive in Vestavia Hills. Representing the work of about 50 artists, this cooperative gallery offers a feast for the eyes. Here, you'll find oils by Les Yarbrough and Troy Crisswell, fiber art by Murray Johnston, bronzes by Frank Fleming, and more. Housed in a former dairy barn built in 1928, the gallery boasts the distinction of being Vestavia's oldest commercial building.

"This gallery offers a great variety of art forms in a wide range of prices," says Bill Charles, a fan and former Birmingham resident. "I'm the proud and happy owner of several works including two affordable Frank Fleming pieces, and I'm glad for the chance to have seen any number of [for me] unaffordable pieces, too. The crew here loves art and delights in sharing that love with their customers, be they buyers or browsers."

Hours are Tuesday through Thursday from 10 a.m. to 5 p.m.; Friday 10 a.m. to 8 p.m.; Saturday 10 a.m. to 4:30 p.m. A reception, featuring artists, food, wine, and sometimes music, takes place from 5:30 to 8:30 p.m. on the first Friday of every month—and you're invited.

coffees and espresso, fresh pastries, muffins, fruit, and cereals from 7 until 10 a.m. daily. Moderate to deluxe. Check out thehotelhighland.com.

While sightseeing in the Magic City, be sure to visit towering **Vulcan** (205-933-1409), the world's largest cast-iron statue, at 1701 Valley View Drive. To reach Vulcan Park atop Red Mountain, take 20th Street South and watch for the sign. An observation deck affords a panoramic view of Birmingham and surrounding Jones Valley. Cast from Birmingham iron, *Vulcan* represents the mythological god of metalworking, fire, and forge. Designed for the 1904 St. Louis Exposition by Italian sculptor Giuseppe Moretti, *Vulcan* lifts his torch in tribute to the city's iron industry. At the base of the 55-foot statue, a museum presents *Vulcan's* history along with an overview of steel production. Admission. For a virtual tour, visit vulcanpark.com.

Consider stopping by **Birmingham Botanical Gardens** (205-414-3950; bbgardens.org) at 2612 Lane Park Road, on the lower southern slope of Red Mountain. Stroll through the Japanese garden complete with a 14th-century teahouse reproduction. Also on the grounds, *Southern Living* magazine maintains demonstration gardens with plantings that might be duplicated at home. The museum's gift shop offers a fine selection of items, from note cards and prints to unusual plants and garden statuary—great for giving or keeping. Free admission. The gardens are open year-round, from dawn to dusk each day. The gift shop is open 9:30 a.m. to 5:30 p.m. Monday through Saturday, and 1 to 4 p.m. Sunday.

The Gardens Cafe by Kathy G at the gardens offers a lovely lunch from 11 a.m. to 2 p.m. on Tuesday through Friday. Inspired by local greens and

Solving Crimes with the Southern Sisters

Before Anne George wrote her critically acclaimed novel, *This One and Magic Life,* she penned award-winning poetry and became a Pulitzer Prize finalist. But her legion of mystery fans most miss the zany antics of Patricia Anne and Mary Alice, an unlikely pair of sleuths who live in Birmingham. As the "Southern Sisters" go about their crime solving, the reader gets a light-hearted look at the local landscape and a lot of laughs. Buy a book in this series, pour yourself a tall glass of iced tea, and enjoy an easy summer afternoon.

produce, the menu changes seasonally. A favorite is the pan-seared tilapia with steamed rice, sautéed green beans, pan sauce, and fried capers for $12.

The Tutwiler (205-322-2100 or 866-850-3053) at 2021 Park Place North makes a comfortable and convenient base for seeing Birmingham's attractions. The staff at this charming historic hotel will make you glad you came to the Magic City. With its rose-marble foyer, original coffered ceilings, moldings, plasterwork, and brass hardware, the hotel recaptures the elegance of another era. Your room or suite, which might come with a balcony or a marble fireplace, features high ceilings, restored woodwork, marble bathrooms, and custom-designed antique reproductions. Built in 1913 as a prestigious apartment/hotel, the redbrick, Italianate Tutwiler underwent a renovation. The Tutwiler's meticulous restoration resulted in charter membership in Historic Hotels of America, a select group recognized for preserving historic architectural quality and ambience. The original Tutwiler, the hotel's namesake, made news in 1974 when it became one of the country's first structures to be leveled by "implosion" (also the inspiration for the hotel's specialty drink by the same name).

The first Tutwiler hosted such dignitaries and celebrities as Eleanor Roosevelt, President Warren G. Harding, Charles Lindbergh, Will Rogers, Nelson Eddy, Tallulah Bankhead, Rocky Marciano, and Marilyn Monroe. Carrying on tradition, the current Tutwiler counts former President George Bush, Dan Quayle, Henry Kissinger, Colin Powell, Casper Weinberger, Mick Jagger, Billy Joel, and Henry Mancini among its honored guests. As another honored guest of the Tutwiler, you can enjoy such amenities as complimentary shoeshines and newspapers, airport transportation, and valet parking. Rates are moderate to deluxe.

For a glimpse of the city's Iron Age, take First Avenue North over the viaduct to 32nd Street toward the towering smokestacks of *Sloss Furnaces* (205-324-1911). Designated a National Historic Landmark, the ironworks that served Birmingham from 1881 to 1971 now serve as a massive walk-through museum portraying the city's industrial past. Near the park gate, a visitor center features exhibits on the various aspects of combining coal, limestone, and ore at high temperatures to produce iron. In its prime, Sloss turned out 400 tons of finished pig iron a day. Hours are Tuesday through Saturday from 10 a.m. to 4 p.m. and Sunday from noon to 4 p.m. Admission is free. Free hour-long guided tours are offered on Saturday and Sunday at 1, 2, and

3 p.m. The museum also offers self-guided and cell phone tours. Guests are asked to wear closed-toe shoes for safety.

For some down-home country cooking, head for **The Irondale Cafe** (205-956-5258)—the inspiration for the Whistle Stop Cafe in the movie *Fried Green Tomatoes*. Located at 1906 First Avenue North in the historic area of Irondale, the cafeteria offers a variety of meats and fresh vegetables including that Southern favorite, fried green tomatoes, that actress/writer Fannie Flagg put in the spotlight. Lunch is served from 11 a.m. to 2:30 p.m. daily. Supper is ready from 5 to 7 p.m. Monday through Saturday. Check the website at irondalecafe.com

Heading toward the Birmingham International Airport, you'll find the **Southern Museum of Flight** (205-833-8226; southernmuseumofflight.org). Look for the big McDonnell-Douglas F-4N Phantom II on the front lawn of the museum at 4343 73rd Street North, two blocks east of the airport. Aviation buffs can spend hours here delving into the mystery and history

---

Irondale Cafe Corn Bread

When you can't stop by the famed Irondale Cafe in Irondale, cook up a batch of the cafe's popular corn bread at home.

1½ teaspoons baking powder

2½ teaspoons vegetable oil

2½ teaspoons melted butter

2 beaten eggs

1½ cups fat-free cultured buttermilk

1½ cups whole milk

1½ cups self-rising white cornmeal

1½ cups self-rising White Lily flour

Combine all ingredients and mix well. Let batter rest under refrigeration for 1–2 hours. Pour batter into a well buttered 9x13 pan. Bake at 350°F in convection oven for 17–20 minutes or until knife inserted into center comes out clean. Brush top liberally with melted butter. Can also bake in a pre-heated, cast iron skillet for a dark and crunchy bottom crust.

of flying. This outstanding facility features a reproduction of a 1910 Curtis "Pusher," the second powered plane to follow on the heels of the Wright brothers' success; a 1925 crop duster that launched Delta Airlines; a dozen Cold War aircraft from the F-84 and F-86 through the A-12 Blackbird, including a MiG-15 and MiG-21; and hundreds of models that trace aviation's history. You'll see decades of memorabilia relating to Amelia Earhart, Gen. Claire Chenault's Flying Tigers, and the infamous Red Baron.

"We've doubled our collection during the last four years," said a staff member, and expansion continues. Visitors can view short movies, shown continuously, on such subjects as the Tuskegee Airmen and women in aviation as well as humorous newsreels on early attempts to fly. Take time to look through the Alabama Aviation Hall of Fame and the Air Force's 50th Anniversary Collection of Aircraft Art on the second floor. The museum, which also offers an aviation reference library, is open from 9:30 a.m. to 4:30 p.m. Tuesday through Saturday. Admission: adults $7, senior citizens and students $6, children (age 3 and under) free, and free for active military members and families.

Afterward return downtown to the Birmingham-Jefferson Civic Center for a spectator outing at the *Alabama Sports Hall of Fame* (205-323-6665). Located at 2150 Richard Arrington Jr. Boulevard, this unique two-floor facility focuses on some of the state's greatest sports figures. Walls of bronze plaques pay tribute to athletes from Olympic diving champion Jenni Chandler to Joe Louis, who boxed his way to the world heavyweight title. You'll also see displays on such sports luminaries as John Hannah, Joe Namath, Bo Jackson, Pat Sullivan, Bart Starr, Ozzie Newsome, Hank Aaron, Willie Mays, Jesse Owens, Hubert Green, Bobby Allison, Pat Dye, and Bear Bryant. Wall cases and displays feature trophies, uniforms, photographs, and other memorabilia from the sports world.

Even though exhibits cover Hall of Fame inductees who made names for themselves in archery, auto and harness racing, golf, baseball, boxing, track, and waterskiing, the name of the game in Alabama is Football (and yes, with a capital F). A black-and-white photo exhibit, depicting unhelmeted players in skimpy uniforms, captures some historic moments during the first Alabama–Auburn clash on February 22, 1893, in Birmingham. Football fever rages in many other parts of the country, but the intensity seems several degrees higher in the South and reaches a boiling point in Alabama

Christmas in Nauvoo

When Gene McDaniel planned a Christmas celebration in *Nauvoo,* population 249, he expected maybe 250 to 500 people. Between 2,000 to 3,000 people showed up for that first holiday festival in 1989, and that's how it's been ever since. Christmas in Nauvoo takes place the first Saturday in December with an open house at the *Old Harbin Hotel* (205-697-5652), myriad lights, attendant festivities, and a parade led by Miss Alabama, who makes the hotel her overnight base.

Other special events in Nauvoo include an Antique Car and Truck Show in June.

Once a booming coal-mining town, Nauvoo takes its name from a Hebrew word meaning "pleasant." A railroad worker, who said the place reminded him of his hometown in Illinois, christened it Nauvoo. After two mines and a lumber mill closed in the 1950s, Nauvoo started to shrivel and dry up. The town's largest structure, the two-story brick Old Harbin Hotel, stands on the corner of McDaniel Avenue and Third Street. Built in 1923 at a cost of $24,574, the hotel boasted 16 furnished rooms and 76 electric lights. The structure, which retains its original pine walls, downstairs pressed-tin ceilings, and four center rooms with skylights, was added to the Alabama Landmark Register in 1990.

Owners Gene and Earlene McDaniel, who live on the premises, have collected a variety of furnishings, antiques, and memorabilia to decorate each of the nine guest rooms individually.

"We don't advertise for customers," said Gene, a retired union coal miner and hardware store owner. "Don't expect a person on duty at the desk. Most weekends in summer, we're booked with family reunions because the whole clan can gather here." Gene, who owns several other buildings in Nauvoo, said he's had from 20,000 to 25,000 visitors at the hotel since 1989. Breakfast is included, and rates are standard. Visit www.nauvooalabama.com to check out special events in town.

during the annual collegiate battle between the Crimson Tide and the War Eagles. You can visit the Hall of Fame Monday through Friday from 9 a.m. to 5 p.m. Check out ashof.org for more information. Admission: adults $5, senior citizens $4, students $3.

Nearby at 2000 Reverend Abraham Woods Jr. Boulevard stands the *Birmingham Museum of Art* (205-254-2565), noted for its excellent Wedgwood collection, the finest outside England. The museum houses a diverse collection of more than 25,000 paintings, pieces of sculpture, prints, drawings, and examples of the decorative arts dating from ancient to modern times. You'll see works by Monet, Sargent, Corot, Cassatt, Bierstadt, Motherwell, Stella, Chihuly, and others.

Other museum treasures include the Kress collection of Renaissance paintings and the largest collection of Asian art in the South.

Check with the staff regarding current offerings. Don't miss the multilevel Charles W. Ireland Sculpture Garden, which provides a splendid backdrop for outdoor exhibits. Oscar's at the Museum restaurant serves lunch from 11 a.m. to 2 p.m. Tuesday through Saturday and features a musical brunch on select Sundays. Stop by the Museum Store for an extensive selection of books, posters, jewelry, crafts, and unique gift items. Except for major holidays, the museum is open from 10 a.m. to 5 p.m. Tuesday through Saturday and noon to 5 p.m. Sunday. Check on current exhibits and other happenings at artsbma.org. Free admission.

Continue south on 21st Street to University Boulevard and take a right to reach the *University of Alabama at Birmingham* campus. One of the nation's top-ranked medical centers, UAB practices a triple-thrust program of education, research, and service. Tucked in the heart of this much-trodden complex on the third floor of the Lister Hill Library Building, you'll find the *Alabama Museum of Health Sciences* and the *Reynolds Historical Library* (205-934-4475). (But you probably won't find a nearby parking place, so wear your walking shoes.) With a rare and valuable collection of medical books and manuscripts (some predate the printing press), the library houses one of the country's foremost collections of its type—on par with similar collections at Harvard, Yale, Johns Hopkins, and other prestigious institutions. Incredible as it sounds, you can read actual letters (pertaining to dental matters) handwritten by George and Martha Washington. The library also owns original correspondence of Louis Pasteur, Sir William Osler, Pierre Curie, and Florence Nightingale. These letters, of course, are safely locked up, but you can ask the curator to don white gloves and show them to you.

The library owes its existence to radiologist Lawrence Reynolds, an Alabamian who grew up in a family of physicians and devoted much of his lifetime to acquiring rare medical books and manuscripts (once spending a month's salary of $600 on a single volume). In 1958 Dr. Reynolds donated his impressive collection of some 5,000 items (now doubled in size) to his alma mater. The library's collection features richly illustrated vellum manuscripts, rare first editions such as Vesalius's 1543 textbook on human anatomy, the earliest known treatise on wine, and a 1517 handbook of surgery (written in German instead of Latin) with extraordinary hand-executed illustrations. Another work, William Harvey's 1628 *De motu cordis,* accurately describes the body's blood circulation for the first time. Also, the library owns a comprehensive collection of primary and secondary resource material relating to Civil War medicine. Other interesting items include antique maps, a sizable collection of Nobel Prize Papers, and a set of two Chinese anatomical charts that date to 1668 and delineate the body's acupuncture points. Don't miss the display of exquisite ivory miniature mannequins (physicians' dolls used for medical instruction) dating from the 17th and 18th centuries. Another room contains displays of various medical instruments and equipment along with changing exhibits. The library and museum are open from 9 a.m. to 5 p.m. Monday through Friday, and admission is free. You can find more information at uab.edu/historical with links to the Reynolds Historical Library, the Alabama Museum of Health Sciences, and the UAB Archives.

Don't miss the **Birmingham Civil Rights Institute** (205-328-9696), located at 520 16th Street North. The focal point of the Civil Rights District, which also embraces historic 16th Street Baptist Church and Kelly Ingram Park, the facility features innovative exhibits, which re-create in graphic fashion a sad chronology of segregation's inequities. Visitors start their journey through darkness with a film, followed by a startling entrance to the "Barriers" Gallery, where exhibits trace the struggle that led to the passage of civil rights laws. The Richard Arrington Jr. Resource Gallery offers an interactive multimedia experience and creates a "living library" honoring persons who participated in the civil rights struggle. Video segments from the institute's Oral History Project interviews are available for learning and research. Admission: adults $12, senior citizens $5, college students $6, children (grades 4 to 12) outside Jefferson County $3, children (age 17 and under) living in Jefferson County free. Hours are 10 a.m. to 5 p.m. Tuesday through Saturday and 1 to 5 p.m. Sunday. Visit bcri.org for more information.

While exploring the Magic City, take in nearby Homewood, where you'll find a delightful neighborhood market and cafe specializing in Mediterranean fare. **Nabeel's Cafe** (205-879-9292) at 1706 Oxmoor Road offers a menu with a global theme and a market filled with imported herbs, coffees, teas, olive oil, beans, nuts, and more. Vats of olives, bins of spices, and wedges of Greek, Italian, Bulgarian, Russian, and Lebanese cheeses tempt the shopper here.

The Krontiras family, John and Ottavia with their son Anthony, own and operate this establishment, housed in the white-painted brick building with an exterior wall mural and green canopies. The cafe evokes the intimacy of a European dining experience with a leisurely sharing of food and drink. Wine barrels and a wooden rack for wine storage along the dining-room wall suggest the old country. Anthony, Nabeel's chef, focuses on family recipes and prepares food with home-cooked flavor. Nabeel's numerous awards include "Birmingham's Favorite Restaurant" in a former readers' poll conducted by *Birmingham Magazine*. "We try to treat customers as if they were guests at our home," said John.

Sip some of the cafe's celebrated and refreshing mint tea and scoop up some taramasalata dip, made of red caviar and salted carp roe, with a pita wedge while you decide what to order. From homemade soups and piquant Greek salads to sandwich specialties like *fior di latte* (made with fresh mozzarella cheese, roasted peppers, and fresh basil), Nabeel's crew prepares everything fresh daily. Favorites include eggplant parmesan and a spinach pie (*spanakopita*). Made of fresh spinach and layered with phyllo, Greek feta cheese, and herbs, *spanakopita* is served with a salad and pita bread. Other popular menu items include grouper Greek style and filet mignon. End your meal on a sweet note with baklava, cannoli, butter cookies, or honey crescents. Restaurant hours are Monday through Wednesday 11 a.m. to 8 p.m., Thursday through Saturday 11 a.m. to 9:30 p.m. Market hours are Monday through Saturday 8 a.m. to 6 p.m. Click on nabeels.com for more information and some mouth-watering recipes.

Another interesting dining experience awaits at 1500 First Avenue North #45 in Homewood. Here, at **The Cafe at Innovation Depot** (205-314-3456; culinardcafe.com), you can dip into progressive American cuisine prepared by aspiring chefs and gourmands as they perfect their skills in chopping, whisking, sautéing, and serving their way through a two-year culinary course—longer if they add a baking stint to the core curriculum. Someday, you might say, "I knew that chef when . . ."

Menus, prepared by senior-level students, change seasonally, and feature wholesome down-home cooking for breakfast and lunch. A popular choice is the salmon and brie—fresh spring greens topped with grilled Atlantic salmon topped with melted brie cheese, vanilla poached pears, fire roasted bell peppers, candied walnuts, crumbled bleu cheese, and sun-dried cranberries with lavender honey dressing. The cafe is open Monday through Friday from 7 a.m. to 4 p.m. Before leaving the Birmingham area, stop by *The Bright Star* (205-424-9444) in nearby Bessemer. Housed in a tall brick building at 304 North 19th Street, this restaurant beckons diners with an extensive menu prepared with Greek flair. Brothers Jimmy and Nicky Koikos continue a family culinary tradition that started in 1907.

The attractive interior features roomy brass and glass-topped booths and murals dating from 1915, painted by a European artist traveling through the area. The Bright Star offers daily luncheon specials, such as fresh trout amandine or Greek-style beef tenderloin tips with such side dish choices as fresh fried eggplant, corn on the cob, and candied yams.

For dinner start with a cup of the restaurant's scrumptious gumbo. (All fish dishes here feature fresh seafood straight from the coast.) For the main course, you might choose broiled snapper (Greek style) or the beef tenderloin. Other enticing entrees include lobster and crabmeat au gratin, a broiled seafood platter, and a tasty blackened snapper, prepared New Orleans style, with a creamy wine sauce. Top off your meal with a slice of fresh homemade pineapple-cheese or lemon icebox pie. Economical to moderate prices. Lunch hours are 11 a.m. to 3 p.m. daily. Dinner is served 4:30 to 9 p.m. Sunday through Thursday and 4:30 to 10 p.m. Friday and Saturday. View the property at thebrightstar.com.

The Capstone

Traveling southwest from Birmingham about 50 miles takes you to *Tuscaloosa.* This college town, rich in tradition, served as Alabama's capital from 1826 to 1846.

Before exploring the area's many attractions, you might like to fortify yourself with a slab of ribs at *Dreamland Bar-B-Que* (205-758-8135; dreamlandbbq.com), two miles from the intersection of US 82 and I-59, off Jug Factory Road in Jerusalem Heights at 5535 15th Avenue East. Here you don't have to agonize over what to order—the choice is ribs along with slices of white bread to sop up the sauce. You'll also get a bib that says AIN'T

NOTHIN' LIKE 'EM—NOWHERE, a stack of napkins, and a wet paper towel to assist you in this gustatory project that must be performed with no inhibitions. If you want more variety in your meal, get a bag of potato chips. Beer or soft drinks, followed by toothpicks, complete the feast.

True, Dreamland stays crowded and the noise level runs high, but regulars say these things add to the place's appeal. Dreamland's hours are 10 a.m. to 10 p.m. Monday through Thursday. On Friday and Saturday the restaurant is open from 10 a.m. to 11 p.m. and Sunday from 11 a.m. to 9 p.m. Rates are economical to moderate.

Continue to nearby *Cypress Inn* (205-345-6963; cypressinnrestaurant .com) at 501 Rice Mine Road North. Located on the Black Warrior's banks, this restaurant offers fresh seafood, prime steaks, and traditional Southern fare as well as a relaxing river view. House specialties include Hoppin' John (a combination of black-eyed peas, rice, scallions, and bacon), smoked chicken with white barbecue sauce, crispy fried catfish, and fresh broiled red snapper. Also popular are the homemade yeast rolls, fresh raisin-bran muffins, and peanut butter

alabamatrivia

Founded in 1819 near the site of an early Indian village, Tuscaloosa occupies the highest navigable point on the Black Warrior River.

pie. The Cypress Inn serves lunch from 11 a.m. to 2 p.m. daily; dinner hours run from 5:30 to 9:30 p.m. Monday through Thursday, 5 to 10 p.m. Friday and Saturday, and 5 to 8 p.m. Sunday. Economical to moderate prices.

Art lovers will want to search out a rare museum at 1400 Jack Warner Parkway Northeast. The *Tuscaloosa Museum of Art: Home of the Westervelt Collection* (205-562-5280; tuscaloosamoa.org) showcases Jack W. Warner's remarkable assemblage resulting from four decades of collecting. In addition to paintings and sculpture, the collection includes American decorative arts and antiques such as furniture by Duncan Phyfe, silverware by Paul Revere, exquisite porcelain, early American firearms, and more. Most of the furniture dates to the period between 1820 and 1840, and every piece is museum quality.

Here, you'll view portraits of Washington, Jefferson, and Lafayette all painted from life as you wend your way through galleries and color-coordinated suites in the Blue, Yellow, Green, and Salmon rooms. Visitors to the Gulf States Paper offices will remember seeing some of the works previously exhibited there. The extensive collection, which has been called an "unparalleled assembly of 18th, 19th and 20th century American art," was moved to the facility in 2011.

Artists represented include Andrew Wyeth, Frederic Remington, George Catlin, Mary Cassatt, and Georgia O'Keeffe. Also, you'll see works by John Singer Sargent, Winslow Homer, Albert Bierstadt, James McNeil Whistler, Childe Hassam, James Peale, Thomas Cole, Asher B. Durand, and many others.

The world-class collection can be viewed by the public 10 a.m. to 6 p.m. Tuesday through Saturday; Admission is free. Afterward head for the **University of Alabama campus,** the site of a beautiful historic district as well as the home of the Crimson Tide. Since student William Gray Little organized the college's first football club in 1892, Alabama has celebrated "A Century of Champions." A good place to learn about the school's more than 100-year football history is the **Paul W. Bryant Museum** (205-348-4668; bryantmuseum.com). To reach the museum from US 82, take the University Boulevard exit and follow the signs. If you arrive via I-59, exit onto I-359, take the 35th Street exit to 10th Avenue, go north to Bryant Drive, and then turn east. You'll find the museum on campus at 300 Paul W. Bryant Drive.

For some background on the legendary figure called "The Bear," the man who became college football's most acclaimed coach, start your museum visit by viewing *The Bryant Legacy,* a film narrated by sports commentator Keith Jackson. While browsing among the displays, you'll see a replicated setting of Bear Bryant's office and a dazzling version of his famous hat. Sculptor Miraslav Havel translated the familiar crimson-and-white houndstooth pattern into a multifaceted Waterford crystal showpiece. A courier transported the real hat from Tuscaloosa to Ireland for its magic rendering—and back again.

alabamatrivia

Educator Julia Tutwiler, born in 1841 in Tuscaloosa, worked to secure the admission of women to the University of Alabama.

Although dedicated to the memory of Bryant, who headed Alabama's football teams from 1958 to 1982, the museum also pays tribute to other coaches and players prominent in the school's history. You'll see photos, memorabilia, and audiovisual displays pertaining to such superstars as Joe Namath, Kenny Stabler, Cornelius Bennett, and Bart Starr. To supplement vintage film clips, montages, and recordings, the museum offers taped highlights of recent games.

In addition to the large exhibit hall, the museum houses a comprehensive library of media guides, game programs, photographs, books, films, scrapbooks, and other materials covering Southeastern Conference and college sports. Admission: adults $2, senior citizens and children $1. Except for major holidays, hours run from 9 a.m. to 4 p.m. daily.

While exploring the campus, stop by the **Gorgas House** (205-348-5906) at 810 Capstone Drive. One of four university buildings to survive the Civil War, this 1829 two-story brick federal-style cottage with a curving cast-iron staircase originally served as a college dining hall. Inside you'll see period furnishings, an outstanding collection of Spanish colonial silver, and memorabilia of William Crawford Gorgas, who was noted for his work in the prevention and cure of yellow fever. Free admission. The Gorgas House is open Monday through Friday from 9 a.m. to noon and 1 to 4:30 p.m. with tours by appointment. Tap into gorgashouse.ua.edu for more details.

Housed at nearby Smith Hall at 427 Sixth Avenue Northeast, the **Alabama Museum of Natural History** (205-348-7550) features extensive fossil and mineral collections. Entering this 1909 classical revival building, you'll see a spacious hall and a sweeping marble staircase with iron railings. Exhibits include pottery, tools, weapons, and various artifacts from South Pacific and Central and South American cultures.

On display in the gallery upstairs, you'll find the Hodges meteorite—an outer-space missile weighing 8.5 pounds that struck a Sylacauga woman in 1954. Featured fossils include mammoth, mastodon, mosasaur, and marine turtle, along with a 65-foot whale fossil. You'll also see a Studebaker buggy from the 1880s and a free-standing exhibit illustrating the research methods used by Professor Eugene Allen Smith, for whom the building is named, in gathering his geological and biological collections. Except for major holidays, you can visit the museum Monday through Saturday from 10 a.m. to 4:30 p.m. Admission: adults $2, children and seniors $1. Check amnh.ua.edu for more background.

Downtown at 2300 University Boulevard in a building that dates to the 1890s, you'll find **DePalma's Italian Cafe** (205-759-1879;

depalmasdowntown.com). This Italian cafe is noted for its pizzas, cal-
zones, and dishes such as pine nut–crusted salmon, veal Marsala, or pasta
DePalma—angel-hair pasta baked in a cream sauce with garlic, cheeses, and
Italian herbs and topped with mushrooms, mozzarella, and a choice of ham,
Italian sausage, artichokes, and more. Tiramisu ranks at the top of the dessert list, and the crew offers a great wine selection, too. In fact, the owners
make regular scouting trips to Italy for their selections. Here, messages don't
come in a bottle—but *on* a bottle—because the staff invites you to sign and
date your wine label and pen an appropriate message. Then your special
bottle joins a long line of others on the booth-level shelf. DePalma's is open
from 11 a.m. to 10 p.m. Monday through Thursday and until 11 p.m. Friday
and Saturday, on Sunday from 11 a.m. to 9 p.m. Prices are economical to
moderate. Reservations not accepted.

After your campus tour take time to explore Tuscaloosa (a Choctaw
name that means "black warrior"). While downtown, stop by the ***Battle-
Friedman House*** (205-758-6138; historictuscaloosa.org), a handsome Greek
revival mansion located at 1010 Greensboro Avenue. Built in 1835, this structure now serves as a house museum and city cultural center. The home may
be visited Tuesday through Saturday between 10 a.m. and noon and 1 to 4
p.m. Admission: adults $5, children (under age 12) free.

Continue to 1512 Greensboro Avenue, where you'll find ***The Waysider
Restaurant*** (205-345-8239) in a small early-20th-century house. Because
this is the place for breakfast in Tuscaloosa, you may have to stand in line,
so bring along a newspaper to read while you wait for a table. No wimpy
affair, breakfast at The Waysider means homemade biscuits (with a deserved
reputation), eggs, grits (get the cheese version), and a meat of your choice:
from sugar-cured ham to grilled pork chops or steak. An order of real
country-cured ham with two eggs and red-eye gravy runs in the economical
range. You can also opt for pancakes.

The Waysider opens at 5:30 a.m. Tuesday through Saturday. Sunday
breakfast hours run from 6:30 a.m. to 1 p.m. Lunch hours are 11 a.m. to 1:30
p.m. Tuesday through Friday.

Next, head to nearby ***Northport,*** just a short drive across the Black
Warrior River. Once called Kentuck, Northport has developed into an important craft center with a complex of studios and galleries. The third weekend of October the ***Kentuck Festival of the Arts*** features more than 300

selected artists and craftspeople from all over the country. Kerry Kennedy, Steve Davis, Ann Betak, Robby Roberts, Daniel Livingston, and a number of other artists maintain individual studios at the **Kentuck Museum Association** (205-758-1257), located at 503 Main Avenue. The gift shop, which offers photography, pottery, glass, jewelry, musical instruments, textiles, baskets, and other items, is open Tuesday through Friday from 10 a.m. to 5 p.m. and Saturday from 10 a.m. to 4:30 p.m. Call for information on the center's artists, exhibits, or Kentuck Museum's gallery or visit kentuck.org.

If you have a green thumb, be sure to stop by the **Potager** (205-752-4761; adamsantiques.com), next door at 428 Main Avenue. The shop offers everything from books and tools to gardening accessories. Zebra finches provide the chirping background music. Afterward step through the connecting door to **Adams' Antiques** (205-758-8651; adamsantiques.com) for more browsing. Both shops are open from 10 a.m. to 5 p.m. Tuesday through Saturday.

After your Northport excursion, head for **Moundville,** named "the Big Apple of the 14th century" by *National Geographic*. To reach **Moundville Archaeological Park** (205-371-2234), located about 15 miles south of Tuscaloosa, take State Route 69 South to 634 Mound Park. Said by archaeologists to be the best preserved prehistoric settlement east of the pueblos, Moundville is an internationally known archaeological site with more than 20 flat-topped earthen mounds, plus other less prominent ones, spread over a 317-acre setting on the Black Warrior River. For a sweeping overview of the grounds, you can climb to the top of a 60-foot ceremonial mound. The **Jones Archaeological Museum** spotlights a re-created marriage ceremony from 500 years ago featuring life-size figures. You'll also see hundreds of Mississippian artifacts, ceremonial vessels, and tools made by the advanced group of prehistoric people who occupied this area between AD 1000 and 1450. Don't miss the Rattlesnake disc, the most famous artifact ever found at Moundville. Although scholars disagree on the meaning of the entwined rattlesnakes on the disc, the hand with the eyelike motif in the palm is common in Mississippian art. The Edward T. Douglass Nature Trail winds through ½ mile of scenic woodlands. The level boardwalk offers a fascinating trek that takes visitors from ground level to treetop height. The ring road at the park is also a great place to ride a bike.

For a welcome break, the **Black Warrior Coffee Company** (205-371-2572; moundville.ua.edu) is a good cafe to enjoy a variety of Native

American specialty coffees and teas along with cakes, pies, pastries, and homemade cream sodas. The park, open daily, may be visited from 9 a.m. to dusk. Except for major holidays, the museum is open 9 a.m. to 5 p.m. The museum closes at 4 p.m. from November through February. Camping, hiking, and picnicking facilities are available. Admission: adults $8, senior citizens $7, students $6, children (under age 5) free; Native Americans free with tribal membership card. The annual four-day *Moundville Native American Festival,* featuring southeastern Native American crafts and cultural activities, takes place during the first week in October. For more information, click on moundville.ua.edu.

Afterward return north to US 82, and travel west toward Pickensville and the Tennessee-Tombigbee (Tenn-Tom) Waterway, which offers exceptional fishing, hunting, and recreational facilities.

Tenn-Tom Terrain

Don't miss the *Tom Bevill Visitor Center* (205-373-8705) at Pickensville, ½ mile south of the junctions of State Routes 14 and 86. The white-columned Greek revival–style mansion you see here looks as if it dates from the mid-1800s but actually was completed in 1986. Definitely not your average rest stop, this facility primarily represents a composite of three historical homes in the vicinity, and you'll see portraits of these grand mansions in the central hall. Ascend the sweeping stairway to the second floor, where various exhibits interpret the Tennessee-Tombigbee Waterway's history. A 22-foot relief map illustrates the waterway's course through several locks and dams,

---

Strange as It Sounds

Carrollton offers a unique site—a face imprinted on a windowpane at the *Pickens County Courthouse.* To learn the strange story behind the image of a prisoner's face preserved here since 1878 (the visage remains despite repeated scrubbings and harsher attempts at removal), step inside the courthouse and pick up a leaflet that provides some background information. You can also read an intriguing account of the mysterious face in Kathryn Tucker Windham's book *13 Alabama Ghosts and Jeffrey* (published by the University of Alabama Press in Tuscaloosa).

and a model display demonstrates the lockage process. Even better, you can climb to the roof level and perhaps watch a vessel pass through the Tom Bevill Lock and Dam. Whether or not said event happens during your visit, the splendid view from the cupola justifies the climb.

After your house tour, stop by the US Snagboat *Montgomery* near the visitor center. A National Historic Landmark, this steam-powered stern-wheeler once kept Southern rivers navigable by removing tons of debris, such as fallen trees and sunken logs that impeded river traffic. Except for some federal holidays, and weekends during November through March, the center is open daily year-round. Summer hours are 9 a.m. to 5 p.m., and winter hours are 8 a.m. to 4 p.m.

Next, head south to *Aliceville,* home of a unique museum, a lovely bed-and-breakfast, and fine Southern fare at **Plantation House Restaurant** (205-373-8121; plantationhouse.8k.com). The eatery, located at 102 Memorial Parkway on the State Route 17 bypass, features two homemade soups daily and plenty of ethnic variety with Cajun, Italian, and Mexican selections. You'll enjoy a variety of homemade desserts at this restaurant, which dates to 1905 and is listed on the Alabama Register of Historic Landmarks and Heritage. The restaurant serves lunch Tuesday through Friday 11 a.m. to 2 p.m., and dinner Thursday through Saturday 5 to 9 p.m. Prices are moderate.

Don't miss the *Aliceville Museum* (205-373-2363), downtown at 104 Broad Street. During World War II some 6,000 German prisoners—most from Field Marshall Erwin Rommel's Afrika Korps—were interned at Camp Aliceville, site of the present-day *Sue Stabler Park* about 2 miles due west of town on State Route 17. In 1993 the city hosted its 50-year Prisoner of War Reunion. During this three-day event, officials, residents, and visitors—including 15 German ex-POWs and their families—gathered to dedicate the only World War II German POW museum in the US. The last Prisoner of War Reunion was in 2007. A 15-minute video, featuring first-person interviews with the camp guards and prisoners, provides background on the museum's focus. Historians will want to view a 45-minute video produced by the History Channel. Exhibits include drawings, paintings, sculpture, musical instruments, furniture, newspapers, photos, and other artifacts from Camp Aliceville. Also, visitors can see an American military collection from World War II in the adjacent building and a 1948 Coca-Cola bottling works. Museum hours are 10 a.m. to 4 p.m. Monday through Friday and by appointment only on Saturday. Admission: adults $5, senior citizens and students $4.

From Aliceville you can either dip southeast via State Route 14 to Eutaw (a charming town covered in the Southwest section of this book) or return east to tour Tannehill, about midway between Birmingham and Tuscaloosa.

Peach Country

To reach **Tannehill Ironworks Historical State Park** (205-477-5711; tannehill.org) near McCalla, take exit 100 off I-59 and follow the signs to 12632 Confederate Parkway. This 1,500-acre wooded park spills into Tuscaloosa, Jefferson, and Bibb Counties. On the grounds you'll see the remains of the Tannehill Iron Furnaces and more than 40 pioneer homes and farm outbuildings. A cotton gin, blacksmith shop, and gristmill (that grinds cornmeal one weekend a month from March to November) add to the authenticity of this mid-1800s re-creation. Exhibits at the Iron and Steel Museum of Alabama spotlight the history of technology prior to 1850. The facility offers hiking trails and camping. The park is open from 7 a.m. to dark year-round. Museum hours run from 8:30 a.m. to 4:30 p.m. weekdays, 10 a.m. to 3 p.m. Saturday, and 12:30 to 4:30 p.m. Sunday. Admission: adults $3, senior citizens $2, children (ages 6 to 11) $1, children (age 5 and under) free.

Afterward you might like to shift south to **Montevallo,** located in the middle of Alabama. Here the **University of Montevallo,** situated on a beautiful campus complete with brick streets, tree-lined drives, and historical buildings such as the 1823 King House and Reynolds Hall, makes a pleasant stopover. An arbor walk features a variety of trees labeled by their common and scientific names. Better yet, pick up a *Red Brick Walking Tour* guide, available in versions highlighting several interests—from architectural and horticultural to ghosts. These guides and other information on local sites are available at the Montevallo Chamber of Commerce office (205-665-1519; montevallocc.com) and the Montevallo Welcome Center based at the historic Will Lyman House at 720 Oak Street, adjacent to the campus. The public can also attend campus concerts, plays, films, lectures, art exhibits, and sporting events; most activities are free. Call the university's public relations office at (205) 665-6230 to check on current happenings during the time of your visit or check out montevallo.edu.

For overnighters, the on-campus *Ramsay Conference Center* (205-665-6280) offers double rooms on a space-available basis, seven days a week during the school term, at bargain rates. The rooms feature TVs and private bathrooms. A short stroll away you'll find the college dining hall with cafeteria-style meals. Pay-at-the-door prices for breakfast, lunch, and dinner are economical.

While in Montevallo, the *Eclipse Coffee* (205-665-4234, eclipsecoffee.com) also offers a quick pick-me-up at 1032 Main Street. Free Wi-Fi is available inside or on the wraparound porch. With a spacious dining room and three rooms of books, Eclipse is a pleasant place to dine, read, listen to music, or just sit around. Open Monday through Wednesday 7 a.m. to 10 p.m., Thursday and Friday 7 a.m. to midnight, and Saturday 8 a.m. to midnight.

For a lovely overnight, stay at the *Fox and Pheasant Inn* (205-665-3080; foxandpheasantinn.com) at 540 Shelby Street. Innkeeper Janice Seaman rescued the historic home and turned it into the luxurious inn it is today.

A 1915 English manor-style home, the Fox and Pheasant offers four suites with private baths, cable TV, luxury bedding, towel warmers, and much more. Days start with a gourmet breakfast, maybe eggs Benedict or blueberry pancakes with applewood smoked bacon. Guests also can order a lunch to enjoy on the premises or to pack in a hamper for a picnic in the countryside. Dinner menus also are available with such popular items as steak Diane and honey-roasted pork tenderloin stuffed with apricots, walnuts, and shiitake mushrooms. For dessert, it is difficult to pick a favorite between the delicious chocolate pecan bourbon pie and flourless chocolate cake.

Before leaving town, visit *Orr Park,* where you can stroll along Shoal Creek, a natural habitat for Tim Tingle's life-size wood carvings of birds, animals, and wizard faces.

Continuing south to *Clanton* in the heart of peach country, you'll find several places to purchase this locally grown fruit. *Peach Park,* for instance, features fresh peaches (in season) along with homemade peach ice cream, milk shakes, yogurt, and other delicious desserts as well as pecans and boiled peanuts.

A Revolutionary Experience

Prepare yourself for a revolutionary experience and step into the action at **The American Village** (205-665-3535 or 877-811-1776), located 4 miles off I-65 at exit 234 in Montevallo at 3727 State Road 119. Actually, you don't have to do much preparation if your visit coincides with that of school groups because their teachers have already primed them to participate and appreciate the exciting turn of events that brought about a struggling young nation's independence.

Authentically costumed interpreters bring to life the fervor of that time when our forebears made choices that formed the fabric of our lives today. You'll get caught up in such events as the Stamp Act Rally and interact with colonial residents expressing their growing resentment against the mother country. You'll hear Patrick Henry's fiery oratory and attend the 1787 Philadelphia Convention to form a new national government. You'll voice your opinions, vote, and maybe even sit behind the desk in the Oval Office.

The backdrop for this revolutionary experiment is a complex of various colonial buildings including the centerpiece Washington Hall, inspired by Mount Vernon, and a Williamsburg-style courthouse. But this 113-acre development is not about buildings—handsome though they are—it's about ideas. And the dreamer who envisioned this place, Tom Walker, wants citizens of today and tomorrow to realize they also have choices—just as our early leaders did. The village's mission of strengthening and renewing the foundations of American citizenship can be witnessed in action weekdays from 10 a.m. to 4 p.m. with public tours at 10 a.m., noon, and 2 p.m. The village is closed Saturday and Sunday. You can pay a virtual visit via americanvillage.org. Admission: adults $8.50, senior citizens and children (ages 5 to 17) $8, children (age 4 and under) free.

Village visitors can see a Southern Living Showcase House replica of the Philadelphia residence occupied by George and Martha Washington and then John and Abigail Adams, adding another facet to the on-site history lesson.

To learn about the area's history, visit the new **Aldrich Coal Mine Museum** (205-665-2886) housed in the former Montevallo Coal Mining Company at 137 Highway 203. Owners Henry and Rose Emfinger are proud to tell visitors about the only monument in Alabama dedicated to all coal minters. The museum is located in the old company store and features a simulated coal mine. Open Thursday through Saturday from 10 a.m. to 4 p.m., Sunday 1 to 4 p.m., and other times by appointment. Admission: adults $5, children $3.

While in the area, plan a visit to **Confederate Memorial Park** (205-755-1990), just off US 31 near I 65 at County Road 63 in Marbury. The site of a former home for Confederate veterans and their widows, the park features a museum with historical displays, Civil War relics, flags, Confederate uniforms, and weaponry. On the grounds you'll also find two cemeteries, a chapel, the old Mountain Creek Post Office, picnic pavilions, and hiking trails. Except for major holidays, the museum is open from 9 a.m. to 5 p.m. The park may be visited year-round from 6 a.m. to dusk. Admission: adults $5, college students and senior citizens $4, children (ages 6 to 18) $3; and children (under age 6) free.

Head back north to **Calera** to see several antiques shops and the **Heart of Dixie Railroad Museum** (205-668-3435). From I-65 take exit 228 and travel less than a mile west on State Route 25, following signs to the museum at 1919 Ninth Street. Exhibits include World War II photos, framed timetables, waiting room benches, old railroad lanterns, signal equipment, special tools used to repair steam locomotives, a caboose stove, and an arrival/departure board from the demolished Birmingham Terminal. A glass case contains dishes made by Marshall Field and Company in 1925 for the Rock Island Lines. You'll see a centralized train control board (CTC) with which one person, a railroad counterpart of the airline's air traffic controller, managed a large section of tracks and the trains that traveled it. Locomotives, guard cars (the museum owns four of only six in existence), passenger and freight cars, and the state's largest railroad crane stand outside the green depot museum. Hours are 9 a.m. to 4 p.m. Tuesday through Saturday. The museum sponsors train rides and special events. Call for more information on the museum and train ride schedule with excursion rates. Trains generally run from mid-March until the weekend before Christmas. Museum admission is free, but donations are accepted. Visit hodrr.org for more information.

Continue a few miles northeast via State Route 25 to **Columbiana,** where you'll discover hundreds of prized possessions from the country's first First Family. People can't believe that all these things belonged to George Washington, and they are amazed to find such a collection in central Alabama at the **Karl C. Harrison Museum of George Washington** (205-669-8767). Housed in a modern building that adjoins the Mildred B. Harrison Library's right side, the facility provides spacious quarters for the extensive collection and permits previously stored pieces to be exhibited. Located at 50 Lester Street, the museum stands behind the handsome Shelby County Courthouse.

The foyer's focal point, a commanding bust of George Washington, was created by French sculptor Jean Antoine Houdan from a life mask. Nearby, a glass case topped by a handsome pair of pink Sevres vases contains family correspondence, documents, jewelry, and a writing instrument from Washington's survey case. Martha Washington's prayer book ranks among the museum's rarest possessions. Two dining room tables feature beautiful settings with exquisite porcelain pieces and coin-silver utensils used at Mount Vernon. A prized 207-piece set of Minton porcelain is displayed on a table and buffet and also fills the shelves of a walnut cabinet signed by William Elfie.

Other treasures include family portraits, various personal items, an original 1787 Samuel Vaughn sketch of Mount Vernon's grounds, and some 70 letters and documents dating to the Revolutionary War period. You can read correspondence from James Madison, Lord Cornwallis, John Adams, Aaron Burr, and other historic figures. The collection's oldest item is the 1710 handwritten will of Col. Daniel Parke, the grandfather of Martha Washington's first husband. You'll also see an original tintype made by Civil War photographer Mathew B. Brady that depicts Robert E. Lee in uniform for the last time.

Amassed by Eliza Parke Custis Law, Martha Washington's granddaughter, the collection passed through six generations of Washington heirs down to Shelby County's Charlotte Smith Weaver. After giving her grandchildren selected items, Mrs. Weaver offered the remainder of the family collection for public preservation. Columbiana banker Karl Harrison acquired two-thirds of it for this museum, and the rest went to Mount Vernon. The Columbiana museum procured additional family pieces from the estate of George Washington's half brother, Augustin, in 1989. Except for major holidays, the museum is open 10 a.m. to 3 p.m. Monday through Friday. Admission is free. Visit online at washingtonmuseum.com.

Woodland & Water

Continue east to **Sylacauga,** sometimes called Marble City. While many cities contain marble monuments and buildings, here the entire town rests on a marble bed about 32 miles long and more than a mile wide. Sylacauga marble was used in the US Supreme Court Building in Washington, DC, Detroit's General Motors Building, and in many other distinctive edifices. "The Sylacauga area has some of the whitest marble in the world," says a local quarrying company official.

Stop by the **Isabel Anderson Comer Museum and Arts Center** (256-245-4016; comermuseumweebly.com) at 711 Broadway Avenue North. At the museum, housed in a former library building dating from the 1930s, you'll see a big chunk of calcite quartz, unusual because it came from the middle of a local marble quarry. The museum owns several pieces by Giuseppe Moretti, the Italian sculptor who designed Birmingham's statue of *Vulcan*. Moretti came to Sylacauga in the early 1900s to open a marble quarry.

The museum's displays cover everything from beaded evening bags and Victorian hat pins to a reproduction of the Hodges meteorite that hurtled down on Sylacauga from outer space and struck a local woman in 1954. Here, you'll find a gallery of Native American artifacts, antique toys, handmade fabrics from the 1830s, and an extensive collection of photos and scrapbooks on local history. Pioneer exhibits are housed in the basement. One section features albums, awards, photos, costumes, and other memorabilia of native son Jim Nabors, who starred as TV's Gomer Pyle on *The Andy Griffith Show*.

The museum is open 10 a.m. to 5 p.m. Tuesday through Friday or by appointment. Although there's no admission charge, donations are accepted.

For fine dining with a Southern accent, visit **Buttermilk Hill Restaurant & Bar** (256-207-1001) at 300 East Third Street. Housed in a Victorian home built in 1904, the restaurant's name comes from its historic location. The interior features original

alabamatrivia

More than two dozen albums showcase the singing talent of Sylacauga native Jim Nabors of *The Andy Griffith Show* and *Gomer Pyle, USMC* fame. Nabors also is well known for singing "Back Home Again in Indiana" to kick off the Indy 500 race held each year in Indianapolis over the Memorial Day weekend. Nabors's tradition continued for more than 30 years. Nabors announced that, because of declining health, the 2014 Indy 500 would be the last one for which he sang.

floors, fireplaces, ornate woodwork, antique chandeliers—and maybe some ghosts, hints Kara McClendon Bacchi, who owns the property.

Depending on the weather, you may opt for lunch or dinner on the marble patio or front wraparound porch. For lunch, try the sautéed buttermilk chicken breast over romaine, tomatoes, locally made goat cheese,

Meteorite From Outer Space Brings Rude Awakening to Alabama Woman

Taking a nap on her couch, a Sylacauga woman got an unexpected awakening. Crashing through the roof of her home, an 8.5-pound meteorite ricocheted off a console radio and smashed into the woman's hand and hip. It is the only confirmed occurrence of an extraterrestrial hitting a human.

The event on November 30, 1954, caused a flurry of media coverage and an Air Force investigation. Today the hunk of space stone—known as the Hodges meteorite—is on display at the *Alabama Museum of Natural History at the University of Alabama* (427 Sixth Ave. NE, Tuscaloosa; 205-348-7550; amnh.ua.edu).

When 31-year-old Ann Hodges was jolted awake by the noise and the pain, she first thought a gas space heater had exploded and hurled something at her. Then she saw the grapefruit-size rock on the floor. And a gaping hole in the roof.

People in Alabama and nearby states reported seeing a fireball streaking through the sky at about the same time. Neighbors said they saw the falling star, followed by an explosion and billowing smoke. Most onlookers thought it must have been an airplane crash. Geologists said the loud noise was likely a sonic boom created by the meteorite as it traveled many times the speed of sound.

Examined by a local doctor, Hodges was found to have no permanent damage. Her hip and hand were swollen and painful, with a grapefruit-size bruise on her hip, but the hoopla surrounding the event soon engulfed her. Besieged by the media, Hodges was featured in *Life* magazine, as well as many other newspapers and magazines around the nation. She also appeared on Gary Moore's popular TV show, *I've Got a Secret.* Hodges eventually donated the meteorite to the Alabama Museum of Natural History.

Hodges died of kidney failure in 1972 at age 49.

The meteorite itself is still on display underneath a glass case at the Alabama Museum of Natural History. The 7-inch-by-5-inch-by-5-inch rock is covered with a thick black coating from its blazing entry. It has several chips and a patch of tar from the Hodges' roof.

toasted walnuts, and sweet onions with Balsamic molasses vinaigrette. A dinner choice might be the pork tenderloin roulade with lavender, sage, Parmesan, and sundried tomatoes drizzled with truffle oil and served with buttermilk mashed potatoes (a signature dish here) and assorted vegetables. Or select from the two or three daily specials. As for dessert, you'll want to try a seasonal treat like the chef's sublime take on strawberry shortcake with sliced berries, whipped cream, sweet corn bread, and a splash of sorghum syrup. Hours run 11 a.m. to 2 p.m. Tuesday through Friday and 5 to 9 p.m. Tuesday through Saturday. Moderate to expensive. Visit buttermilkhill restaurant.com.

Don't leave town without treating yourself to some ice cream at *Blue Bell Creameries* (256-249-6100 or 888-573-5286; cnd.bluebell.com) at 423 North Norton Avenue. What's your pleasure? Choices range from lemon, triple chocolate, chocolate chip, caramel pecan fudge, and banana split to pecan praline and cream, cherry vanilla, and black walnut—and the list goes on. In addition to watching ice cream being made, you can relax (after you finish agonizing over which flavor to order) in the old-fashioned ice-cream parlor or browse in the Country Store. Tours, which last about 45 minutes, take place Monday through Friday. Call ahead for information on how to schedule or join a tour. The Country Store is open from 9 a.m. to 5 p.m. Monday through Friday.

After leaving Sylacauga, follow US 280 southeast to *Alexander City,* home of the Russell Corporation. Employing about four-fifths of the local workforce, Russell outfits the sports world all the way from Little League through hundreds of college teams to most of the National Football League. This company handles every step of the process from cotton production to finished product. The sweat suit you don for your jog around the block may well have come from Alex City, as the locals call it.

The *Russell Retail Store* (256-397-1757), a big cheese-wedge of a building at 3562 US 280, sells sweatpants and tops, T-shirts, cardigans, and other leisure wear—maybe even your favorite team's togs. In addition to a university section (that carries mostly Atlantic Coast Conference and Southeastern Conference athletic apparel), the outlet offers casual clothing for men, women, and children. The Cross-Creek line features an array of items in both heavyweight and lightweight knits. You may want to personalize your purchases with selected transfers—from save the earth to holiday and hunting themes—that can be applied by heat press in 15 seconds. The store also carries a wide line of Spaulding products. Also, a back room contains discounted items. The store's hours are 10 a.m. to 6 p.m. Monday through Friday, 9 a.m. to 6 p.m. Saturday, and 1 to 5 p.m. Sunday.

While in the Alex City area, you might like to explore nearby *Horseshoe Bend National Military Park* (256-234-7111; nps.gov/hobe), the site of the final battle of the Creek War, which made a national hero of Andrew Jackson. Located about 12 miles north of Dadeville on State Route 49, the 2,040-acre park features a visitor center with exhibits on the battle, Creek Indian culture, and frontier life. The visitor center is open daily 9 a.m. to 4:30 p.m. Free admission.

Other local options include boating, swimming, and fishing at *Lake Martin,* which offers a 750-mile shoreline against a backdrop of wooded hills. This body of water spills over the southern half of Tallapoosa County and even splashes into neighboring Elmore and Coosa Counties. Depending on the season and local weather conditions, anglers haul in largemouth and striped bass, bream, bluegill, crappie, and catfish from this lake. For more outdoor recreation continue south to Elmore County.

Places to Stay in Central Alabama

ALEXANDER CITY

Baymont Inn & Suites
4335 US 280
(800) 337-0300

Days Inn
3146 US 280
(256) 234-6311

Mistletoe Bough
497 Hillabee St.
(256) 329-3717
mistletoebough.com

Quality Inn
2945 US 280
(256) 234-5900 or

ANNISTON

The Victoria
1600 Quintard Ave.
(256) 236-0503 or
(800) 260-8781
thevictoria.com

BIRMINGHAM

Birmingham Marriott
3590 Grandview Pkwy.
(205) 968-3775 or
(800) 627-7468

The Historical Redmont
2101 Fifth Ave. North
(205) 324-2101
theredmonthotel.com

**The Hotel Highland
Five Points South**
1023 20th St. South
(205) 933-9555
thehotelhighland.com

FOR MORE INFORMATION ABOUT CENTRAL ALABAMA

**Alexander City
Chamber of Commerce**
120 Tallapoosa St.
PO Box 926
Alexander City 35010
(256) 234-3461
alexandercitychamber.com
info@alexandercitychamber.com

**Anniston/Calhoun County
Chamber of Commerce**
1330 Quintard Ave.
PO Box 1087
Anniston 36201
(256) 237-3536 or
calhounchamber.com
info@calhounchamber.com

**Greater Birmingham
Convention & Visitors Bureau**
2200 Ninth Ave. North
Birmingham 35203-1100
(205) 458-8000 or (800) 458-8085
birminghamal.org
info@birmingham.org

Montevallo Chamber of Commerce
845 Valley St.
Montevallo 35115
(205) 665-1519
montevallocc.com
montevallochamber@gmail.com

**Tuscaloosa Tourism & Sports
Commission**
1900 Jack Warner Pkwy.
Tuscaloosa 35401
(205) 391-9200 or (800) 538-8696
visittuscaloosa.com

**Hyatt Regency
Birmingham**
1000 Riverchase Galleria
(205) 705-1234

**Renaissance Ross
Bridge Golf Resort &
Spa**
4000 Grand Ave.
(205) 916-7677 or (800)
593-6419

**Sheraton
Birmingham Hotel**
2101 Richard Arrington Jr.
Blvd. North
(205) 324-5000 or
(888) 627-7095

The Tutwiler
2021 Park Place North
(205) 322-2100 or
(866) 850-3053

DELTA

Cheaha State Park
2141 Bunker Loop
(256) 488-5115 or
(800) 610-5801
alapark.com/cheaharesort

MONTEVALLO

**Ramsay
Conference Center**
University of Montevallo
24 Vine St.
(205) 665-6280

NAUVOO

Old Harbin Hotel
131 Third St.
(205) 697-5652

OXFORD

Holiday Inn Express Hotel & Suites
160 Colonial Dr.
(256) 835-8768 or
(888) 465-4329

PELHAM

Oak Mountain State Park
200 Terrace Dr.
(205) 620-2524 or
(800) ALA–PARK
alapark.com/oakmountain

SYLACAUGA

Quality Inn
89 Gene Stewart Blvd.
(256) 245-4141 or
(800) 526-3766

TUSCALOOSA

Hotel Capstone
320 Paul Bryant Dr.
(205) 752-3200 or
(800) 477-2262
hotelcapstone.com

Centerstone Inn
4700 Doris Pate Dr.
(205) 556-3232 or
(800) 311-3811
centerstonehotels.com

Courtyard by Marriott
4115 Courtney Dr.
(205) 750-8384 or
(800) 321-2211

VINCENT

Blue Spring Manor
2870 Hwy. 83
(205) 672-9955
bluespringmanor.com

Places to Eat in Central Alabama

ALEXANDER CITY

Sinclair's Kowaliga
295 Kowaliga Marina Rd.
(256) 215-7035

ALICEVILLE

Plantation House Restaurant
102 Fifth St. SE
(205) 373-8121
plantationhouse.8k.com

ANNISTON

Betty's Bar-B-Q Inc.
401 South Quintard Ave.
(256) 237-1411

Classic on Noble
1024 Noble St.
(256) 237-5388
classiconnoble.com

Top O' the River
3330 McClellan Blvd.
(256) 238-0097
topotheriverrestaurant
.com

The Victoria
1604 Quintard Ave.
(256) 236-0503
thevictoria.com

BESSEMER

The Bright Star
304 North 19th St.
(205) 424-9444
thebrightstar.com

BIRMINGHAM

Bottega
2240 Highland Ave. South
(205) 939-1000
bottegarestaurant.com

Cafe at Innovation Depot
1500 First Ave. North
(205) 314-3456
culinardcafe.com

Cafe Dupont
113 20th St. North
(205) 322-1282
cafedupont.net

Chez Fonfon
2007 11th Ave.
(205) 939-3221
fonfonbham.com

Highlands Bar & Grill
2011 11th Ave. South
(205) 939-1400
highlandsbarandgrill.com

Hot & Hot Fish Club
2180 11th Court South
(205) 933-5474
hotandhotfishclub.com

Arlington Antebellum Home & Gardens

331 Cotton Ave. SW
Birmingham
(205) 780-5656
This circa 1850 Greek revival mansion contains a fine collection of period antiques.

Birmingham Zoo

2630 Cahaba Rd.
(205) 879-0408 or (205) 879-0409
Both big and little kids enjoy outings to this facility, the home of some 900 animals from all over the globe. A new 3,000-square-foot Butterfly Encounter is home to hundreds of butterflies, more than 20 species all native to Alabama. The Rhino Encounter lets visitors get up close and personal with two 4,000-pound rhinos. Check the website at birminghamzoo.com.

International Motorsports Hall of Fame & Talladega Superspeedway

3198 Speedway Blvd.
Talladega
(256) 362-5002
This unique facility, which occupies a complex of circular-shaped buildings, captures the speed of movement and thrill of competitive racing. You'll see the Budweiser Rocket Car, a missile on wheels that broke the sound barrier, and record-breaking vehicles once guided by Richard Petty, Bill Elliott, Bobby Allison, and other racing greats. Additional exhibits include vintage autos, drag racers, motorcycles, trophies, photos, and a simulator that puts you in the driver's seat. You can also tour the adjacent Talladega Superspeedway, the world's fastest

speedway. For more information check out motorsportshalloffame.com and talladegasuperspeedway.com.

McWane Science Center

200 19th St. North
Birmingham
(205) 714-8300
Definitely not off the beaten path, this science-adventure museum occupies the historic Loveman's department store building in the heart of downtown. Youngsters will especially enjoy the IMAX theater's presentations and simulated space-flight experiences offered by the Challenger Center for Space Science Education, a nonprofit organization founded by the families of the seven Challenger crew members who died in the tragic 1986 space shuttle explosion. The Ocean Pool, World of Water, and various interactive science exhibits all add to the excitement. Visit the museum's website at mcwane.org.

Splash Adventure

4599 Alabama Adventure Pkwy.
Bessemer
(205) 481-4750
This fun-filled family park offers water adventure galore in Bessemer, just southwest of Birmingham. Choose from watery fun on Acapulco Drop, Castaway Island, Kahuna Waves, and a zipline. Or pick the world's first 360-degree interactive water-based obstacle course. The Wipeout Adventure Course features a series of ropes, bridges, and towers along with hand- and foot-activated water elements. Visit the park's website at splashadventurewaterpark.com.

The Silvertron Cafe
3813 Clairmont Ave.
(205) 591-3707
silvertroncafe.com

CALERA

Zapopan Restaurant
4416 US 31
(205) 668-4008

HOMEWOOD

Nabeel's Cafe
1706 Oxmoor Rd.
(205) 879-9292
nabeels.com

HOOVER

Brock's
Renaissance Ross Bridge
Resort
4000 Grand Ave.
(205) 949-3051

IRONDALE

The Irondale Cafe
1906 First Ave. North
(205) 956-5258
irondalecafe.com

MAYLENE

Fox Valley Restaurant
County Rd. 17
(205) 664-8341

MONTEVALLO

Zapopan Restaurant
4551 State Rte. 25
(205) 665-7404

MOUNDVILLE

Pappy's Bar-B-Q
39616 State Rd. 59
(205) 371-4171

MOUNTAIN BROOK

Chez Lulu
1909 Cahaba Rd.
(205) 870-7011
chezlulu.us

NORTHPORT

Wintzell's Oyster House
1 Bridge Ave.
(205) 247-7772
wintzellsoysterhouse.com

OXFORD

China Luck
503 Quintard Dr.
(256) 831-5221

SYLACAUGA

**Buttermilk Hill
Restaurant & Bar**
300 East Third St.
(256) 207-1001
buttermilkhillrestaurant
.com

**LaCosta Mexican
Restaurant**
215 North Broadway Ave.
(256) 249-3360

TRUSSVILLE

**Chocolate Biscuit
Tearoom**
335 Main St.
(205) 655-0119
thechocolatebiscuit.com

TUSCALOOSA

Cypress Inn
501 Rice Mine Rd. North
(205) 345-6963
cypressinnrestaurant.com

DePalma's Italian Cafe
2300 University Blvd.
(205) 759-1879
depalmasdowntown.com

Dreamland
5535 15th Ave. East
(205) 758-8135
dreamlandbbq.com

Evangeline's
1653 McFarland
Blvd. North
(205) 752-0830
evangelinesrestaurant.com

**The Waysider
Restaurant**
1512 Greensboro Ave.
(205) 345-8239

The Plains

On your way to "The Plains" (home of Auburn University) in the historic Chattahoochee Trace's upper section, you might want to strike out east to **Tuskegee.** Stop by the **Tuskegee Human & Civil Rights Multicultural Center** (334-724-0800), which also serves as a welcome center. Located in a former bank building at 104 South Elm Street, the facility houses exhibits on the history of Macon County, including one on the Tuskegee Syphilis Study and local civil rights activities. Here, you can pick up tourist information. The staff will answer your questions and suggest nearby off-the-beaten-path spots to visit. Hours are Tuesday through Saturday from 10 a.m. to 3 p.m. Admission is free.

Next make your way to West Montgomery Road and **Tuskegee Institute National Historic Site** (334-727-3200), where even peanut-butter buffs will be amazed to learn about the peanut's potential. The Carver Museum pays tribute to the creative genius of the agronomist, artist, and inventor who helped change the course of Southern agriculture. George Washington Carver's agricultural

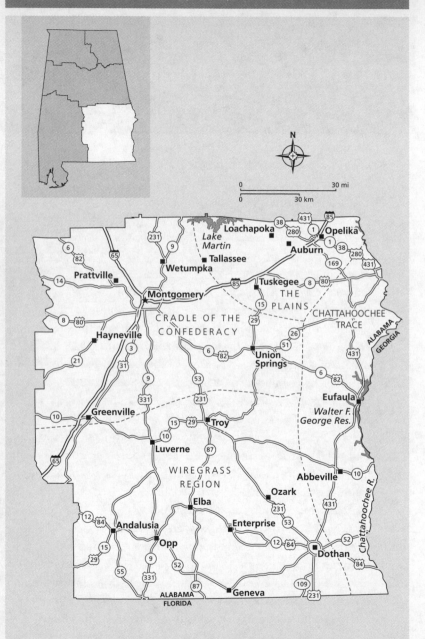

experiments with peanuts, pecans, sweet potatoes, and cotton resulted in a more educated approach to farming—not to mention hundreds of new products, many featured among the museum's exhibits. You'll also see some of Carver's artwork and a model of the first lab he used to launch research that resulted in the transformation of sweet potatoes into after-dinner mints, a coffee substitute, lemon drops, starch, synthetic ginger, tapioca, library paste, medicine, writing ink, and a multitude of other items. As for the multipurpose peanut, the legendary scientist's list of possible uses ranges from beverages, foods, cosmetics, dyes, and medicines to diesel fuel, laundry soap, and insecticide. Before you leave the museum, be sure to visit the gift section. I bought a copy of a booklet (first published in June 1925) entitled *How to Grow the Peanut and 105 Ways of Preparing It for Human Consumption,* containing recipes from peanut bisque to peanut pudding. Museum admission is free. Except for Thanksgiving, Christmas, and New Year's Day, the museum is open Monday through Saturday from 9 a.m. to 4:30 p.m.

Later take a campus stroll to see some of the handmade brick buildings, which students constructed during the institute's early years. You'll also want to tour *The Oaks* at 905 W. Montgomery Road, home of Booker T. Washington, who served as first president of Tuskegee Institute, which was founded in 1881. The home is furnished as it was during the time the Washington family lived there. Admission is free. Tours are available. Call (334) 727-3200 for information. Head north to the "land where turtles live"—a former Creek Indian settlement called *Loachapoka* that once also thrived as a stagecoach junction. Seven miles west of Auburn on State Route 14, you'll find the *Loachapoka Historic District,* which features several structures dating from the decade 1840 to 1850. *The Lee County Historical Society Museum* (334-887-3007, leecountyhistoricalsociety.com), housed in the old Trade Center building at 6500 Stage Road, contains items ranging from a unique hand-carved cedar rocking chair and an 1840s accounting desk to an oak map case, an antique medical bag, and a punch bowl and dipper made from gourds.

alabamatrivia

George Washington Carver invented peanut butter during his experiments at Tuskegee Institute.

The Intrepid Tuskegee Airmen

During the early 1940s, Moton Field served as the training grounds for the Tuskegee Airmen, who overcame formidable odds to serve their country with bravery and distinction in a segregated America. As escorts to World War II bombing missions in North Africa and Southern Europe, these African-American aviators compiled an enviable combat record and ranked among the military's best pilots. The 332nd Fighter Group never lost a bomber to enemy fighters while escorting the 15th Air Force on bombing missions. Revered by American bomber crews (who called them the "Red-tail Angels" because of their aircrafts' distinctive markings), these flying heroes also commanded the respect of the German Luftwaffe.

At the US Air Force Academy, the Tuskegee Airmen statue acknowledges their extraordinary contribution: "They rose from adversity through competence, courage, commitment, and capacity to serve America on silver wings, and to set a standard few will transcend."

Lending her support to Tuskegee Institute's civilian pilot training program, First Lady Eleanor Roosevelt visited here in March 1941. She requested to be taken on a flight by Charles Alfred "Chief" Anderson, who inspired the founding of Tuskegee's School of Aviation, and newspapers across the country carried a photo of this unprecedented event.

The Tuskegee group's achievements represent a turning point in the role of African-Americans in the US military and factored into President Harry S. Truman's signing Executive Order 9981 in 1948, setting the stage for the military's desegregation and later the Civil Rights Movement.

In 1998, Congress designated the Tuskegee Airmen National Historic Site as a unit of the National Park System. Along with the remaining hangar, visitors can see the airfield taxiway, control tower, reservoir, gasoline pits, and fuel storage facilities from the World War II era. The modest airport terminal also features exhibits of photos that chronicle the history of Black aviation and the Tuskegee Airmen.

The National Park Service Visitor Center is located on the outskirts of Tuskegee at 1616 Chappie James Avenue. Except for major holidays, the site is open Saturday 9 a.m. to 4:30 p.m. Free admission. To reach the "Home of Black Aviation," take exit 38 off I-85. For more information call (334) 724-0922 or visit nps.gov/tuai.

Upstairs, rooms with individual themes feature vintage costumes such as an 1877 wedding dress, an exhibit on Ella Smith's Roanoke doll creations, antique quilts, and a melodeon. Other displays include military uniforms and equipment, kitchen utensils and gadgets, and an almost complete section of Auburn annuals that date to the 1890s.

On the grounds you'll see a steam-powered cotton gin, gristmill, working blacksmith shop, bandstand, doctor's buggy, and dogtrot cabin (moved here from rural Tallapoosa County and reconstructed). If you visit in October, don't miss the **Historical Fair and Ruritan's Syrup Sopping** in Loachapoka. Folks at this event, harking back to yesteryear, demonstrate the entire process of converting sugar cane into syrup—from cane crushing by mule-drawn press to syrup sampling on homemade sweet potato biscuits (sometimes called "cat head biscuits" because of their large size). For information on making an appointment to see the museum, call the Auburn-Opelika Tourism Bureau at (866) 880-8747 or (334) 887-8747, stop by at 714 Glenn Avenue, or visit aotourism.com.

Afterward continue east to "sweet Auburn, loveliest village of the plain." This line from Oliver Goldsmith's poem "The Deserted Village" inspired the university town's name. Founded by the Alabama Methodist Conference in 1856, the school later became a land-grant institution. (Incidentally, if you enter **Auburn** by way of I-85, a trail of big orange tiger paws takes you all the way to the university campus.)

Start your tour of the **Auburn University Historic District** at Toomer's Corner, a busy intersection that gets layered so deeply with toilet tissue after each Tiger victory that sometimes vehicles cannot pass through for an hour or two while a celebration takes place. (Auburn is the only city in the world to have a line item in the city budget for the removal of toilet paper.) Toomer's Corner is named in honor of former state senator Sheldon "Shell" Toomer, a halfback on Alabama's first football team in 1892. Local lore says that the tradition of papering Toomer's Corner can be traced back to the days when Toomer's Drugs had the only handy telegraph for fast (in those days) news delivery. When Auburn played away games, fans would wait to hear results from the drugstore telegraph. If the team won, the ticker tape would be thrown on power lines in celebration.

Before embarking on your campus trek, you might like to step into **Toomer's Drugstore** (334-887-3488; toomersdrugs.com), a local landmark

BEST ATTRACTIONS IN SOUTHEAST ALABAMA

Alabama Shakespeare Festival,
Montgomery

First White House of the Confederacy,
Montgomery

The Jule Collins Smith Museum of Art,
Auburn

Landmark Park,
Dothan

Lovelace Athletic Museum and Hall of Honor,
Auburn

Old Alabama Town,
Montgomery

Pioneer Museum of Alabama,
Troy

Rosa Parks Library and Museum,
Montgomery

State Capitol,
Montgomery

Town of Eufaula

Tuskegee Institute National Historic Site,
Tuskegee

US Army Aviation Museum,
Fort Rucker

at 100 North College Street, to see the antique marble soda fountain and to order a lemonade. Shell Toomer established the store in 1896. Hours are Monday through Friday 10 a.m. to 6 p.m., Saturday 10 a.m. to 5 p.m., and Sunday noon to 5 p.m. This section of campus features several buildings that date from the 1850s to the early 1900s. You'll see the Gothic revival University Chapel, Langdon Hall, and Samford Hall. The latter, a four-story brick structure of Italianate design, dates to 1888 and stands on the site of Old Main, a building that burned the year before.

To explore a tucked-away corner on campus, search out the *Donald E. Davis Arboretum,* with pavilion, lake, and some 200 labeled botanical specimens ranging from red Japanese maples and chinquapin oaks to Southern magnolias and chinaberry trees. The 13.5-acre arboretum is open daily from sunrise to sunset. Restrooms are located on the east side of the pavilion.

Don't miss the *Lovelace Athletic Museum and Hall of Honor* (334-844-4750), located at the corner of Samford and Donahue in the Athletic

Complex when it reopens in 2010 after major renovations. Honoring Auburn's athletes, the museum recognizes such athletes as Heisman Trophy winner and football/baseball hero Bo Jackson, NBA star Charles Barkley, star baseball player Frank Thomas, Heisman Trophy winner/coach Pat Sullivan, and legendary coaches Pat Dye and Shug Jordan. Check out auburntigers .com to see some Auburn legends and keep up with the renovation project.

To visit a jewel of a museum, head to 901 South College Street. Here you'll find *The Jule Collins Smith Museum of Art* (334-844-1484) overlooking a three-acre lake. Constructed of travertine stone from Italy, the handsome facility features eight exhibition galleries, a museum shop, an auditorium, and a cafe. On entering, you'll see a stunning glass chandelier created for the vaulted rotunda by internationally known glass artist Dale Chihuly.

Other treasures include one of the world's largest collections of Victorian Belleek porcelain, outstanding Tibetan bronzes, and more than 100 of Audubon's most acclaimed prints. But the big story here centers on a collection of 36 paintings and drawings that had remained homeless for more than half a century.

Originally assembled by the US State Department in 1946, the collection features works by John Marin, Georgia O'Keeffe, Ben Shahn, Arthur Dove, Ralston Crawford, Yasuo Kuniyoski, and others. Because of its abstract nature and the political leanings of a few of the artists, the traveling exhibit met with so much criticism on the home front that it was recalled, stored, and labeled government "surplus property," thus allowing tax-supported institutions like Auburn to receive a 95 percent discount when the collection was subsequently offered at auction. An Auburn professor with foresight, Frank Applebee, spearheaded "the art bargain of the century" when he persuaded art department instructors to pool their yearly salary increase and enter the announced auction. As a result, Auburn University's Advancing American Art Collection was acquired in 1948 for an unthinkable $1,072. Experts call this body of works, now valued somewhere between $7 and $10 million, one of the most important collections of American art from the post–World War II era.

After viewing the exhibits, take time to enjoy the museum's botanical gardens with walking paths. The Museum Cafe is a great place to relax and recharge. The menu changes weekly and specials are posted on the website.

TOP ANNUAL EVENTS IN SOUTHEAST ALABAMA

Bridge Crossing Jubilee
Selma, first full weekend in March
(334) 526-2626
bcjubilee.org

Rattlesnake Rodeo
Opp, first Saturday and Sunday
in April
(334) 493-4572 or (800) 239-8054
cityofopp.com

Azalea-Dogwood Trail and Festival
Dothan, late March or early April
(334) 615-3000

Auburn Floral Trail
Auburn, late March or early April
(334) 501-3085

Spring Pilgrimage
Eufaula, first weekend in April
(888) 383-2852
eufaulapilgrimage.com

A-Day Football Game
Auburn, April
(334) 844-4040 or (800) AUB-1957

Auburn CityFest
Auburn, April
(334) 501-2936
auburncityfest.com

On the Tracks Food & Wine Festival
Opelika, October
(334) 745-0466
onthetracks.org

Historical Fair and Ruritan's Syrup Sopping in Loachapoka
Loachapoka, October
syrupsopping.com

Alabama Coastal BirdFest
Fairhope, October
alabamacoastalbirdfest.com

National Peanut Festival
Dothan, November
(334) 793-4323 or (888) 449-0212
nationalpeanutfestival.com

A favorite is the delicious crab bisque and the fried goat cheese salad with grapes and pecans. The cafe is open for lunch Tuesday through Friday from 11 a.m. to 2 p.m. and for dinner on Thursday from 5 to 8 p.m.

Museum hours are 8:30 a.m. to 4:30 p.m. Tuesday through Saturday, and 1 to 4 p.m. Sunday. On Thursday nights, hours are extended to 8 p.m. Free admission. For more information, click on jcsm.auburn.edu.

While in Auburn consider headquartering at *Crenshaw Guest House* (334-821-1131 or 800-950-1131), 2 blocks north of Toomer's Corner. Shaded by giant oak and pecan trees, this blue Victorian gingerbread–style house stands at 371 North College Street in Auburn's Old Main and Church Street

Historic District. Owners Lynn and George Postell, who furnished the two-story 1890 home with lovely antiques, offer five units for overnight guests. The Postells wanted to start a small family business and purchased the house in July 2008 knowing it is a lovely bed-and-breakfast facility. The Crenshaw also offers two guest cottages on the property—the Coach Dye Cottage with two bedrooms and two baths, and the Thach Cottage with a loft and bedroom. Guests receive a bountiful hot breakfast. See crenshawguesthouse .com. Standard to moderate rates.

While in the area, golfers will want to tee off at *Auburn Links at Mill Creek* (334-887-5151, auburnlinksgolf.com), a $5 million facility that occupies 274 acres located about 3 miles south of town near the intersection of US 29 and I-85 at exit 51 at 826 Shell Toomer Parkway. (The 18th hole's sand traps form a giant tiger paw print.)

Auburn's sister city, *Opelika,* makes a good place to continue your area exploration. In Opelika's "olden days," passengers traveling through by train sometimes saw shootouts across the railroad tracks. Fortunately, today's visitors don't have to dodge stray bullets, so you can relax as you explore the Railroad Avenue Historic District.

As a result of Opelika's participation in Alabama's Main Street program (a project of the National Trust for Historic Preservation), many once-forgotten structures have been rescued and reincarnated as charming shops such as *Easterday Antiques* at 805 South Railroad Avenue. Helen Easterday, who's been called "the quintessential town person," and her husband, Kenneth, have embraced the local downtown revitalization program to the point of converting the enormous upper level of their shop into a wonderful home. Mrs. Easterday's passion for art may be observed in the exquisite antique furnishings, oriental rugs, paintings, and accessories displayed in her shop. The shop is open 9:30 a.m. to 4 p.m. weekdays. Appointments are suggested. For more information or an appointment, call (334) 749-6407 or visit easterdayantiques.com.

After your Railroad Avenue stroll, head to *The Museum of East Alabama* (334-749-2751; eastalabama.org), located nearby at 121 South Ninth Street. Here you'll see a dugout canoe of white cypress that dates back as far as 3,500 BC, as well as glass milk bottles, baby bonnets, Shirley Temple and Roanoke dolls, toys, collections of vintage typewriters, pianos, farm implements, war memorabilia, and surgical instruments. Notice the interesting foot X-ray machine (typical of those once used in shoe stores) and the bicycle-propelled ice-cream cart. The museum's collection also includes an early-20th-century kitchen and a full-size fire truck. Hours are 10 a.m. until 4 p.m. Tuesday through Friday and 2 to 4 p.m. on Saturday. Admission is free.

Looking to the right as you exit the museum, you'll see the lofty clock tower of the *Lee County Courthouse,* a half block away. Listed on the National Register of Historic Places, the handsome, white-columned, two-story brick structure dates to 1896 and features marble floors and decorative arched windows.

Take time to drive around a bit to see Opelika's lovely homes, which exemplify a wide range of architectural styles. While in the area, golfers will enjoy playing the *Grand National,* one of Alabama's fine courses on the Robert Trent Jones Golf Trail at 3000 Robert Trent Jones Trail. For more information on this award-winning course, built on 1,300 acres encompassing a 650-acre lake, call (334) 749-9042 or (800) 949-4444 or visit rtjgolf.com/grandnational.

Chattahoochee Trace

After touring War Eagle country, continue south toward Eufaula, sometimes called the "Natchez of Alabama." You may want to make your base at lovely *Lakepoint Resort* (334-687-8011 or 800-544-5253; alapark.com/lakepoint resort), about 7 miles north of town just off US 431 at 104 Old Highway 165. Located on the shores of Lake Eufaula (also known as Lake George), this complex offers accommodations ranging from campsites, cabins, and cottages to resort rooms and suites along with a restaurant, coffee shop, lounge, and gift shop. Recreation options include swimming, golfing, tennis, hiking, picnicking, biking, waterskiing, and boating—not to mention fishing in a 45,200-acre lake known as the Big Bass Capital of the World. Room rates are standard.

Continue to Eufaula, a city filled with multiple versions of the perfect Southern mansion. Located on a bluff above the Chattahoochee River, Eufaula boasts the state's second-largest historic district and offers a feast for architecture aficionados. During the *Eufaula Pilgrimage,* an annual event that takes place the first full weekend in April, visitors can enjoy home tours, antiques shows, concerts, and other festivities. For more information, contact the Eufaula Heritage Association at (888) 383-2852 or go to eufaula pilgrimage.com.

Stop by the **Hart House** (334-687-9755) at 211 North Eufaula Avenue, an 1850 Greek revival structure that serves as headquarters for the Historic Chattahoochee Commission. Here you can pick up visitors information about the Trace, a river corridor running through portions of Alabama and Georgia. Throughout this bistate region, travelers will discover a wealth of historic sites, natural attractions, and recreation facilities. Except for holidays, the Hart House may be visited from 8 a.m. to 5 p.m. Monday through Friday.

Continue to **Shorter Mansion** (334-687-3793 or 888-383-2852) at 340 North Eufaula Avenue. This elegant structure dates to 1884 and features 17 Corinthian-capped columns and an elaborate frieze of molded acanthus leaves and scrolls beneath its lofty balustraded roof. Be sure to notice the front door's beveled leaded glass and the entrance hall's parquet floor and molded plaster cornices. This Neoclassical revival mansion, furnished in fine Victorian period pieces, houses the Eufaula Historical Museum and serves as headquarters for the Eufaula Heritage Association.

One upstairs room contains portraits of six state governors who were either born in or later lived in Barbour County. Another upstairs room pays tribute to retired Adm. Thomas H. Moorer, a Eufaula native who served two terms as chairman of the Joint Chiefs of Staff. Displays include Admiral Moorer's portrait, uniform, awards, and mementos from his naval career.

You'll also see Waterford crystal and cut-glass chandeliers, antiques, Confederate relics, period wedding dresses, Alabama memorabilia, and decorative arts. You may browse through the mansion at your leisure or take a guided tour. Admission: adults $5, children (ages 3 to 12) $3. Except for major holidays, the home is open Monday through Saturday from 10 a.m. to 4 p.m.

Before leaving Eufaula be sure to visit **Fendall Hall** (334-687-8469), at 917 West Barbour Street. Built between 1856 and 1860, the home features stenciled walls and ceilings painted by a 19th-century Italian artist, and the original decor with high Victorian colors remains relatively unchanged. Also noteworthy are the entrance hall's striking black-and-white marble floor and the home's early plumbing system, supplied by attic cisterns. Rumor has it that a ghost named Sammy makes his presence known here from time to time. Currently the house is open for tours Monday through Friday from 10 a.m. to noon and 1 to 4 p.m. and the first Saturday of the month. Admission:

adults $5; college students, senior citizens and military $4; children (ages 6 to 18) $3.

After touring this town of lovely mansions, head to **Clayton**, a small town with some unique attractions, such as the **Octagon House** at 103 North Midway Street. Listed on the National Register of Historic Places, this unusual structure, also known as the Petty-Roberts-Beatty House, is the state's sole surviving antebellum octagonal house. The ground floor served as the original kitchen (and also as the setting for a mystery, *The Rusty Key,* written by one of the home's owners). Four chimneys extending above the cupola enclose the staircase of this eight-sided structure. The first floor features four main rooms, two small rooms, and two halls that open to the surrounding porch. To arrange a tour call (334) 775-3254. Modest admission.

At nearby Clayton Baptist Church Cemetery (also on North Midway Street), you'll find the **Whiskey Bottle Tombstone,** once featured on *Ripley's Believe It or Not!* television show. The bottle-shaped headstone and footstone, which mark the final resting place of William T. Mullen (1834–1863), still contain their original removable stone stoppers. Such a memorial obviously tells a story, and the story behind the stone goes something like this: Mr. Mullen, a local accountant, acquired a reputation as a heavy drinker. His wife, Mary, a devout teetotaler, threatened that if he drank himself to death, she would let the world know by erecting an appropriate memorial. The Whiskey Bottle Tombstone testifies that she kept her promise.

Wiregrass Region

Continuing south along the Chattahoochee Trace takes you to **Dothan,** in the state's southeastern corner. Here, in a region called the Wiregrass, early settlers battled the odds to cultivate this large stretch of land once completely covered by clumps of stiff, dry grass growing under longleaf pines. To learn more about the Wiregrass region's roots, stop by **Landmark Park** (334-794-3452; landmarkpark.com), in Dothan on US 431, about 3 miles north of Ross Clark Circle at 430 Landmark Drive. At this living-history farmstead, you may be greeted by sheep, goats, pigs, chickens, cows, and a mule. You'll see a blacksmith shop, pioneer log cabin, smokehouse, cane-mill syrup shed, and other authentic outbuildings of an 1890s farm.

"We want to preserve the natural and cultural heritage of the Wiregrass region," says William Holman, Landmark Park's executive director, who calls the 100-acre park an outdoor classroom. The cozy clapboard farmhouse looks as if its occupants just stepped out to milk the cows and may return any minute. An apron hangs on a cupboard door, and a shaving mug and brush wait beside the washstand.

The park offers a full schedule of special events with demonstrations of seasonal farming activities, pioneer skills, and various crafts. In addition to the farmstead, you'll see a country store, church, one-room schoolhouse, drugstore, gazebo, interpretive center, planetarium, nature trails, board-walks, beaver ponds, and picnic areas. Youngsters will especially enjoy the playground with its barnyard theme. Admission: adults $4, children (ages 3 to 12) $3. Hours are 9 a.m. to 5 p.m. Monday through Saturday and noon to 6 p.m. Sunday. Continue to downtown Dothan, the area's major trade center. Proclaimed "Peanut Capital of the World," this region produces one-fourth of the nation's peanuts. Each fall Dothan stages the *National Peanut Festival* (334-793-4323; nationalpeanutfestival.com) with a full calendar of events, from demonstrations of square dance rounds by the Goober Gambo-leers to a contest for prize-winning peanut recipes. Look for the large peanut sculptures, individually decorated and placed throughout town.

Across the street from the Civic Center, you'll see the *Wiregrass Museum of Art* (334-794-3871; wiregrassmuseum.org) at 126 Museum Avenue. This three-level facility features a full schedule of rotating exhibits attractively displayed in various galleries. The museum contains a classroom/studio and a children's hands-on gallery. Youngsters will find the activity area entertaining as well as educational. The museum's hours are 10 a.m. to 5 p.m. Tuesday through Saturday. Admission is free, but donations are accepted.

First known as Poplar Head, Dothan took its present biblical name in 1885. Around that time, concerned citizens decided to tone down the town's rowdy image and hired a marshal and deputies to enforce new laws designed to terminate the saloons' regular Saturday-night brawls.

While driving around town, you'll see local history depicted in colorful murals on various city buildings. The *Mule Marker* in Poplar Head Park pays tribute to the animal that played a major role in the Wiregrass region's early development. Nearby at 115 North Saint Andrews Street, you'll notice the impressive **Dothan Opera House,** a neoclassical revival structure that dates from 1915. Another downtown historic site, **Porter Hardware** (334-792-3158; ircusa.com/porter), at 136 East Main Street with its rolling ladders, still exudes the nostalgic flavor of its late-1800s origin.

Afterward head to nearby Ozark, home of the **Claybank Church** on East Andrews Avenue just off State Route 249. This 1852 log church with hand-split board shingles and original pews is open daily during daylight hours.

Carry on your exploration of the Wiregrass region with a visit to **Enterprise** and don't miss the **Boll Weevil Monument.** Actually, you can't miss this memorial because it stands in the middle of Main Street. And if you aren't sure you'd recognize a boll weevil (a bug about a quarter-inch long with a snout half the length of its body), just watch for a statue of a woman clad in classic drapery who stands on an ornamented pedestal and holds a magnified version of the pest high above her head. A streetside plaque explains that in 1919 the citizens of Enterprise and Coffee County erected the statue in profound appreciation of the boll weevil and what it has done as the herald of prosperity. After the boll weevil demolished two-thirds of Coffee County's cotton in 1915, local farmers started to diversify, planting other crops such as sugar cane, corn, hay, potatoes, and peanuts. Particularly suited to the Wiregrass, peanuts played a primary role in saving the local economy after the boll weevil's destruction and soon became the region's principal cash crop.

About half a block from the Boll Weevil Monument stands the venerable **Rawls Hotel** (334-308-9387) at 116 South Main Street. Listed on the National Register of Historic Places, the hotel dates to 1903 and makes a great headquarters while checking out the local sites. A hub for civic and social events until it closed in the early 1970s, the refurbished property once again lures travelers. In addition to several businesses, the hotel houses a fine dining restaurant, meeting rooms, tavern, and four handsome rooms and suites. The Rawls Restaurant offers farm-to-table cuisine with a contemporary Southern touch. The restaurant is open Tuesday through Friday from 11 a.m. to 2 p.m. with dinner served Tuesday through Saturday from 5 to 10 p.m. Keep a lookout for the ghost of founder Japheth Rawls, who is said to walk the halls keeping an eye on his beloved hotel. Visit the website at rawlsbandb.com. Rates are standard to moderate.

Behind the hotel on Railroad Street, you'll find the Pea River Histori-cal Society Depot Museum at 106 Railroad Street. In railroad's golden days, passengers simply stepped off a train here, and a short stroll took them to the Rawls. Today's visitor can browse through the depot's rooms and large freight area filled with historical artifacts. "Many of the arrow and spear points in the Indian Room were discovered by local farmers, while plowing their land," said a volunteer.

History buffs can dip into more local lore at *Pea River Genealogical Library* (334-393-2901) at 108 South Main Street. A stroll along Main Street takes you past eateries like the *Magnolia Room Cafe* and antiques shops.

Before or after exploring downtown, stop by the *Enterprise Welcome Center* and Little Red Schoolhouse (complete with pot-bellied stove and slate boards) near the US 84 bypass.

At the *Boll Weevil Soap Company,* you'll find Southern Belle, Camellia Flower, High Cotton, Gardener's Love, Southern Romance, and other herbal products made by Rosemary Howell, a nurse by profession. Visit bwsoap .com, call (334) 393-7627, or stop by 600 Boll Weevil Circle, Suite 3, and make someone happy with a fine selection of soaps. The shop is open Monday through Saturday from 10 a.m. to 6 p.m. Golfers will want to play *Tartan Pines,* a challenging 18-hole course on the town's west side. The facility, with a restaurant on the premises, opened in 2000 and offers club memberships but also welcomes the public.

Opp, in neighboring Covington County, hosts a unique annual event: the *Rattlesnake Rodeo.* This spring festival, scheduled the first full week-end in March, features the world's only rattlesnake race along with arts and crafts (including several made from rattlesnake skins), a buck dancing con-test, and programs on rattlesnake education and safety. For specific informa-tion call (334) 493-4572. You can also visit cityofopp.com. To reach *Troy* follow State Route 87 north from Enterprise. On the southern outskirts of this town, the home of Troy State University, you'll find the *Mossy Grove School House Restaurant* (334-566-4921) just off US 231 at 1902 Elba Highway. Set among moss-draped trees, this rustic structure started out as a one-room schoolhouse in 1856. Later enlarged and renovated, the building still contains its original stage, now part of the back dining room.

Diners can order fried dill pickles to nibble on while waiting for their entrees and admire memorabilia ranging from Confederate money, swords, and a cannonball to antique tools, barrels, and even bear teeth. Also displayed here are an old-fashioned telephone, cheese cutter, barber chair, and many other items.

Popular entrees include broiled shrimp scampi, charbroiled chicken tenders, and charbroiled rib eye. All dinners include hush puppies, coleslaw or salad, wedge fries or baked potato, and white beans with a special pepper relish. Moderate prices. Hours are 5 to 9 p.m. Tuesday through Saturday.

Continuing north through Troy takes you to the ***Pioneer Museum of Alabama*** (334-566-3597), located at 248 US 231. Situated on 30 wooded acres, this fascinating folk museum contains some 18,000 items from the past two centuries. You'll find extensive collections, all well organized and attractively displayed, plus 15 outbuildings. Household items range from lemon squeezers, sausage stuffers, and butter molds to cookware, fluting irons, spittoons, and an Edison phonograph with a morning glory–shaped speaker. Although the lovely period furnishings of the three Bass Rooms reflect an upper-class lifestyle, the museum's collections focus on items that played a part in the daily existence of the community's middle- and lower-class members.

Other exhibits include newspaper typesetting and printing machines, an enormous collection of farm equipment, blacksmith and carpenter shop displays, and several horse-drawn vehicles, including an antique hearse. One exhibit, "When Cotton Was King," features a mule with "a lean and hungry look." Upon seeing the sculptor's interesting armature, museum officials had the artist stop working at once to preserve the unique look of the unfinished piece. Other objects on display include a portable boll weevil catcher, a peanut sheller, and a moonshine still.

Don't miss the early-20th-century street setting featuring storefronts of barber and millinery shops, a bank, and offices for a dentist, doctor, and lawyer—all appropriately equipped. Save plenty of time for exploring the grounds, too. On your way to see the furnished dogtrot log cabin and nearby tenant house, you'll pass a loblolly pine known as the Moon Tree—the seed from which it grew journeyed to the moon and back with the Apollo astronauts. Before leaving the museum, stop by the country store stocked with essentials such as snuff, castor oil, patent medicines, and bone buttons. You'll also find a restored 1928 schoolhouse, a working gristmill, a corncrib made of hand-hewn logs, a covered bridge, a nature trail, and a picnic area on the grounds. Other interesting exhibits include Native American artifacts and a coal-burning train engine. Thursday visitors can watch quilters at work, and weaving demonstrations take place Friday and Saturday. Except for major holidays, hours are 9 a.m. to 5 p.m. Tuesday through Saturday. Admission: adults $6, senior citizens $5, students (age 6 to college) $4, children (age 5 and under) free. Preview the property at pioneer-museum.org.

Cradle of the Confederacy

For a hearty meal at **Red's Little School House** (334-584-7955), located at blink-and-you've-missed-it Grady, travel north from Troy on US 231, then turn onto State Route 94 in the direction of Dublin and Ramer. At the intersection of Route 94 and Gardner Road, look for a tall water tower, labeled Pine Level, with a small red structure beside it. Or leave the directions up to your GPS. At this restaurant, housed in a former school and owned by Debbie Deese, you'll find a buffet selection of all-you-can-eat, fresh, home-cooked vegetables such as sweet potato soufflé, fried okra, and collards. (Red, Debbie's father and the former owner, grows acres and acres of vegetables each season and reaps a huge harvest.) The menu also features fried corn bread, chicken and dumplings, barbecue, and fried chicken. If you manage to save room for dessert, the choices are listed on the blackboard.

Even though the nation's presidents look sternly from their frames over the chalkboard and old maps suggest geography-test anxiety, this is a place to relax. Schoolmarm Debbie banters with the customers, who obviously enjoy both the food and the friendly surroundings. Debbie, who calls herself "a half-decent guitar player," sometimes sings for the crowd. "Everyone brags on the food, and laughs at the entertainment," she writes in the preface of her cookbook.

Debbie converted two school buses into traveling kitchens and takes her catering show on the road for large gatherings. She has cooked for five governors and one president. "I think food is the answer to everything," she says. School starts at 11 a.m. and ends at 9 p.m. Wednesday through Saturday and closes at 3 p.m. on Sunday. Prices are economical to moderate.

Afterward continue north on one of several roads that lead to **Montgomery,** about 30 minutes away. Montgomery offers a wealth of attractions appealing to all interests. In the past the city has been home to such luminaries as Tallulah Bankhead, Hank Williams, and Nat King Cole. Montgomery served as a launching ground for the Wright brothers, who gave early flying lessons here; a playground for Zelda and F. Scott Fitzgerald; and a battleground in the Civil Rights Movement. This city also pioneered the nation's first electric trolley system, the Lightning Route, which made its successful trial run in 1886.

alabamatrivia

Nat King Cole was born at the Cole-Samford House on St. John Street in Montgomery.

Make the ***Montgomery Area Visitor Center*** (334-262-0013; visiting montgomery.com) at 300 Water Street your first stop in the city. Housed in historic Union Station that dates to 1898, the center offers a handsome medley of exhibit panels on area attractions along with maps and information on accommodations, restaurants, festivals, and more. Take a virtual 13-minute city tour in the minitheater and collect some souvenirs in the gift shop. Hours are 8:30 a.m. to 5 p.m. Monday through Saturday and noon to 4 p.m. Sunday.

On the city's southeast side, you'll find the ***Alabama Shakespeare Festival (ASF)*** (334-271-5353 or 800-841-4273). Just off East Boulevard on Woodmere Boulevard in the Wynton M. Blount Cultural Park, ASF presents works ranging from familiar classics to world-premiere Southern Writers' Project productions. You can take in a performance of works by such writers as Sir Noel Coward, Anton Chekhov, Eugene O'Neill, George Bernard Shaw, Tennessee Williams, and, of course, the Bard. The only American theater invited to fly the same flag as that used by England's Royal Shakespeare Company, ASF attracts more than 300,000 visitors annually from all 50 states and 60 foreign countries and is the world's fifth-largest Shakespeare festival.

Situated in a 250-acre, landscaped, English-style park, the $21.5 million performing arts complex houses two stages, rehearsal halls, and a snack bar along with costume, prop, and gift shops. The grounds, perfect for strolling or picnicking, feature a reflecting lake complete with gliding swans. Wend your way through Shakespeare Gardens, with a 325-seat amphitheater against a setting that brings to life the Bard's botanical references to flowers and herbs, such as rosemary "for remembrance" (and great as a garnish for most meat dishes, too). Linger awhile and enjoy the park's various colors, textures, and smells. For information, brochures, or tickets, call or write to Alabama Shakespeare Festival, One Festival Drive, Montgomery 36117-4605. You can visit asf.net to check on current productions.

Before leaving the park, take time to browse through the *Montgomery Museum of Fine Arts* (334-240-4333). Located at One Museum Drive, this facility features the fine Blount Collection with works representing more than 200 years of American art. Also, you'll see Old Master prints, outstanding porcelain and glass collections, 19th- and 20th-century American paintings and sculpture, and art of the American South. View mmfa.org for current exhibitions and more information on the museum's holdings. Admission is free. Except for major holidays, the museum's hours are 10 a.m. to 5 p.m. Tuesday through Saturday. Thursday hours extend to 9 p.m. The Sunday schedule is noon to 5 p.m. Enjoy a lunch break in the museum at Cafe M, an artful bistro that serves from 11 a.m. to 2 p.m. Tuesday through Saturday. Sample the Mediterranean chicken salad and flourless fudge cake. Then save a bit of bread to toss to the ducks, who cruise by regularly with great expectations. Rates are economical to moderate.

Back in downtown Montgomery, across the street from Cloverdale Park, stands the former home of a famous couple who personified the Jazz Age. Housed in the lower right section (Apartment B) of a circa-1910 two-story brown structure at 919 Felder Avenue, you'll find the *F. Scott and Zelda Fitzgerald Museum* (334-264-4222; fitzgeraldmuseum.net). Francis Scott Key Fitzgerald met Zelda Sayre, a native of Montgomery and daughter of an Alabama Supreme Court judge, at a local dance in 1918. The couple married in 1920, soon after Scott published his first novel, *This Side of Paradise*.

The Fitzgeralds and their daughter, Scottie, lived here from October 1931 to April 1932. While here Scott worked on his novel *Tender Is the Night* and the screenplay for a Jean Harlow movie. At the same time Zelda, whose writings include a play as well as several short stories and articles, started her only novel, *Save Me the Waltz*. Beautiful, flamboyant, and driven, Zelda also excelled at painting and ballet. Unfortunately, her recurring

alabamatrivia

The Wallace Foundation in Montgomery honors Lurleen Wallace, the third woman ever elected governor of a state.

mental collapses played havoc with the family's lives and prevented her from realizing more of her creative potential.

You'll see eight pieces of Zelda's original artwork including paintings and a self-portrait in pencil along with her personal cigarette holder, family photos, autographed books, letters, and other memorabilia. Plans were afoot to tear down this historic home until local attorney Julian McPhillips and his wife, Leslie, purchased it and set about creating this museum. In the sunroom you can watch a 25-minute video that provides some glimpses into the lives of the author of *The Great Gatsby* and his talented but tormented wife. A donation of $5 per adult is requested, with $3 for adults and senior citizens, $2 for students, children (5 and under) free. Hours are 10 a.m. to 2 p.m. Wednesday through Friday and 1 to 5 p.m. Saturday and Sunday. Visit the website at fitzgeraldmuseum.net.

Afterward head downtown to Montgomery's capitol complex, where you can easily spend a full day. If you enjoy digging into the past, you'll find this area fascinating to explore. From here Jefferson Davis telegraphed his "Fire on Fort Sumter" order, and the country suddenly found itself embroiled in the Civil War. Rising impressively above its surroundings on Dexter Avenue, the 1851 capitol reflects the period's prevailing architecture—Greek revival. In this building Jefferson Davis took his presidential oath for the Confederacy, and a six-pointed brass star now marks the spot.

At 644 Washington Avenue, just across the street from the capitol, stands the *First White House of the Confederacy* (334-242-1861; firstwhitehouse .org). Occupied by the Jefferson Davis family during the early days of the War Between the States, this Italianate-style home built by William Sayre dates to the early 1830s. Elegant downstairs parlors and second-floor bedrooms (including a charming nursery) contain Davis family possessions and period antiques. Other displays include Civil War relics, letters, and glass-cased documents. Hours are 8 a.m. to 4:30 p.m. Monday through Friday, 9 a.m. to 4 p.m. on Saturday. Admission is free.

Next door to the Davis home, you'll find a treasure-filled museum, the *Alabama Department of Archives and History,* archives.state.al.us. This building houses an enormous manuscript collection and exhibits spanning the gap from the Stone Age to the Space Age. On February 15, 2014, the Museum of Alabama opened with its new centerpiece exhibit on "Alabama Voices." The permanent Smithsonian-quality exhibit covers nearly 11,000 square feet on the museum's second floor and details Alabama history from the dawn of the 1700s to the present. The archives are open Monday through Saturday from 8:30 a.m. to 4:30 p.m.

A short jaunt takes you to the *Dexter Avenue King Memorial Baptist Church* (334-263-3970; dexterkingmemorial.org). Located at 454 Dexter Avenue, the church became a National Historical Landmark in 1974. It was at this church, pastored by Dr. Martin Luther King Jr., that the Montgomery bus boycott was organized on December 2, 1955, launching the American Civil Rights Movement.

An hour-long tour covers the church's early history as well as the more recent role it played as a rallying place for civil rights activists. On the ground floor, a six-section folk mural illustrates major events from Dr. King's life. Hours are 10 a.m. to 4 p.m. Tuesday through Friday and 10 a.m. to 2 p.m. on Saturday. Admission.

To learn more about Dr. King's life and family, visit the Dexter Parsonage Museum, where Dr. King and his family lived between 1954 and 1960. Built in 1912, the nine-room clapboard parsonage at 309 Jackson Street has been restored to its appearance when Dr. King and his family lived there. Much of the furniture was used by Dr. King and his family. Adjacent to the parsonage is an interpretive center with photos of the 12 pastors who lived there, plus a wall of Pastoral Wisdom with inspirational quotes from pastors.

Nearby, in front of the Southern Poverty Law Center at 400 Washington Avenue, stands the *Civil Rights Memorial.* Designed by Maya Lin, who also served as the architect for the Vietnam Memorial in Washington, DC, this black granite memorial documents major events in the struggle for civil rights.

Don't miss the *Rosa Parks Library and Museum* (334-241-8615), a state-of-the-art facility at 252 Montgomery Street. This site marks the spot where Mrs. Parks was arrested in 1955 and offers an in-depth look at the event that started the Montgomery bus boycott. A project of Troy State University Montgomery, the interpretive museum features original exhibits, including historical papers from that era and a replica of the public bus, complete with a unique treatment of the scene in which Mrs. Rosa Parks played her significant role in shaping history to become "Mother of the Civil Rights Movement." The new Children's Wing features the Cleveland Avenue Time Machine, which takes riders on a unique trip to the past with an overview of events that led to the modern day Civil Rights Movement. On the second floor visitors will find extensive historical information with kiosk, panel, and computer presentations detailing events before and during the Montgomery Bus Boycott. For more background on this pivotal event in the city's (and nation's) civil rights heritage, visit troy.edu/rosa-parks-museum. Museum hours run from 9 a.m. to 5 p.m. Monday through Friday and from 9 a.m. to 3 p.m. on Saturday. Admission: adults $7.50, children (age 12 and under) $5.50.

Also downtown, at 301 Columbus Street, you can step back into the 19th century at *Old Alabama Town* (334-240-4500 or 888-240-1850). This fascinating concentration of historically restored buildings provides glimpses of city and country living in the 19th and early 20th centuries. Start your tour at the *Loeb Center,* where you can also visit the museum store. Continue your excursion into the past at *Lucas Tavern* and other buildings in this history-filled complex. You'll see an 1850s dogtrot house (a dogtrot is a form of Southern architecture that features an open central hall connecting two rooms, sometimes called pens). Other stops include such buildings as a carriage house, grocery store, church, country doctor's office, and a one-room schoolhouse—complete with *McGuffey's Readers* and slates.

You'll also see the nearby Rose-Morris House, where you can enjoy music on the dogtrot, and the *Ordeman House,* a handsome townhouse with elegant furnishings and backyard dependencies. Except for major holidays, the center's hours are 9 a.m. to 4 p.m. Monday through Saturday. Check out oldalabamatown.com to learn more. Admission: adults $10, children (ages 6 to 18) $5, children (age 5 and under) free.

alabamatrivia

A life-size statue of Hank Williams stands in Montgomery's Lister Park across from the City Auditorium, where Williams's funeral service took place.

"Your Cheatin' Heart" immediately brings Hank Williams to mind for all country music lovers, and fans from throughout the world travel to Montgomery to pay tribute at his grave site. Set in *Oakwood Cemetery,* the marble memorial is sculpted in the shape of two large music notes and a cowboy hat. You can also see a life-size bronze statue of the musician in Lister Hill plaza, across from City Hall.

Hank Williams's Funeral

Shortly after celebrating the New Year of 1953, mourners began flocking to Montgomery. They lined the streets and congregated outside a boardinghouse where a silver casket sat. So many people came to pay tribute that the funeral couldn't be held in a church. The service had to be moved to the biggest facility in town, the Municipal Auditorium.

Ironically, that was the very auditorium where the fallen star had performed so many times. Now it was where Hank Williams, the Drifting Cowboy, would be bade farewell for his last journey. On Sunday afternoon, January 4, 1953, an estimated 25,000 came to Montgomery for the funeral of Hank Williams.

Grand Ole Opry stars arrived in a special chartered plane. Among the Opry entertainers were Jimmy Dickens, Carl Smith, Webb Pierce, Bill Monroe, Ray Price, and June Carter. Loads of flowers were delivered, including two guitar-shaped floral arrangements that stood on each side of the coffin.

At 1 p.m. the casket was brought in and opened at 1:15. Dressed in a white cowboy stage outfit, Williams clutched a tiny white Bible in his hand. His band, the Drifting Cowboys, stood by as a guard of honor. Hundreds filed by to pay their respects.

At 2:30 p.m. the auditorium doors were closed and the service started with Ernest Tubb singing "Beyond the Sunset." A gospel quartet, the Statesmen, who would later sing at Elvis Presley's funeral, sang "Precious Memories." Possibly the only black quartet to perform at a prominent white funeral in Alabama prior to the civil rights era, the Southwind Singers sang "My Record Will Be There."

Roy Acuff performed Hank's popular song, "I Saw the Light." Red Foley's voice wavered and tears flowed down his face as he sang "Peace in the Valley." Foley and Williams had made a promise that whoever died first, the other would sing at his friend's funeral.

Hank Williams was only 29 years old when he died. Slumped in the backseat of a baby-blue Cadillac speeding through a dark night, Hank Williams drew his last breath. The country music legend was on his way to a concert in Canton, Ohio. Somewhere in West Virginia, Williams's young driver became worried about the lifeless body draped in a navy blue overcoat in the backseat. By then it was too late. Carried into an emergency room, Williams was pronounced dead on January 1, 1953. His heart had given out after years of alcohol and prescription drug abuse. Hank is buried in Oakwood Cemetery in Montgomery

Stop by 118 Commerce Street for an in-depth look at the legacy of Alabama-born Hank Williams. Paying tribute to the memory of this country music legend, the **Hank Williams Museum** (334-262-3600) contains recordings, albums, musical instruments, clothing, a saddle with silver trim, family photos, and other personal items. The museum's focal point is the baby-blue 1952 Cadillac convertible in which the singer/songwriter died while being driven to his scheduled performance in Canton, Ohio, on January 1, 1953. Eight rooms and 35 showcases feature memorabilia of family members and associates. A carved Kowliga, like the wooden Indian that inspired Williams's song, "Kowaliga" and created by the Wood Chippers (with a time investment of 559 hours), looms 8.5 feet tall. Museum hours are 9 a.m. to 4:30 p.m. Monday through Friday, Saturday 10 a.m. to 4 p.m. on Saturday, and 1 to 4 p.m. on Sunday. Admission: $10 for adults (ages 15 and up), $3 for children (ages 4 to 14). Visit thehankwilliamsmuseum.net for more details and some toe-tapping music.

At 551 Clay Street, you'll find a warm welcome at **Red Bluff Cottage** (334-264-0056 or 888-551-2529), a perfect place to headquarter in Alabama's capital city. In fact, the upstairs porch of this raised cottage offers fine views of the state capitol and the Alabama River. Bonnie and Barry Ponstein, who purchased the inn from previous owners Anne and Mark Waldo, share the cooking and dispense Southern hospitality—Alabama style. "We have a good time down here," says Barry, quoting his three rules: No smoking, no pets, and no grumpy people. The Red Bluff offers four rooms with private baths and a full breakfast, perhaps Bonnie's famed wild rice waffles with fresh berries. Pampering their guests, the Ponsteins offer extra amenities such as complimentary soft drinks, snacks, fresh ground coffee, and a large selection of teas. Visit redbluffcottage.com and check for special packages. Moderate rates.

alabamatrivia

Life magazine ranked Hank Williams as Number One in the "100 Most Important People in Country Music."

After exploring the capital of the Old South, head north to **Wetumpka,** a charming town with a unique setting. Not only situated on the Coosa River's banks, Wetumpka also sits in the bowl of a 4-mile-wide crater created by the impact of a meteorite about 83 million years ago. Head first to the

Wetumpka Area Chamber of Commerce (334-567-4811; wetumpkachamber .com), located at 110 East Bridge Street in the heart of downtown. While collecting travel information at the chamber office, housed in a former bank building that dates to 1905, notice the original brass chandelier with a Greek key design that repeats the ceiling motif. Wetumpka comes from an Indian word that means "tumbling waters."

Spanning the Coosa River, you'll see the town's focal point, a picturesque arched bridge built in 1937. Named for a former governor, the Bibb Graves Bridge allegedly is the only one south of the Mason-Dixon Line suspended by reinforced concrete. After crossing the bridge, notice the historic First Presbyterian Church, organized in 1834. It was here that soldiers in the Wetumpka Light Guard gathered on April 16, 1861, before leaving to confront their destinies in the Civil War.

If you saw the movie *Big Fish,* filmed in and around Montgomery and starring Jessica Lange, Albert Finney, Ewan McGregor, and Danny DeVito, then the town might look vaguely familiar although the film crew made several exterior changes.

Before leaving town, be sure to visit **Our Place Cafe** (334-567-8778) for a delectable dinner. Located at 809 Company Street, the restaurant occupies a brick building once owned by the Graham family. Back in the 1930s, the structure housed a grocery store with an apartment above and later served as an office for the family's wholesale gasoline business.

Owners David and Mona Funderburk offer casual elegance in dining and an ambience-filled restaurant with seating on two levels. Try the signature crab cakes, served with a special dill sauce, or the evening special. David describes his cuisine as "more Creole than Cajun," and his menu features six seafood selections nightly as well as steaks. The restaurant opens at 4:30 p.m. Tuesday through Saturday. Prices are moderate.

Save time to explore nearby **Fort Toulouse-Jackson Park** (334-567-3002; fttoulousejackson.org). To reach the park, the site of two forts from different centuries, take US 231 North and watch for the turnoff sign to 2521 West Fort Toulouse Road. Continue 2.4 miles down this road to the main gate. After entering the park you'll see the visitor center on the left. Inside, displays of artifacts unearthed in archaeological digs, from brass uniform buttons and silver earrings to French wine bottles and cannonballs, provide background on the site's history.

The original 1717 French fortress, named for Count Toulouse (son of Louis XIV), served as a trading post where Native Americans exchanged furs and deerskins for European goods. This French outpost also helped keep the British at bay. Gen. Andrew Jackson's forces later built a larger 19th-century counterpart while fighting the Creek Indians. From here Old Hickory plotted his campaign against the British and Spanish that ended with the Battle of New Orleans.

Fort Toulouse and Fort Jackson living-history programs, staged monthly on the park's grounds, permit visitors to dip a bit deeper into the forts' earlier days. The park usually has something going on three out of four weekends.

This 164-acre park also offers a picnic area, campground, and launching ramp. Another attraction is the 30-acre arboretum with walkway, footbridges, and study decks. Nearby, the Coosa and Tallapoosa Rivers—with their cache of bass, bream, catfish, and crappie—beckon anglers. (A state fishing license is required.) Modest admission. Except for major holidays, the park is open from sunup to sundown year-round, and the visitor center hours run from 9 a.m. to 4 p.m. daily. For more information visit fttoulouse jackson.org.

After your park outing follow State Route 14 west to *Prattville.* Daniel Pratt, for whom the town was named, came here from New Hampshire in the 1830s and established an industrial center—still the site for the manufacture of cotton gins. A drive through *Old Prattvillage* takes you past a section of restored 19th-century buildings. For a driving tour map, which highlights about 40 homes in the historic district along with area churches and industrial sites, stop by the Prattville Chamber of Commerce (131 North Court Street; 334-365-7392; prattvillechamber.com) or City Hall at 101 West Main Street.

Better yet, set off on a walking tour of the village. At Prattvillage Gardens you'll see a small 1800s plantation chapel surrounded by a profusion of plants and a butterfly walk. Open the gate and stroll past theme gardens devoted to herbs, perennials, and old-fashioned favorites like hollyhocks, dianthus, and oak-leaf hydrangeas.

Stop by the *Prattaugan Museum* (334-361-0961; autaugaheritage.org), which houses the Heritage Center. Located at 102 East Main Street, this circa 1848 home showcases antiques, exhibits on area history, Indian artifacts, and genealogical records. In the backyard, notice the artesian well with a dipper hanging nearby. Prattville acquired its "Fountain City" title because it boasts a number of artesian wells. Except for city holidays, hours are Tuesday through Friday from 10 a.m. to 4 p.m. and Saturday 10 a.m. to 2 p.m. Admission is free, and donations are accepted.

Heritage Park, which features a three-tiered fountain, overlooks the town's focal point, Daniel Pratt's big brick gin factory. From this scenic spot, you can watch water spilling over the dam into Autauga Creek. Wander along historic West Main Street past **Red Arrow Hardware** at 119 West Main Street (334-358-1525) with its nostalgic inventory. Across the street at 131 First Street, you can see all sorts of timepieces awaiting repair at **The Village Clocksmith** (334-491-8463). Check out **Fancy Free** with an impressive inventory of "antiques, boutiques, and uniques."

Nature lovers will enjoy trekking through **Wilderness Park** on Upper Kingston Road. Located inside the city limits, the park could be a world

alabamatrivia

Alabama's forest acreage ranks as third largest in the nation and second largest in the South.

away—in central China by the looks of it. Instead of a typical Southern forest's foliage, the paved half-mile path leads through a thick stand of towering bamboo.

Search out nearby **Buena Vista** (334-365-3690 or 334-361-0961; autaugaheritage.org/buenavista), an early plantation home, located on Autauga County Road 4 between US 31 and State Route 14. Fronted by four Ionic columns and constructed of heart pine, the Greek revival–style structure stands on a sweeping lawn studded with camellias and magnolias. A striking circular staircase spirals from the large entrance hall to the third-floor banquet room. Originally built in the federal style and known as Montgomery House, the home is listed on the National Register of Historic Places. Some historians claim the house dates to 1822, but other sources say circa 1830 would be more accurate. You'll see some period furnishings and memorabilia. Owned by a local corporation and operated by the Autauga County Heritage Association, Buena Vista is open to the public for tours on Tuesday between 10 a.m. and 2 p.m. or by appointment. Admission is $5.

Want to visit the best little town in Alabama? Then head about 40 miles (or minutes) south of Montgomery, take the Greenville exit 130 off I-65, and turn left. Ditto if you're looking for the best small town in America.

It's true—*Greenville,* with a population of some 8,000—outscored every other US city with fewer than 100,000 residents in a national home towns index that measures the power of place using statistical data compiled by academic researchers.

Known as "Camellia City," Greenville promises plenty for flower lovers, history buffs, and golfers. Founded in 1820, the town boasts lovely homes, churches, and public buildings, many on the Register of Historic Places. Cambrian Ridge, one of the award-winning courses on the Robert Trent Jones Golf Trail, beckons only minutes away, with the more famed RTJ course, Capitol Hill, in easy driving distance.

Stop by the *Greenville Area Chamber of Commerce* (334-382-3251; greenville-alabama.com), housed in the old CSX depot on Bolling Street to pick up a brochure called *Historic Main Street Greenville,* which details a self-guided tour of the town's interesting sites. Shady streets, brick paving, and gas lights make Commerce Street an attractive place to stroll.

A jaunt takes you past a local landmark, the *Ritz Theatre.* Dating to 1935, the former movie house built in the then-popular Art Deco style later fell into disrepair. Now rescued and restored, the Ritz serves as the venue for a variety of productions from theater to music and dance. Other sites of interest include Greenville's circa-1936 City Hall, a WPA project and the city's best example of colonial revival civic architecture. Continue your stroll through Confederate Park, established in 1897. With a fountain as its centerpiece, this block-size space is sometimes the setting for evening concerts.

You'll see several handsome churches such as First Presbyterian, Greenville's oldest brick church. Search out the Pioneer Cemetery with its ornate cast-iron fence and elaborate monuments. Unusual cast-iron covers, an invention patented in 1874 by Greenville native Joseph R. Abrams, top several graves, and others are covered with giant cockleshells, a Victorian custom. Many of the area's early settlers, including Capt. William Butler for whom the county is named, are buried here.

Spend some time browsing through some of Greenville's one-of-a-kind boutiques and gift shops such as *The Pineapple* (334-382-7240) at 132 West Commerce Street, which offers unusual flags and banners, photo frames, hand-decorated clothing, and collectibles. In a beautifully restored building at 112 West Commerce, *Karen Rainey Interiors* (334-382-9486 or 334-382-0936; karenraineyinteriors.com) showcases antiques and accessories and provides decorator services for interiors from Gulf Coast condos to Atlanta townhouses. With a wooded recreation area plus playgrounds and pavilions for picnickers, *Sherling Lake* (334-382-3638 or 800-810-5253; sherlinglake.com), about 4 miles west of Greenville via exit 130 off I-65 at 4397 Braggs Road, offers plenty of recreation options, including camping and fishing. August visitors can take in the annual Watermelon Jubilee with arts, crafts, food, and fun.

From Greenville, a short drive south takes you to Georgiana and the *Hank Williams, Sr., Boyhood Home and Museum* (334-376-2396; hank museum.com). Located at 127 Rose Street, the home contains six rooms filled with walls of family photos, original posters, albums, 78 rpm recordings, a church pew, piano, and 1923 Victrola. Also, visitors will see one of the singer's Stetson hats and two suits. Fans from all over the world donated many of the items on display. Draperies, custom made for the musician's Nashville home, feature an overall design of lyrics and music from "Your Cheatin' Heart." Hours are 10 a.m. to 4 p.m. Monday through Saturday. Admission: adults $3, students $2, children (age 6 and under) free. Each June, Georgiana hosts an annual Hank Williams Day Celebration with country music concerts, food concessions, and street dances.

Places to Stay in Southeast Alabama

AUBURN/OPELIKA

Auburn Marriott Opelika Hotel & Conference Center at Grand National
3700 Robert Trent Jones Trail
(334) 741-9292 or
(866) 846-4655

Auburn University Hotel and Dixon Conference Center
241 South College St.
(334) 821-8200 or
(800) 228-2876
Auhcc.com

Chewacla State Park
124 Shell Toomer Pkwy.
(334) 887-5621 or
(800) 252-7275
alapark.com/chewacla

Crenshaw Guest House
371 North College St.
(334) 821-1131 or
(800) 950-1131
crenshawguesthouse.com

Hilton Garden Inn
2555 Hilton Garden Dr.
(334) 502-3500

DOTHAN

Best Western Dothan Inn & Suites
3285 Montgomery Hwy.
(334) 793-4376 or
(800) 780-7234

Courtyard by Marriott
3040 Ross Clark Circle
(334) 671-3000 or
(800) 321-2211

Hampton Inn & Suites
4684 Montgomery Hwy.
(334) 671-7672

Holiday Inn South
2195 Ross Clark Circle
(334) 699-6868 or
(800) 777-6611

ENTERPRISE

Rawls Hotel
116 South Main St.
(334) 308-9387
rawlsbandb.com

EUFAULA

Comfort Suites
12 Paul Lee Parkway
(334) 616-0114

Lakepoint Resort
104 Old Hwy. 165
(334) 687-8011
alapark.com/
lakepointresort

GREENVILLE

Baymont Inn & Suites
71 Jameson Lane
(334) 382-6300 or
(800) 337-0300

MONTGOMERY

Drury Inn and Suites
1124 Eastern Blvd.
(334) 273-1101

Embassy Suites
300 Tallapoosa St.
(334) 269-5055 or
(800) 362-2779

Extended Stay America
5115 Carmichael Rd.
(334) 273-0075

Holiday Inn East
1185 Eastern Blvd.
(800) HOLIDAY

Quality Inn
5601 Carmichael Rd.
(334) 226-5537

Red Bluff Cottage
551 Clay St.
(334) 264-0056 or
(888) 551-2529
redbluffcottage.com

**Renaissance
Montgomery Hotel
& Spa at the Convention
Center**
201 Tallapoosa St.
(800) 468-3571

Wingate Inn
2060 Eastern Blvd.
(334) 244-7880

PRATTVILLE

**Montgomery Marriott
Prattville Hotel and
Conference Center**
2500 Legends Circle
(888) 250-3767 or
(334) 290-1235

Places to Eat in Southeast Alabama

AUBURN/OPELIKA

Ariccia
241 South College St.
(334) 821-8200 or
(800) 228-2876

The Lakeview Room
3700 Robert Trent Jones
Trail
(334) 741-9292

Mellow Mushroom
128 North College St.
(334) 887-6356
mellowmushroom.com

Warehouse Bistro
105 Rocket Ave.
(334) 745-6353
warehousebistro.com

DOTHAN

**Hunt's Seafood
Restaurant
and Oyster Bar**
177 Campbellton Hwy.
(334) 794-5193
seafoodsteakoysters
dothan.com

Old Mexico
2920 Ross Clark Circle
(334) 712-1434

The Old Mill Restaurant
2557 Murphy Mill Rd.
(334) 794-8530
oldmilldothan.com

FOR MORE INFORMATION ABOUT SOUTHEAST ALABAMA

Auburn/Opelika Tourism Bureau
714 East Glenn Ave.
Auburn 36830
(334) 887-8747 or (866) 880-8747
aotourism.com
info@aotourism.com

Dothan Area Convention & Visitors Bureau
3311 Ross Clark Circle
PO Box 8765
Dothan 36304
(334) 794-6622
dothanalcvb.com

Enterprise Chamber of Commerce
553 Glover Ave.
PO Box 310577
Enterprise 36331-0577
(334) 347-0581 or (800) 235-4730
enterprisealabama.com
chamber@enterprisealabama.com

Eufaula/Barbour County Chamber of Commerce
333 East Broad St.
Eufaula 36027
(334) 687-6664 or (800) 524-7529
eufaulachamber.com
info@eufalachamber.com

Historic Chattahoochee Commission
PO Box 33
Eufaula 36072-0033
(334) 687-9755 or (877) 766-2443
chattahoocheetrace.com
trace@eufaula.rr.com

Montgomery Convention & Visitors Bureau
300 Water St.
PO Box 79
Montgomery 36101
(334) 261-1100 or (800) 240-9452
visitingmontgomery.com
tourism@visitingmontgomery.com

Tuskegee Area Chamber of Commerce
121 South Main St.
PO Box 831034
Tuskegee 36083
(334) 727-6619
tuskegeeareachamber.org
info@tuskeegeeareachamber.org

MAINSTREAM ATTRACTIONS WORTH SEEING IN SOUTHEAST ALABAMA

Montgomery Zoo
2301 Coliseum Pkwy.
Montgomery
(334) 240-4900
montgomeryzoo.com
Observe more than 800 animals from five continents in the zoo's naturalistic settings and take a train ride around the park. Relocated from its former home in Opelika and housed next to the zoo, the Mann Museum allows you to get acquainted with bears, wolves, moose, and more mounted specimens of North American wildlife, all presented in realistic settings. The natural history museum's life-size exhibits numbered more than 300 at last count. Both attractions are open from 9 a.m. to 5:30 p.m. daily. December hours are 9 a.m. to 5 p.m. Admission: adults $12 for zoo, $6 for museum, or $18 for both; senior citizens $10 for zoo, $5 for museum or $14 for both; children (ages 3 to 12) $8 for zoo, $4 museum, or $11 for both.

US Army Aviation Museum
6000 Novosel St.
Fort Rucker
(334) 255-3036, (334) 598-2508, or (888) 276-9286
This museum is in Fort Rucker, a training base for military helicopter pilots located 5 miles west of Ozark. Covering the complete history of Army Aviation, this complex contains one of the world's largest collections of helicopters. Exhibits include maps and photos of Army Aviation's role in the Louisiana Maneuvers through Operation Desert Storm, a full-scale model of the Wright B Flyer, and unusual pieces such as a Sopwith Camel and a Nieuport 28. You can even walk through a Chinook (CH-47-A) and view today's high-tech Apache combat helicopter. The Army Aviation Museum is free and open to the public from 9 a.m. to 4 p.m. Monday through Friday and from 9 a.m. to 3 p.m. on Saturday. Visit the museum's website at armyavnmuseum.org.

ENTERPRISE

Cutt's
417 East Lee
(334) 347-1110

Rawls Restaurant
116 South Main St.
(334) 308-9387
rawlsbandb.com

EUFAULA

Cajun Corner
114 North Eufaula Ave.
(334) 616-0816
cajuncorner.com

Lakepoint Resort
104 Lake Point Dr.
(334) 687-8011

Lakeside Restaurant
1720 North Eufaula Ave.
(334) 687-3132
alapark.com/
lakepointresort

Old Mexico
1248 South Eufaula Ave.
(334) 687-7770

River City Grill
209 East Broad St.
(334) 616-6550

GREENVILLE

Bates' House of Turkey
1001 Fort Dale Rd.
(334) 382-6123
batesturkey.com

MILLBROOK

Fantail Restaurant
2060 Downing
(334) 285-7255
fantailrestaurant.com

MONTGOMERY

Bonefish Grill
7020 East Chase Pkwy.
(334) 396-1770
bonefishgrill.com

**The House Restaurant
at Renaissance
Montgomery Hotel**
201 Tallapoosa St.
(334) 481-5166
houserestaurant
montgomery.com

Lek's Railroad Thai
Union Station,
300 B Water St.
(334) 269-0708
thaiemeraldlek.com

Martha's Place
7798 Atlanta Hwy.
(334) 356-7165
marthasplacebuffet.com

**Railyard Brewing
Company**
12 West Jefferson St.
(334) 262-0080
railyardbrewingcompany
.com

Sinclair's East
7847 Vaughn Rd.
(334) 271-7847
sinclairsrestaurants.com

**The Chophouse at
Vintage Year**
405 Cloverdale Rd.
(334) 239-0041
chophousevy.com

PRATTVILLE

**Marriott Legends at
Capitol Hill**
2500 Legends Circle
(334) 290-1235 or
(888) 250-3767

TROY

**Mossy Grove School
House Restaurant**
1841 87 South Hwy.
(334) 566-4921

WETUMPKA

Our Place Cafe
809 Company St.
(334) 567-8778

SOUTHWEST ALABAMA

Black Belt

Alabama's Black Belt, so called because of a strip of dark, rich soil that stretches across part of the state's south-central section, covers 4,300 square miles. This fertile farmland became the setting for a host of plantations prior to the Civil War and you'll see many antebellum structures throughout the area. From *Selma,* which retains a lingering flavor of the Old South's cotton-rich aristocratic past, you can easily make a loop of several small Black Belt towns with their treasure troves of architecture. Situated on a bluff above the Alabama River, Selma served as a major munitions depot, making battleships as well as cannonballs, rifles, and ammunition for the Confederate cause.

US 80 west from Montgomery to Selma leads across the *Edmund Pettus Bridge,* a landmark that figured prominently in the civil rights struggle. In 1965 marchers followed Martin Luther King Jr. across this bridge on their trek to Montgomery during voting-rights demonstrations.

Located near the bridge, the *National Voting Rights Museum* (334-418-0800; nvrmi.com) at 1012 Water Avenue

presents a visual history of the Selma-to-Montgomery march and related events. Upon entering, viewers see themselves reflected in a mirrored "I Was There" wall with a display of cards recording firsthand observations by individuals. A series of rooms focus on reconstruction, suffrage, and other aspects of the voting-rights struggle. A large window, etched with the names Andrew Young, Martin Luther King Jr., Thurgood Marshall, Dick Gregory, and other museum Hall of Fame inductees, provides a fitting vantage point for viewing the historic Pettus Bridge. Hours are 10 a.m. to 4 p.m. Monday through Thursday. Friday, Saturday and Sunday by appointment only. Admission: adults $6.50; senior citizens and students $4.50.

Take time to stroll along historic Water Avenue, a restored 19th-century riverfront warehouse district with brick streets, arcades, and parks overlooking the river. Nearby, at 1124 Water Avenue, you'll find a mini-mall with an eatery and several interesting shops.

Settle into a room at the restored *St. James Hotel* (334-872-3234 or 866-965-2637; historicstjameshotel.com) and map out your Selma itinerary. One of the country's few remaining antebellum riverfront hotels, the St. James occupies a corner at 1200 Water Avenue. Lacy iron grillwork traces the balconies of the camel-colored structure, which surrounds a courtyard with fountain. The original 1837 hotel served passengers from paddle wheelers

BEST ATTRACTIONS IN SOUTHWEST ALABAMA

Battleship USS *Alabama*, Mobile Bay	**Mobile Museum of Art,** Mobile
Bellingrath Gardens and Home, Theodore	**Old Cahawba Archaeological Park,** Cahaba
Dauphin Island	**Town of Demopolis**
Fort Morgan, Mobile Bay	**Town of Fairhope**
Gulf Coast beaches	**Town of Marion**
Mobile's historic districts	**Town of Selma**

and steamboats that plied the Alabama River and also those from the nearby railroad station. Jesse and Frank James (under assumed names) once stayed at the St. James.

Many of the rooms' balconies overlook the historic Edmund Pettus Bridge. Furnished with antebellum and Victorian pieces, the hotel boasts a ballroom; elegant guest rooms and suites; a Drinking Room with handsome, marble-topped mahogany bar; and a white-tablecloth dining room. Standard to moderate.

To dip into more of the city's interesting history, stop by the handsome **Old Depot Museum** (334-874-2197; olddepotmuseum.com), located on the corner of Martin Luther King Street and Water Avenue. Built in 1891 by the Louisville and Nashville Railroad, this arched and turreted two-story redbrick structure stands on the site of the Confederate Naval Foundry, which Union troops destroyed during the Battle of Selma in 1865. The museum houses everything from a 1908 portrait camera used by psychic Edgar Cayce (who once lived in Selma and operated a photography studio here) to Victorian hair combs, plantation records, quilts, Confederate bills, cannonballs, early medical equipment, and antique tools.

In the Black Heritage Wing, you'll see sculpture by Earl Hopkins, nationally recognized for his wood carvings and leather crafts. Hopkins, who uses exotic woods in his creations, worked at Colonial Williamsburg before retiring to his native Selma. A not-to-be-missed rare display of photographs, made between 1895 and 1905 by Selmian Mary Morgan Keipp, depicts daily life on a Black Belt plantation. The series is considered one of the finest and most complete collections of photos covering that period in history.

Behind the museum you'll see a Firefighters Museum plus a boxcar, caboose, and old farm equipment. Monday through Saturday the museum is open from 10 a.m. to 4 p.m. or by appointment. Admission: adults $5, senior citizens $4, children $2.

Nearby at 410 Martin Luther King Street, stands **Brown Chapel African Methodist Episcopal Church,** another significant structure in Selma's history. This 1908 Byzantine-style building served as headquarters for the civil rights activists who played a pivotal role in bringing about the passage of the National Voting Rights Act during the turbulent decade of the 1960s. Visitors may take a self-guided walking tour of the surrounding historic area.

TOP ANNUAL EVENTS IN SOUTHWEST ALABAMA

Mardi Gras
Mobile, February
(800) 566-2453

Arts & Crafts Festival
Fairhope, March
(251) 621-8222

Azalea Trail Run & Festival
Mobile, March
(800) 566-2453

Festival of Flowers
Mobile, March
(251) 639-2050 or (800) 566-2453
festivalofflowers.com

Historic Selma Pilgrimage
Selma, March
(800) 457-3562
selmapilgrimage.com

The Original German Sausage Festival
Elberta, last Saturday in March
and October
(251) 986-5805

Crawfish Festival
Faunsdale, last weekend in April
(unless Easter)
(334) 628-3240

Blessing of the Fleet
Bayou La Batre, May
(251) 824-2415
fleetblessing.org

To Kill a Mockingbird
Monroeville, last weekend of April
and first three weekends in May
(251) 575-7433
monroecountymuseum.org

Alabama Deep Sea Fishing Rodeo
Dauphin Island, July
(251) 471-0025
www.adsfr.com

Alabama Tale Tellin' Festival
Selma, second weekend in October
(334) 878-2787
artsrevive.com

Sometime during your local tour, be sure to stop at 109 Union Street to tour the white-columned, three-story, brick *Vaughan-Smitherman Museum* (334-874-2174), named for the local hospital (once housed here) and in honor of Selma's former mayor, who played an active role in historic preservation. Crowning Alabama Avenue, this impressive building opened its doors in 1848 as the Central Masonic Institute and later served as a hospital for wounded Confederates (escaping the fate of many Selma buildings when Union general John Harrison Wilson's raiders, disobeying orders, embarked on a wholesale campaign of wanton destruction in April 1865). The building later served as a courthouse, military school, and private hospital. Inside

Selma Haunted History Tours
Selma/Dallas County locations,
October
(800) 45-SELMA

Bayfest Music Festival
Mobile, first weekend in October
(251) 470-7730
bayfest.com

Alabama Deep Sea Fishing Rodeo
Mobile, July
(251) 471-0025
adsfr.com

National Shrimp Festival
Gulf Shores, October
(251) 968-6091
myshrimpfest.com

Riverfront Market
Selma, second Saturday of October
(800) 457-3562

Frank Brown International Songwriters Festival
Gulf Shores, November
(850) 492-7664
frankbrownsongwriters.com

Pow Wow
Atmore, November
(251) 368-9136

Magic Christmas in Lights
Bellingrath Gardens & Home
late November through December
(251) 973-2217
bellingrath.org

Christmas on the River
Demopolis, December
(334) 289-0270
demopolischamber.com

you'll see a large collection of Civil War relics, Confederate money, medical artifacts, and period furnishings from the mid-1800s. Hours are 9 a.m. to 4 p.m. Tuesday through Saturday or by appointment. Modest admission.

On a drive through the Old Town Historic District, you'll see block after block of antebellum and Victorian architecture. On the third weekend in March, the *Historic Selma Pilgrimage* provides visitors with opportunities to tour many of the city's outstanding homes (see selmapilgrimage.com for more information). A reenactment of the Battle of Selma is another popular springtime event. On the second Saturday in October, the grand event is the Tall Tellin' Festival.

For a memento of your visit, consider purchasing a cookbook called *Tastes of Olde Selma,* available in several places throughout the city. Compiled by Selma's Olde Towne Association, the book contains line drawings and brief histories of many of the town's significant structures along with a selection of wonderful recipes. The front cover features a color illustration of **Sturdivant Hall** (334-872-5626), a neoclassical mansion located at 713 Mabry Street. Designed by Thomas Helm Lee (Robert E. Lee's cousin), this magnificent home that took three years to build boasts elaborate ceilings and decorative moldings with a motif of intertwined grape leaves and vines. You'll also see a spiral staircase, marble mantels, and servant pulls—each with a different tone. Other treasures include period furnishings, portraits, silver, crystal, china, and a rare French-made George Washington commemorative clock of ormolu and gold—one of only seven in existence.

Coral vines climb the home's back walls, and mock lemons perfume the air. You may be presented with a sprig or cutting of lavender, mint, or sage from the mansion's herb garden outside the backyard kitchen. The home's formal gardens, which feature a variety of native flowers, shrubs, and trees, serve as a lovely backdrop for the pilgrimage's annual grand ball. Except for major holidays, Sunday, and Monday, Sturdivant Hall is open from 10 a.m. to 4 p.m. Admission: adults $5.

By the way, some Selmians say the ghost of John McGee Parkman, one of Sturdivant Hall's former owners, roams the mansion. You may or may not see house ghosts here, but you can certainly find several in Sturdivant Hall's gift shop—sandwiched between the covers of some of Kathryn Tucker Windham's books, such as *13 Alabama Ghosts and Jeffrey* or *Jeffrey's Latest 13.* For a souvenir or gift, you might like to buy *Alabama—One Big Front Porch,* an engrossing collection of stories compiled by Alabama's famous storyteller Mrs. Windham, who died in 2011. To hear other famous Southern storytellers, plan your visit to coincide with the **Alabama Tale Tellin' Festival,** an annual fall event staged in Selma. Driving along Dallas Avenue (which becomes State Route 22), you'll pass the **Old Live Oak Cemetery,** filled with ancient trees festooned by Spanish moss. During spring, dogwoods and azaleas make this site even more spectacular. A number of Confederate graves and unique monuments may be seen here, including the mausoleum of William Rufus King, who named Selma and planned its layout. King, on the Democratic ticket with Franklin Pierce, died shortly after being elected vice president of the US.

For dinner strike out for the **Tally-Ho Restaurant** (334-872-1390), located at 509 Mangum Avenue, just off Summerfield Road in the northern section of town. Owner Bob Kelley's entrees run the gamut from seafood and chicken to prime rib au jus. A board features daily specials, which might include grilled pork chops with Thai sauce. Homemade zucchini muffins accompany entrees. For dessert try the chocolate cheesecake or amaretto soufflé. The restaurant's hours are Monday through Thursday 5 to 9 p.m., Friday and Saturday 5 to 10 p.m. Prices are moderate. The website is tallyhoselma.com.

> ## alabamatrivia
>
> Currency issued in Louisiana before the Civil War ($10 notes bearing the word *dix,* French for the number 10) led to the South being called "Dixie Land" and gave Alabama her nickname, "Heart of Dixie."

During your Selma visit, swing southwest about 9 miles on State Route 22 toward **Cahaba** ("Cahawba" is the historical spelling). Watch for a sign that says TO CAHABA, then turn left and travel 3.5 miles to 9518 Cahawba Road. When you reach a dead end, turn left again and continue 3 miles to **Old Cahawba Archaeological Park** (334-872-8058; cahawba.com), the site of Alabama's first permanent state capital. Here, near the place where the Cahaba and Alabama Rivers merge, once stood a thriving town. Today's visitors will have to use some imagination to visualize the remaining ruins as grand mansions that surrounded a copper-domed capitol, completed in 1820. A large stone monument and interpretive signs in conjunction with old street markers, brick columns, cemeteries, and domestic plants growing wild offer the few clues that this off-the-beaten-path spot once flourished as a political, commercial, and cultural center. You'll also see an artesian well (where watercress grows), the source of water for the elaborate gardens surrounding the Perine family mansion, which once stood nearby.

The visitor and education centers provide information on Cahaba's glory days. In 1825 legislators voted to move Alabama's capital to Tuscaloosa. While local lore holds that frequent flooding caused Cahaba to lose its position as the state's seat of government, evidence suggests that sectional politics probably played a larger role. Gradually Cahaba became a ghost town, and by 1900 most of its buildings had disappeared. The park offers a handicapped accessible nature trail. Except for major holidays, the park is open daily from 9 a.m. to 5 p.m., and the visitor center is open from noon to 5 p.m. Admission is free.

Afterward follow US 80 west from Selma until you reach Dallas County Road 45; then turn north to *Marion,* one of Alabama's oldest towns and a leading cultural center for planter society. The city is home to both *Judson College* and *Marion Military Institute.* The latter's chapel, Old South Hall, and Lovelace House on campus served as hospitals during the Civil War. The graves of more than 100 Southern and Union soldiers were later relocated from campus to *Confederate Rest,* a cemetery behind St. Wilfrid's Episcopal Church. The Old Marion City Hall (moved to MMI's campus from the downtown square) houses the *Alabama Military Hall of Honor.* For an appointment to see the exhibits, call (334) 683-2346.

Downtown you'll see several historical churches and the handsome Perry County Courthouse dating from the early 1850s. Be sure to drive down Green Street, the setting for a number of antebellum residences, including the *Lea-Griffith Home* (circa 1830), where Texas hero Sam Houston married Margaret Lea (their marriage license is recorded in the courthouse). With some 200 sites (in a wide variety of architectural styles) listed on the National Register of Historic Places, Marion promises plenty to see.

During your Marion excursion take a stroll across the Judson College campus and stop by the *Alabama Women's Hall of Fame,* which occupies the first floor of Bean Hall at 302 Bibb Street. Formerly the school's library, this Carnegie-built structure stands on the corner of Bibb and East Lafayette Streets. Bronze plaques pay tribute to Helen Keller, Julia Tutwiler, Lurleen Burns Wallace, Tallulah Bankhead, Zelda Sayre Fitzgerald, her daughter Frances Scott Fitzgerald Smith, and many other women of achievement with Alabama connections. Former first ladies Barbara Bush and Rosalynn Carter have spoken at past induction ceremonies. Except for major holidays, hours are 8 a.m. to 5 p.m. Monday through Friday. For a tour call (334) 683-5100 or visit awhf.org. Admission is free.

Marion's early-20th-century train depot serves as a visitor center complete with walking trail along the former railroad tracks. For more information on Marion, call the chamber of commerce at (334) 683-9622 or stop by 1200 Washington Street.

After exploring Marion follow State Route 14 west to Alabama's Catfish Capital, *Greensboro*. Because this Black Belt town managed to escape the Civil War's ravages, a large number of its antebellum homes and churches have been preserved. In fact the entire downtown district, featuring some 150 19th-century structures, is on the National Register of Historic Places. More than 60 of the town's homes predate the Civil War. Be sure to drive along Main, Tuscaloosa, and South Streets, all of which offer interesting architecture. At Market and South Streets, you'll see the *Noel-Ramsey House*. Built between 1819 and 1821, this is the only remaining residence of French settlers from nearby Demopolis's Vine and Olive Colony.

Don't miss *Magnolia Grove* (334-624-8618), a two-story Greek revival house built around 1840 by a wealthy cotton planter, Col. Isaac Croom. Located at 1002 Hobson Street, the home stands among lovely magnolia trees and landscaped gardens on a 12-acre setting. Magnolia Grove was also the home of Croom's nephew, Rear Adm. Richmond Pearson Hobson, a Congressional Medal of Honor winner. A naval hero in the Spanish-American War, Hobson later served in Congress and introduced legislation (the Hobson Amendment) that became the basis for the Constitution's prohibition amendment. The Museum Room contains memorabilia from Hobson's military and political careers.

The house also features family portraits, heirlooms, and furnishings from the 1830s to the early 1900s. You'll see an 1866 piano, a Persian rug from the late 1800s, a chaperon's bench, and antique quilts. Outbuildings include a kitchen, slave cottage, and a structure that probably served as Isaac Croom's office. Hours are 10 a.m. to 4 p.m. Tuesday through Friday, and 10 a.m. to 2 p.m. the first Saturday of each month, plus other times by appointment. The grounds may be visited from noon to 4 p.m. on Sunday. Admission: adults $5, college students and senior citizens $3, children (ages 6 to 18), children (age 6 and under) free.

From Greensboro head south on State Route 25 toward *Faunsdale,* population 98. Housed in an 1890s mercantile building on the town's main street, *Ca-John's Faunsdale Bar & Grill* (334-628-3240; ca-johns.net) serves great steaks and seafood, and owner John (Ca-John) Broussard, originally from Louisiana, offers a variety of crawfish specialties in season. The food speaks for itself, attracting diners from distant towns. Windows sport red-and-white checkered cafe curtains. A pot-bellied stove and fireplace add to the ambience. Saturday night patrons often can enjoy live music until the wee hours. Hours are 5 to 10 p.m. Friday and 11 a.m. to 10 p.m. on Saturday. From Faunsdale return to US 80 and head west toward Demopolis.

Sometime during your visit to the area, make an outing to *Prairieville,* the site of *St. Andrews Episcopal Church.* Located a short distance off US 80, this red Carpenter Gothic structure dates from 1853 and is a National Historic Landmark. Nearby you'll see a picturesque old cemetery, where many of this area's early settlers are buried.

alabamatrivia

An immense 1833 meteor shower inspired the song, "Stars Fell on Alabama."

Peter Lee and Joe Glasgow, master carpenters and slaves of Capt. Henry A. Tayloe, supervised a crew of slaves belonging to church members in the construction of this edifice, built to serve settlers from the Atlantic seaboard.

Craftspeople created the mellowed appearance of interior wood walls by applying a brew made from the stems of tobacco plants. Pokeberry weeds provided color for some portions of the lovely stained-glass windows. Ragweed, chewed and molded, forms the decorative relief letters of a biblical quotation near the altar. Be sure to notice the pipe organ (which is still playable) and the choir gallery. Closed as a regular parish in 1927, the church hosts a special service the first Sunday in October followed by a picnic dinner on the grounds. Group tours can be arranged by appointment; call (334) 606-9612.

Traveling 9 miles west on US 80 takes you to *Gaineswood* (334-289-4846), a gorgeous cream-colored mansion with white-columned porticos. Once the centerpiece of a huge plantation, the home now stands in the suburbs of the town of *Demopolis* at 805 South Cedar Avenue. Gen. Nathan Bryan Whitfield, a gifted inventor, musician, artist, and architect, started construction on the house in 1843. He spent almost two decades planning and building this elegant Greek revival home and continued to refine it until the Civil War's outbreak.

Stepping into the columned ballroom, you'll see yourself reflected 13 times in the vis-à-vis mirrors. Be sure to notice the glass-ceiling domes and the elaborate friezes and medallions. The home contains its original furnishings, family portraits, and accessories. Don't miss the flutina (invented by Whitfield), a one-of-a-kind musical instrument that sounds something like a riverboat calliope.

In many ways Gaineswood reminded me of Thomas Jefferson's splendid Monticello, and my guide said visitors often make that observation. Every year in September, Gaineswood celebrates Harvest Fest with crafts, food, and music. Except for major holidays, Gaineswood is open Tuesday through Friday from 10 a.m. to 4 p.m. and from 10 a.m. to 2 p.m. the first Saturday of each month. Special tours can be arranged by appointment. Admission: adults $5, senior citizens and college students $4, children (ages 6 to 18) $3.

Continue to downtown Demopolis, "the City of the People," a town with an interesting origin that goes back to 1817 when 400 aristocrats, fleeing France after Napoleon's exile, landed here at the white limestone bluffs overlooking the Tombigbee River. They acquired a large tract of land along the river and set about establishing the *Vine and Olive Colony.* The agricultural experiment, however, yielded little more than frustration for the colonists, who lacked essential farming skills and found the local climate and soil unsuitable for cultivating their imported grape vines and olive trees.

You'll see a display on this early colony in the French Room at *Bluff Hall* (334-289-9644). Located at 407 North Commissioners Avenue next to the Civic Center, this 1832 brick home takes its name from its position overlooking the Tombigbee River. Originally built in the federal style, the home took on a Greek revival appearance after later additions. Furnishings are Empire and mid-Victorian.

As you start upstairs notice the newel post's amity button, symbolizing a state of harmony between the owner and builder. In addition to documents, crystal, silver spoons, cannonballs, portraits, and other memorabilia of the Vine and Olive Colony, you'll see a room filled with period costumes, such as an 1831 wedding dress. Bluff Hall is noted for its extensive collection of vintage clothing.

The kitchen's interesting gadgets range from an egg tin, sausage stuffer, and fluting iron to the "humane" rat trap on the hearth. Adjacent to the home, the Canebrake Craft Corner offers a choice selection of items including posters depicting a European artist's imaginative conception of the early Vine and Olive Colony, handmade split-oak baskets, and eye-catching pottery by Susan Brown Freeman. Bluff Hall is owned and operated by the

Marengo County Historical Society. (The county's name was inspired by Napoleon's victory at the Battle of Marengo in northern Italy.) Except for major holidays, Bluff Hall is open Tuesday through Saturday from 10 a.m. to 5 p.m. and on Sunday from 2 to 5 p.m. Admission: adults $5, students $3.

While sightseeing stop by **New Orleans Bar & Grill** (336-315-5351; neworleansbarandgrill.com) at 4312 Big Tree Way. The restaurant serves a variety of sandwiches, salads, and dinner entrees. Try the Jack Daniel's steak and chicken salad. Hours are 11 a.m. till 10 p.m. Monday through Saturday, Sunday noon to 10 p.m. Prices are moderate.

Demopolis offers more than mansions and water recreation. You'll find plenty of interesting places to shop, too. Downtown, at 110 West Washington Street, **The Mustard Seed** (334-289-2878) offers fine gifts, china, crystal, housewares, collectibles, dolls, and toys. The Mustard Seed also has a coffee shop with gourmet casseroles to go as well as chicken salad, pimiento cheese spread, turtleback cookies, and much more. Local festivals include a July the Fourth celebration, Freedom on the River at City Landing, and December's **Christmas on the River,** which features a weeklong festival of parades, tours, and events culminating in an extravaganza of decorated, lighted boats gliding down the Tombigbee River. For more information on these or other special events, including productions by the Canebrake Players (a local theater group) or on other area attractions, call (334) 289-0270.

Traveling north takes you to **Eutaw,** a charming hamlet situated around a courthouse square that dates from 1838. The town boasts 53 antebellum structures, with many on the National Register of Historic Places. Head first to the chamber of commerce office on the courthouse square, where you'll find information on both Eutaw and Greene County.

Beside the historic Vaughn Morrow House on Main Street stands the First Presbyterian Church. Organized in 1824 as Mesopotamia Presbyterian Church, the congregation's current home dates from 1851. This white-steepled structure looks as if it belongs on a Christmas card (without the snow, of course—a rare commodity in most of Alabama). Original whale-oil lamps, stored for a time in the slave gallery, have been wired for electricity and again grace the church's interior. For a tour, inquire at the church office in the adjacent Educational Building.

Nearby, on the corner of Main Street and Eutaw Avenue, stands St. Stephen's Episcopal Church. The handsome brick structure features a hand-carved lectern, an elegant white marble baptismal font, and beautiful stained glass windows. To see the lovely interior, check with the church office.

After exploring Eutaw head west to *Gainesville,* a delightful piece of the past populated by 307 people. Most places like this charming town have vanished from today's landscape. Here you'll see historic cemeteries and churches like the *First Presbyterian Church,* which dates from 1837 and has been rescued from flames on three occasions—once with a hand-to-hand bucket brigade. Interior features include whale-oil lamps, box pews, the altar's original chairs, and a bell with a tone enhanced by 500 melted silver dollars. Because several denominations share this church (one per Sunday), attendees label themselves "Metho-bap-terians." Other sites of interest include the *1872 Methodist Church; St. Alban's Episcopal Church,* founded in 1879; and the *Confederate Cemetery.* For more local information stop by one of the downtown stores.

Afterward continue south to nearby *Livingston.* The town was named for Edward Livingston, who served as Andrew Jackson's secretary of state.

On your way into town, stop by Sumter County's *Alamuchee Covered Bridge,* across from the Baptist Student Union on the campus of Livingston State University. Capt. W. A. C. Jones of Livingston designed and built this 1861 structure, one of the South's oldest covered bridges. Made of hand-hewn heart pine held together by large wooden pegs, the bridge originally spanned the Sucarnochee River, south of town. In 1924 the bridge was taken down and reconstructed across a creek on the old Bellamy-Livingston Road, where it remained in use until 1958. The bridge was moved to its present location and restored in 1971. You might enjoy seeing more of the campus, which also boasts two lakes.

Downtown you'll see a lovely square surrounding the impressive domed *Sumter County Courthouse* (circa 1900). This area remained Choctaw country until 1830, when the US acquired it in the Treaty of Dancing Rabbit Creek.

Head to *York,* about 11 miles southwest of Livingston. In this small town near the Mississippi border, you'll find a wonderful art museum inside *The Coleman Center* (205-392-2005 or 205-392-2004; colemanarts.org), at 630 Avenue A. The museum, a library, genealogical room, and a cultural center occupy an early-20th-century general store. On an exterior wall of the building, a repainted vintage ad shows silent film star Clara Bow promoting an early brand of gasoline. You'll enter The Coleman Center through a courtyard on the opposite side.

A staff member described the four-building complex as a community effort and the only facility of its kind in Sumter County. Local citizens contributed the land, building, services, and funds for the center. In addition to its permanent collection, which includes an original etching by Renoir, prints, paintings, pottery, and other items, the museum features traveling exhibits. Hours are 10 a.m. to 5 p.m. on Monday through Wednesday and Friday and from 10 a.m. to noon on Saturday or by appointment. Admission is free. Visit York on the first Saturday of each month and take in some special events at local galleries.

Timberland

Timber is big business in this part of the state, and hunting and fishing are popular pastimes. If you're in the mood for a feast, head for *Ezell's Fish Camp* (205-654-2205; ezellscamp.com) near *Lavaca* at 776 Ezell Road. This out-of-the-way restaurant is definitely worth adding some extra miles to your trip. In fact, some customers fly in, and an Ezell's staffer meets them at the airport. The restaurant also gets a lot of river traffic and often provides transportation into town for boating customers who need motel lodging.

To reach the restaurant from Lavaca, take State Route 10 east toward Nanafalia and turn left just before reaching the big bridge. Located on the west bank of the Tombigbee River, this family operation is the granddaddy of "catfish cabins" you might see while driving through the state. Following family precedent, each of the Ezells' three children went into the restaurant business.

As you arrive, you'll see a large rustic structure with a roof of wooden shingles. The restaurant started out as a Civil War–era dogtrot cabin, and the Ezells added more rooms for their brisk business. The rambling structure now seats 400 people. Mounted deer and moose heads line the walls. (Mr. Ezell, an avid angler, hunter, and trapper, used to ship his furs to New York's garment district.)

The back porch, a favorite spot for eating, overlooks the river. Start with an appetizer of onion rings, crab claws, or fried dill pickles. In addition to

Need Some Mama Nems Pepper Jelly?

Then hurry to the *Alabama Rural Heritage Center* (334-627-3388; ruralheritage center.com) in Thomaston, a Black Belt hamlet northeast of Lavaca at 133 Sixth Avenue. Along with batches of the popular pepper jelly, you'll find a wide selection of Alabama art and handmade crafts in the gift shop. A jar of watermelon rind pickles just might make the perfect souvenir. There is also a restaurant on-site. That special Mama Nems Pepper Jelly is homemade at the center using a time-tested local recipe. The center even grows its own peppers for top-notch quality. So how to eat the tasty jelly? It's a great glaze on ham and pork chops, a sweet barbecue sauce for ribs and chicken, and a delicious spread on warm corn bread.

The once-humble facility was renovated in 2006, thanks to the innovative efforts of two teams of fifth-year architecture students from Auburn University, who designed and worked on the project over a three-year period. Annual events include Evening under the Stars, utilizing the Heritage outdoor stage, on Friday and Saturday evenings during Mother's Day weekend, a Pepper Jelly Festival in April, and an annual Rural Fun Day with storytelling, spinning, weaving, quilting, and other crafts demonstrations the fourth Saturday in August. Hours are Thursday and Friday 10 a.m. to 4 p.m., and Saturday 10 a.m. to 1 p.m.

catfish, the restaurant serves seafood specialties such as shrimp and oysters. Entrees come with slaw, potatoes, and hush puppies. Moderate prices. Open every day except Monday, Ezell's has flexible hours, but the typical schedule is 11 a.m. to 9 p.m. Sunday through Thursday and to 10 p.m. Friday and Saturday.

Traveling south from Lavaca takes you through large expanses of timberland. Forestry and related industries play major roles in the area's economy. Clarke County holds the title of Forestry Capital of Alabama, and Fulton, a small town south of Thomasville, pays tribute to this important industry by hosting a *Sawmill Days* celebration each fall.

If you head south from Jackson, you'll pass unusual geographical features known as salt domes. (A salt dome is the tip of a huge mountain of salt forced to the surface from deep within the earth.) According to a local historian, the salt domes in this area are as close as any to the earth's surface, but you probably won't recognize them as such because they're covered

Discover St. Stephens—Alabama's Territorial Capital

No Black Belt ramble is complete without a visit to *St. Stephens Historical Park.* It was here, in 1799, the first US flag flew over what would become Alabama. Executive director Jim Long, sixth-generation grandson of John McGrew, who settled in St. Stephens during the 1770s, can share many anecdotes about the original site of Alabama's territorial capital, the now vanished but once-thriving Old St. Stephens.

Make your first stop the 1854 territorial courthouse, now called the Old Washington County Courthouse, on US 34 West to collect information. A trio of flags fronts this two-story white building, which houses a museum and serves as headquarters for the St. Stephens Historical Commission. Take the tiny grill-fronted elevator or the stairs to the second floor for a look at the exhibits, which include Indian artifacts, a dugout canoe made somewhere between 600 to 1,000 years ago, portraits of early settlers, and the Old Washington County courtroom with its original furnishings. Once a major fossil site, this area shipped fossils to museums in other parts of the country, and you'll see some interesting specimens.

Afterward, head to the 200-acre park, which offers camping, fishing, and other outdoor recreation. Exploring the park, you'll see an architectural site, old cemetery, and the unusual Indian Baths. "They've been called the Indian Baths as far back as anyone knows, but their origin remains unknown," said a staff member, who came across a mention about mineral springs here in 1818 and also heard speculation that this feature might have been part of an early Spanish irrigation system.

For a modest park admission, which you pay at the camp store by the lake, you can spend a full day hiking, swimming, picnicking, and relaxing. Campers will find that the "view of the night sky is fabulous, and you can hear coyotes howling," said Long. The facility opens at sunrise and closes at sunset, and the main gate is locked at 10 p.m. For more information on this intriguing site, located on the west side of the Tombigbee River in Washington County near Jackson, call (251) 246-6790.

with foliage. After Union forces cut off supplies during the Civil War, the local salt mines became extremely important. Many people made their way here for this commodity, essential for curing and preserving meats.

Take your time while discovering the treasures and pleasures of the Black Belt, a region where history still resonates in its stories—the kind best savored on front porches. Kathryn Tucker Windham, Alabama's famous First Lady of Folk Tales and Ghost Stories grew up in Thomasville, located about an hour south of Demopolis on US 43. She died in 2011. "We're not New York City, and we don't want to be," says tourism coordinator Linda Vice, who can direct you to plenty of interesting, off-the-beaten-path spots in this history-rich area. "We have developed a Black History/Heritage Trail, a Native American Trail, an overall History Heritage Trail, and a Foods Trail through this area." Call Linda at (334) 636-5506.

On the outskirts of Thomasville stands Alabama Southern Community College (334-637-3146), located at 30755 Highway 43. The college library houses the *Kathryn Tucker Windham Museum,* which fans enjoy visiting. Hours are Monday through Thursday from 7:30 a.m. to 7:30 p.m. and on Friday from 7:30 a.m. to 12:30 p.m. or by appointment. Free admission.

Continue to *Camden,* where you'll find the *Black Belt Treasures Gallery* (334-682-9878) downtown at 209 Claiborne Street in a handsomely restored old car dealership. The gallery showcases arts, crafts, books, and food from more than 200 artists and craftsmen from this region. Hours are 10 a.m. to 4 p.m. Tuesday through Friday and 10 a.m. to 2 p.m. Saturday. Visit blackbelttreasures.com.

Before leaving town, stop by *Camden Jewelry and Gifts* (334-682-4057; camdenjewelryandgifts.com) on the 47 Camden Bypass. Besides jewelry, you'll find a selection of taste-tempting gourmet food items, a children's section, kitchen section, bath and body products, travel items, and more. The friendly staff will help you choose the perfect souvenir or gift for everyone on your list. Hours are 9 a.m. to 5 p.m. Monday through Friday and 9 a.m. to 2 p.m. Saturday. If you visit Camden during the Wilcox Historical Society's biennial (slated for odd-numbered years) Fall Tour of Homes, you can survey some of the area's antebellum structures. The stately *Wilcox Female Institute,* which dates from 1850, serves as tour headquarters. Located at 301 Broad Street, the former school (open by appointment) houses a small museum of local history.

For a Southern taste treat, make reservations at the *Gaines Ridge Dinner Club* (334-682-9707), located about 2 miles east of Camden on State Route 10. Housed in Betty Gaines Kennedy's two-story circa-1830 family home, the restaurant seats about 100 guests in five dining rooms. From shrimp bisque to spinach salad and steak or seafood, everything on the

The Quilters of Gee's Bend Create a Bridge to the World

To visit the home of the famed quilters whose works captured the imagination of people across the country, head to Camden and board the **Gee's Bend Ferry.** (Senator John McCain did this during his presidential campaign.) Created by four generations of African-American women whose quilts have been called bold, colorful, and unique, the *New York Times* described their designs and needlecraft as "some of the most miraculous works of modern art America has produced."

The quilters work at Boykin Nutrition Center, and a nearby building houses their current inventory of colorful quilts, which sell for prices ranging from $1,500 to $4,000. The Quilts of Gee's Bend exhibit has intrigued gallery goers to Boston's Museum of Fine Arts, Atlanta's High Museum, and others across the country. The women have also been featured in such publications as *House and Garden,* Oprah's *O* magazine, *Newsweek,* and *Country Home* and on National Public Radio and CBS's *Sunday Morning.*

The quilters struck a chord with people everywhere. Why? Anniston travel writer Mary Eloise H. Leake explains it this way: "Amid a landscape of limitations, the women were and still are strongly individualistic and gifted with artistic vision. Forging bonds across generations, each quilt reflects the personality and talent of the particular woman who stitched it together. With no access to definitive quilting patterns, these women made—and continue to make—quilts with lyrical improvisational designs, amazing asymmetrical constructions, and simple minimalist motifs. While a Gee's Bend's quilt can be a vibrant Joseph's coat of many colors, its hue can also be dull and worn like the clothes from which it has been made.

"As they have traveled the country, the quilts—and many of the quilters—have shared the message that art can be created from basic necessities. Their quilts have formed a bridge from their isolated world to the wider world, and the creators have been delighted to see the joy they have brought to others. Since the quilts have been heralded as artistic triumphs by art critics and warmly received by exhibit viewers, this unaccustomed outpouring of respect and admiration have been wonderful return gifts to these ladies."

To reach Gee's Bend, located in a curve of the Alabama River about 30 miles southwest of Selma, forget the long way via Wilcox County Route 29 and take the ferry from Camden. For schedules, rates, and more information on the Gee's Bend Ferry, see geesbendferry.com.

menu is well prepared and tasty. (Ask Betty about the home's ghosts.) Prices fall in the moderate range, and hours are 5:30 to 9 p.m. Thursday through Saturday.

Wilcox County, which promises good fishing, attracts out-of-state deer and turkey hunters, and many make their headquarters at nearby **Roland Cooper State Park** at 285 Deer Run Drive (334-682-4838; alapark.com/ rolandcooper). If you're in the area during harvest season, consider purchasing some fresh-shelled pecans from Joe C. Williams. To order the local product, write PO Box 640, Camden 36726; or call (334) 682-4559. For more information on Camden and the surrounding area, call the Wilcox Area Chamber of Commerce at (334) 682-4929, visit wilcoxareachamber.com, or stop by at 1001 Earl Hilliard Road.

Traveling south from Camden on State Route 265 takes you by **Rikard's Mill,** just north of Beatrice. Stop by to browse through the Covered Bridge Gift Shop and watch the old-fashioned water-powered gristmill in operation. You'll also find a restored blacksmith shop and hiking trails. Modest admission. Open April through mid-December on Saturday from 9 a.m. to 5 p.m. Call (251) 789-2781 or (251) 575-7433.

Continue south to **Monroeville** (where Alabama authors Truman Capote and Harper Lee played as children) for a stop at the **Old Monroe County Courthouse.** This 1903 three-story brick structure served as a model for the courthouse in the film *To Kill a Mockingbird,* based on Harper Lee's Pulitzer Prize–winning novel (and starring Gregory Peck in the role of Atticus Finch). During the last weekend in April and the first three weekends in May, visitors can watch the stage version of *To Kill a Mockingbird* in a bona fide courtroom setting. Produced by the Mockingbird Players, the local stage adaptation boasts the authenticity of the story's actual location plus cultural awareness and genuine Southern accents.

Don't miss this performance, whose first act takes place on the courthouse lawn when a historic automobile and a mule-drawn wagon arrive for the trial. The Mockingbird Players also draw the audience into the play by choosing members from the audience to fill seats of the all-white, all-male jury, which, of course, convicts defendant Tom Robinson. For more information, visit the website at monroecountymuseum.org.

Dip into the town's rich literary heritage at the **Old Courthouse Museum** (251-575-7433; monroecountymuseum.org), which also features changing exhibits related to Monroe County's past and a gift shop with works by area artists. Adjacent to the courtroom, you'll see an informative Harper Lee exhibit with archival photos, quotes, and a continuous video of local citizens sharing anecdotes from the 1930s. Museum folks can share plenty of firsthand information on the town, its celebrated authors, and the Monroe County Heritage Museums. The museum is located at 31 North Alabama Avenue; admission is free. Hours run from 10 a.m. to 4 p.m. Tuesday through Friday and 9 a.m. to noon on Saturday.

Afterward, take a walking tour around town, where several buildings feature murals illustrating scenes from *To Kill a Mockingbird*. While downtown, stop by **Finishing Touches** (251-575-2066) at 18 East Claiborne Street. You'll enjoy browsing through this shop with lovely handmade items, antiques, kitchen accessories, gifts, clothing for children and ladies, customized baskets, and books. Before leaving the area, you might want to visit the **River Heritage Museum,** housed in the old Corps of Engineers building at the Claiborne Lock & Dam. The surrounding region is a great place for camping and fishing, too. Located about 18 miles from the square in downtown Monroeville, the museum can be reached by taking State Route 41 to County Road 17 and then following the signs to the Claiborne Lock & Dam. The museum's exhibits feature fossils, Native American artifacts, and steamboat relics. The museum is open for special events or by appointment

Monroeville—Literary Capital of Alabama

In recognition of the exceptional literary heritage of Monroeville and Monroe County, the Alabama legislature designated this region the Literary Capital of Alabama in a 1997 joint resolution. Author of "A Christmas Memory," *In Cold Blood, Breakfast at Tiffany's,* and other classics, Truman Capote spent idyllic hours roaming the town as a youngster along with friend Harper Lee, who penned the Pulitzer Prize–winning novel *To Kill a Mockingbird.* Other writers who have called Monroeville home include nationally syndicated columnist Cynthia Tucker and novelist Mark Childress. The small town of Monroeville, which packs a rich literary history, hosts an Alabama Writers Symposium the first weekend in May. For more information on this event, contact the Alabama Southern Community College at PO Box 2000, Monroeville 36461; or call (251) 575-8223.

only. A great time to visit is the annual Alabama River Festival in March when reenactors and demonstrators create a frontier encampment from the late 1700s and early 1800s. Admission is free. For more information call (251) 575-7433.

Gulf Coast Delta

After your timberland excursion head south to Escambia County, where traveling pilgrims can spend an authentic Thanksgiving Day with the Poarch Band of Creek Indians at their annual Pow Wow. Tribal members welcome friends, relatives, and visitors to help them celebrate Thanksgiving day on the *Poarch Creek Reservation,* 8 miles northwest of Atmore at 5811 Jack Springs Road. Festivities include exhibition dancing by tribes from throughout the country, a greased pig chase, turkey shoot, and much more. You can feast on roasted corn, Indian fry bread, ham, fried chicken, or traditional turkey and dressing. Booths feature beadwork, basketry, silver work, and other Native American crafts. Take a lawn chair, camera, and your appetite. Modest admission. For more information on this event, call (251) 368-9136.

Continue southwest toward the Eastern Shore and stop by Malbis, 12 miles east of Mobile on US 90. On Baldwin County Road 27, you'll find the *Malbis Plantation Greek Orthodox Church.* This magnificent neo-Byzantine–style structure, built at a cost of more than $1 million, was dedicated to the memory of Jason Malbis. A former monk who emigrated from Greece in 1906, Malbis traveled through 36 states before selecting this Baldwin County site to establish Malbis Plantation (virtually a self-supporting colony that grew to cover 2,000 acres).

The marble in this edifice came from the same Greek quarries used to build Athens' ancient Parthenon. The majestic interior features a dark-blue 75-foot domed ceiling, stained-glass windows, mosaics, and murals. Greek artists spent eight months completing the paintings that extend from the cathedral's entrance to its altar. Except for Christmas Day, the church is open daily, and admission is free. Hours run from 10 a.m. to 4 p.m. For tour information call (251) 626-3050.

Next swing westward to *Daphne,* perched on Mobile Bay's Eastern Shore, where you might hear someone shout "Jubilee!" When you do, people will grab buckets and rush to the water's edge for flounder,

Strange as It Sounds

Whether or not you hear the cry of "Jubilee!" during your visit to the Eastern Shore of Mobile Bay, you can see this strange spectacle depicted in a photo display at *Manci's Antique Club* (251-626-9917; manci.net) in downtown Daphne. Located at 1715 Main Street, this combination bar/museum (originally opened as a gas station in 1924 by Frank Manci, converted to its current status in 1947 by Arthur Manci, and now operated by a third-generation family member, Alex Manci) houses a rickshaw, oxen yokes, and Victrolas. You'll also see collections of antique tools, cowbells, political campaign buttons, and Native American artifacts. The club boasts the biggest assemblage of Jim Beam decanters outside the distillery's own collection. Claiming the title "Bloody Mary Capital of the Eastern Shore," the house serves its specialty garnished with a pickled string bean. A sign over the bar promises free beer tomorrow.

Those who visit the ladies' room at Manci's will see the wooden figure of a man—dressed only in a fig leaf. The observant will notice the fig leaf is hinged, and the curious might go even further. Unrestrained curiosity can soon turn to horror, however, because a blaring alarm alerts all within hearing distance that one possesses an inquisitive nature. One then must make the uncomfortable choice of exiting—red-faced—to the merriment of Manci's patrons or occupying the ladies' room till closing time. Manci's hours are 11 a.m. to 9 p.m. daily.

shrimp, and crabs—theirs for the scooping. Although not unique to the area, this "shoreward migration of bottom-living organisms"—to put it in technical terms—surprises most visitors. This natural phenomenon might occur several times a summer, usually during the wee morning hours. Some natives claim they can predict an approaching jubilee by watching weather conditions and studying certain indicators in the moon, tide, and winds.

After exploring Daphne continue south to *Fairhope,* a charming flower-filled town founded about 1894 on the "single tax" concept of economist Henry George, who considered land the source of all wealth. The Fairhope Single Tax Colony still functions today, one of the country's few model communities operating on George's taxation theories. A percentage of the town's property is held by the Fairhope Single Tax Colony office, and a resident can lease his or her land for 99 years (or perpetuity). The resident pays a single annual tax on the land only—not on improvements—and this yearly payment covers school district, city, county, and state taxes as well as community services.

Save plenty of time for strolling through the pages of this storybook town with baskets of colorful blossoms cascading from every street corner and rose gardens galore in its bayfront park. Downtown art galleries, boutiques, and eateries beckon browsers. Indulge your whims as you pass restaurants featuring coastal cuisine fresh from the Gulf and shops offering everything from antiques, toys, and custom-designed clothing to nautical gear.

Wander to the *Eastern Shore Art Center* (251-928-2228; esartcenter .com) at 401 Oak Street and view its current exhibits. Top that off with individual galleries that call your name. At Fairhope's monthly First Friday Artwalk, you can hop a free trolley or stroll a 5-block area to visit galleries like Lyons Share and Summit. For a great local souvenir, stop by the *Christine Linson Gallery* (251-929-2015) at 386 Fairhope Avenue and pick up a pack of note cards depicting local scenes.

On a trip to Alabama in 1998, Christine painted the town (in watercolor) and fell in love with its charms. She promptly returned to her lifelong home in Cleveland, Ohio, packed her belongings, moved to Fairhope, and opened her gallery. In addition to her popular Fairhope and Eastern Shore prints and limited edition Christmas cards, you'll see original floral and figurative art work. Also, you might meet felines Matisse and Kahlo (not aloof—only shy). Hours run 10 a.m. to 5 p.m. Monday through Saturday. Check out christinelinson.com for a peek at the artist's portfolio.

Hosts Becky and Bill Jones also welcome visitors to *Bay Breeze Guest House* on historic Mobile Bay, where they can watch the glorious sunsets, go beachcombing or fishing, and feed the resident ducks. Ask Becky, a former biology teacher, about the local jubilee phenomenon. From May through September, guests can enjoy breakfast served on Bay Breeze's pier. Moderate rates. For reservations at either property, call (866) 928-8976.

South of Fairhope at Point Clear (designated "Punta Clara" on 16th-century maps of Spanish explorers), you'll find the *Grand Hotel Marriott Resort, Golf Club & Spa* (251-928-9201 or 800-544-9933) on scenic US 98. This legendary resort on Mobile Bay offers facilities spreading over 550 lovely acres studded with moss-festooned oaks more than 300 years old. The locale has long attracted generations of wealthy Southern families—the site's first resort dates from the mid-1800s. Today's guests continue to enjoy "the Grand's" traditions, such as afternoon tea.

If hotels possess survival instincts, the Grand's got an instinct second to none. The Queen of Southern Resorts refused to accept Hurricane Katrina's ravages and soon regrouped, rebuilt, and refurbished. No stranger to adversity, the grande dame emerged from her own tsunami in the same manner she rebounded after Civil War shelling and fire during the past century and a half.

So settle in and set off on a stroll or Segway tour to see the glorious grounds. Look for the life-size bronze statue of local legend, Bucky Miller. Known for his incredible photographic memory, Bucky (as he was fondly

The Hut of the Poet of Tolstoy Park

Founded in 1894 by a group of utopian dreamers, Fairhope has a way of inviting folks to be themselves, to quietly look inside and see what makes them special. One of those unusual characters has left a strange sort of tourist attraction that still draws visitors today.

Henry Stuart moved to Fairhope from Idaho because he was told he was dying, that he only had a year to live. The doctor was wrong.

Diagnosed with consumption in the 1920s, Stuart lived another two decades after moving to Fairhope. Known as the Hermit of Montrose (a neighborhood in Fairhope), Stuart built himself a small round hurricane proof hut out of concrete. He made all the bricks himself and put the date on each one.

An admirer of famed author Tolstoy, Stuart named his patch of ground Tolstoy Park. It took him over a year to build his hut, which was shaped somewhat like a beehive. He decided he wasn't going to wear shoes but then he found out he needed one shoe to use a shovel so he went to a store and tried to buy one shoe for his right foot. When they said they couldn't sell just one shoe, he bought the pair and told them to keep the left shoe for someone who needed it.

Stuart was said to have earned a living by weaving rugs. Stuart died in 1946 at 88 years old. His hut still stands, now surrounded by office buildings. It rests just off the parking lot of a real estate office. If you can't find it, ask townsfolks and they can probably point you in the right direction. For a fascinating read, look for Sonny Brewer's 2006 novel, *The Poet of Tolstoy Park*. The hut is open to the public any time. Guests can visit and take a book or leave a book. Guests often leave a few coins as well.

known) called hotel guests by name even when years had lapsed between their visits. He greeted everyone warmly and personified the Grand's legendary hospitality during his 64-year tenure. Presiding over the Bird Cage Lounge, he delighted guests with his famous mint juleps. Though Bucky died in 2002, his spirit lives on at the Grand, and his statue was dedicated on Kentucky Derby Day in 2005.

The resort has consistently earned Four Diamond status each year since 1977 when AAA tourism editors started their awards for excellence. With so much to enjoy, from fine dining and a world-class spa to water recreation, tennis, and challenging golf courses, you'll want to check out marriott.com and check in soon after. Call for current vacation packages and reservations at this family-friendly historical hotel. Deluxe.

Be sure to visit a candy shop called *Punta Clara Kitchen* (251-928-8477; puntaclara.com), located in an 1897 gingerbread house 1 mile south of the Grand Hotel at 17111 Scenic Highway 98. Here you can sample confections from pecan butter crunch and divinity to chocolate-covered bourbon balls and buckeyes (balls of creamy peanut-butter confections hand-dipped in chocolate). The shop also sells jellies, recipe books, pickles, and preserves. Before leaving, take a few minutes to look around this historic home, furnished as it was during the late 1800s. Hours are 9 a.m. to 5 p.m. Monday through Saturday and 12:30 to 5 p.m. Sunday.

Behind the Victorian home stands a weathered cedar and cypress structure that originally served as a laundry and wine cellar. It now houses *The Wash House Restaurant* (251-928-4838; washhouserestaurant.com) at 17111 Scenic Highway 98, a great place to savor Southern coastal cuisine. The restaurant features the original working fireplace and wash pot, nowadays in the softly lit bar. Behind the building, a large deck under ancient live oaks makes a romantic setting for dinner.

Owners Wade Selsor and Robert Yarbrough learned their way around the kitchen as kids growing up in Camden, a small town south of Selma. "Wade develops the recipes, but we both play around with them," said Robert, noting they also draw from a broad spectrum of family favorites. The recipe for Sissy's crab cakes, a popular appetizer here, came from his wife's grandmother.

Entree options include savory rack of lamb, seared tuna steak, and chateaubriand, a succulent cut from the heart of the tenderloin, served with potato casserole and blackened asparagus. Green Goddess dressing makes Wade's salads memorable, and his delicious key lime bread pudding offers a different twist. Dinner hours start at 5 p.m. daily; closing time depends on the crowd. Reservations are encouraged. Moderate.

Ready for an anti-stress kind of place? Then head for nearby **Magnolia Springs,** where you can unwind in a serene setting of dappled sunlight and live oaks. In its heyday as a resort area during the early part of the 1900s, Magnolia Springs lured visitors with twice-a-day train service from Chicago, St. Louis, and Cincinnati. "Many a consumptive, rheumatic, nervous, worn-out and over-worked person whose case was thought hopeless by the physicians has found health and a new lease on life by spending a few months at Magnolia Springs," states an early promotional pamphlet.

Once known as the Sunnyside Hotel, the **Magnolia Springs Bed & Breakfast** (251-965-7321 or 800-965-7321) at 14469 Oak Street exudes a friendly aura with its welcoming wraparound porch accented by a swing, wicker furniture, rocking chairs, and ferns. One of the county's three remaining hotels from the resort era, the historic structure is painted a buttery yellow with white trim. Committed to providing warm hospitality, innkeepers David Worthington and Eric Bigelow welcome guests to their 1867 home, nourish them with a delicious breakfast, and recommend local excursions. If you go cruising down the river, you'll see mailboxes at the water's edge. Magnolia Springs's first postmaster launched a mail service by water in 1915, and many residents still get their mail delivered by boat. "It's one of only a few places in the country with a water mail route," says David.

You may have seen Magnolia Springs Bed and Breakfast featured on Bob Vila's *Restore America,* a home-and-garden TV program, in *Southern Living* magazine, or maybe on a past Alabama Public Television special. See magnoliasprings.com. Moderate to deluxe rates.

A short stroll down tree-lined Oak Street takes you to **Moore Brothers Village Market** (251-965-3826), a great place to catch up on local news. The market houses a bakery, deli, butcher shop, gourmet foods, and plenty of nostalgia. You can enjoy lunch daily from 11 a.m. to 4 p.m. and dinner Monday through Thursday from 5 to 9 p.m. and Friday and Saturday from 5 to 10 p.m. at **Jesse's Restaurant** (251-965-3827), also on the premises.

The original Moore Bros. Gen'l Merchandise opened in 1922 and remained a family business until it closed in 1993. Then, in 1997, Charlie

Houser (who spent childhood days here) returned and purchased the neighborhood store and adjacent post office. With the help of an architect and contractor, he connected and rejuvenated the two buildings to implement his image of the perfect neighborhood gathering place.

Paintings depicting local scenes, old photos, and news articles line the walls of the restaurant and also the entryway, where an antique pie safe displays freshly made pastries. Nearby, you can check your weight on the penny scales. If you find yourself penniless, there's usually a spare coin on top of the machine. By the way, it's best to weigh before dining at Jesse's, where the evening special might mean prime rib, shrimp scampi, or whiskey steak. Other popular entrees include crab cakes, Cajun fettuccine, stuffed flounder, and chicken Pontalba. Moderate prices.

Across the road from Jesse's stands Magnolia Springs Park, which showcases one of the town's springs and makes an inviting shady retreat.

After basking in Magnolia Springs's serenity, head for **Foley,** situated around the intersection of US 98 and State Route 59. The town offers not only factory-outlet shopping but a host of attractions such as antiques malls, arts centers, and charming eateries.

Start your tour at 111 West Laurel Avenue with the **Baldwin Museum of Art** and the **Holmes Medical Museum** (251-970-1818), housed in a building that dates to the early 1900s. After viewing the current downstairs art exhibits, climb to the second floor for a close-up look at instruments and memorabilia from medicine's earlier years. Once a hospital for Baldwin County residents, the rooms contain an operating suite complete with table, bone-breaking apparatus, Kelly pad, ether container, and attendant tubes. Also on display are X-ray equipment and medical cabinets filled with delivery forceps, tonsil guillotine and snare, and other instruments. In addition to patient quarters, you can inspect a room devoted to quackery paraphernalia—a color spectrum device for treating everything from headaches to kidney infections, barber bowl for bleeding patients, and diagrammed phrenology skull. Hours are 10 a.m. to 4 p.m. Monday through Friday. Admission is free.

Take a break next door at **Stacey Olde Tyme Soda Fountain** (251-943-7191), with its sweet drinks from the past. In this delightful pharmacy at 121 West Laurel Avenue, you can savor a banana split, slurp on an ice-cream soda, cherry Coke, or chocolate milk shake, and listen to old favorites from the jukebox or player piano while watching a toy train make its rounds above the soda fountain. A penny scale reveals your weight and fate. Hours run from 9 a.m. to 6 p.m. Monday through Friday and 9 a.m. to 5 p.m. on Saturday. Economical rates.

Continuing to the next block, you'll find *The Gift Horse* (251-943-3663; gifthorserestaurant.com), located at 209 West Laurel Avenue. Beyond the restaurant's leaded-glass doors, you'll see a grand banquet table with a buffet of salads, vegetables, meats, breads, and desserts. House specialties include fried biscuits, spinach soufflé, mystery crab-shrimp salad, and the restaurant's famous apple cheese—all prepared from owner Jackie O. McLeod's recipes. Lunch is served from 11 a.m. to 4:30 p.m. daily. Dinner hours run from 4:30 to 9 p.m. or when the crowd thins out. Monday through Saturday, and Sunday hours run from 11 a.m. to 8 p.m. Rates are moderate. Jackie's cookbook, available in the gift shop, makes a great souvenir and divulges some of her culinary secrets. While in Foley you may want to visit the Gift Horse Antique Centre, too.

Follow US 98 east to *Elberta.* During the first half of the century, this fertile area attracted families from central, northern, and southern Europe, as well as Quebec. At Elberta's *German Sausage Festivals,* staged in March and October, descendants of early settlers dress in native attire to perform Old World dances. Call (251) 986-5805 for more information.

To learn more about the ethnic diversity and lifestyles of the county's early settlers, stop by the *Baldwin County Heritage Museum* (251-986-8375), ½ mile east of Elberta at 25521 US 98. In front of the five-acre wooded setting called "Frieden Im Wald," you'll see a working windmill and several outdoor agricultural exhibits.

Displays inside the museum feature the Kee tool collection and vintage farm equipment, a printing press, and an interior section of a post office from Josephine, Alabama. Household items include an Edison phonograph, antique sewing machines, stoves, cooking utensils, and washing machines. Also on display are old-fashioned school desks, folk sculpture, and a moonshine still. You'll also find a blacksmith shop and a church that dates to 1908. The museum is staffed entirely by volunteers, many of them snowbirds from Minnesota, Wisconsin, Michigan, New York, and other northern states, as well as Canada, who contribute their time and skills to restoring artifacts and putting old machinery in running order again. Admission is free. Hours are 10 a.m. to 3 p.m. Wednesday through Saturday. Weekday tours can be arranged by appointment.

At 12695 County Road 95 in Elberta, you can study carnivorous plants like Venus's-flytrap, pitcher plants, and other unusual botanical specimens native to the area at **Biophilia Nature Center.** "Different kinds of wildlife can be seen in season," said Carol Lovell-Saas, who promotes environmental education and takes you on a walk through her "open book of nature" that spreads across 20 acres. Tours offer a minicourse in butterfly gardening for the South or the Midwest and include free pamphlets on each plus literature on ecogardening.

From spring through early winter, several kinds of showy native butter-flies are raised indoors and outdoors, allowing visitors to observe all stages from egg to adult. You'll see forest wildflower meadows and swamp, now being restored with 300 native species, and can stop by a plant nursery and bookstore on the premises. Contact Carol at (251) 987-1200 for specific directions. Tours are offered by appointment only. Check out biophilia.net.

Afterward make your way back to Foley, then follow State Route 59 south to the glistening white sands of **Gulf Shores.** Although a Diners' Club publication once conferred highest honors on the stretch of shoreline along the Florida panhandle between Destin and Panama City, calling it "the world's most perfect beach," fewer people know about the other end of the Southern Riviera—Alabama's toehold on the Gulf of Mexico. In fact, the relatively new town of Gulf Shores did not appear on Alabama's official highway map until the 1960s. But a retreat offering sugar-sand beaches and a balmy climate cannot remain a secret forever, and this 32-mile crescent known as Pleasure Island (once a peninsula) now attracts vacationers from across the country.

Each year, *Southern Living* magazine gives some 16 million readers the chance to vote for their favorite places in the Best of the South Read-ers' Choice Awards. And Gulf Shores always ranks among the favorites in the Beach Town/Resort category. Renourishment programs have made the white-sand playground even wider and just as enticing as before the hurri-cane visitations. You can check out the new Alabama Gulf Coast for yourself at gulfshores.com.

Situated on the shores of the Intracoastal Waterway at **Orange Beach, The Wharf** is a 200-acre resort and entertainment center less than 2 miles from the area's beckoning beaches. Here, in a holiday atmosphere, you can stroll along the boardwalk and browse through boutiques, local shops, and major retail stores. You can take in an exciting concert at the amphitheater or take a spin on the Southeast's largest Ferris wheel. The complex offers restaurants, upscale accommodations, a much-acclaimed destination spa, an outfitter's center, and a marina with public and private boat slips. Condominiums at Levin's Bend stretch for half a mile. The Wharf lures locals and visitors alike with something for everyone. Visit thewharfal.com for a look at what's happening this season on Alabama's Gulf Coast.

Some 100 charter boats dock at nearby Orange Beach marinas, offering outings from sunset cruises to fishing excursions. Surrounding waters feature world-class fishing throughout the year. (For information about state fishing licenses, call 334-242-3829 or 888-848-6887, or check out outdoor alabama.com.)

While in Orange Beach, consider signing up for a cruise aboard the **Blue Dolphin** at Alabama Point to view this stretch of the Gulf Coast's spectacular inland waterways. You'll view other native wildlife and pass beautiful Ono Island, where several celebrities own luxury homes. Call (251) 981-2774 for reservations on this 51-foot, 45-passenger air-conditioned pontoon boat with inside and outside seating. Passengers board at 29603 Perdido Beach Boulevard just across the road from the Flora-Bama. Passengers see dolphins almost every time they go out. And because the boat sits so low in the water, passengers feel like they can almost reach out and touch the dolphins. Check out bluedolphincruises.com for more information.

To see some secluded portions of the area, sign up for a barefoot cruise aboard the **Daedalus.** Based at 5749 Bay La Launch, you'll find the 50-foot sailboat at Bear Point Marina in Orange Beach. Because the big vessel performs in shallow water, passengers can visit hidden bayous and bays and even venture onto an uninhabited beach. Also, you'll enjoy watching cavorting dolphins, ospreys, blue herons, and other wildlife. To book your passage call (251) 987-1228 or click on sailthedaedalus.com for more information.

While exploring Orange Beach, once home to myriad orange trees, search out *Shipp's Harbour Grill* (251-981-9891; shippsrestaurant.com) at Sportsman Marina. Located at 27842 Canal Road, the eatery promises lunch, dinner, and sunsets on the deck. Owners Matt and Regina Shipp feature Gulf

Flora-Bama—Home of the Annual Mullet Toss

Jimmy Buffett used to come here and jam. John Grisham wrote about it in a novel. It's the area's hottest hangout—the *Flora-Bama,* boasting an identity all its own. Located 10 minutes from Gulf Shores on the Alabama/Florida line, the place bills itself as "one of the nation's last great roadhouse watering holes."

"You never know what'll be going on here," says a local. The crowd is mixed, and so is the music—everything from country to rock and roll—and mostly original music. Flora-Bama offers entertainment every day of the year and attracts throngs including now-and-future-famous musicians and songwriters.

The party heats up after five, and the parking lot gets full fast. Though success often invites duplication, Flora-Bama's idiosyncratic style and haphazard floor plan make cloning a remote possibility. A No Tears in the Beer demolition and rebuilding party took place after Hurricane Ivan dealt the place a big blow. Then, in 2005, along came Katrina dumping sand. In spite of it all, they have continued to function, and have had music every day.

You can also take in the annual Interstate Mullet Toss, held the last full weekend in April. (What's a mullet toss? An event on the beach where people vie for the dubious distinction of pitching a dead fish the greatest distance—from Florida to Alabama.)

If your April calendar is too full to fit in the Mullet Toss, there's always next January 1 and the Polar Bear Dip. After testing the Gulf of Mexico's cold waters, you can warm up with a serving of black-eyed peas—the traditional Southern dish declared to bring good luck throughout the year. (The luck intensifies if you consume collards or other greens, and adding hog jowl almost guarantees more luck than you can stand.)

Otherwise you can meander around, buy souvenirs, consume beverages, visit the Beach Oyster Bar, eat crab claws or Royal Reds (the very best of steamed shrimp), purchase lottery tickets, or converse with other patrons. The person standing next to you might have a total of five dollars in his jeans pocket or five million on his net worth statement.

Located at 17401 Perdido Key Drive, with a Pensacola zip, Flora-Bama (850-492-0611 in Florida or 251-980-5118 in Alabama) opens daily at 9 a.m. and shuts down in the wee hours.

seafood and steak and a long list of made-to-order sushi in a casual setting. Ask about the fresh catch of the day with several choices, grilled to perfection. Moderate prices. Open daily at 11 a.m.

You'll find more good eating at *King Neptune's Seafood Restaurant* (251-968-5464; kingneptuneseafoodrestaurant.com) at 1137 Gulf Shores Parkway. Al Sawyer, known as the King of Crustaceans and the Prince of Prawns, owns the popular dining spot. Because Sawyer knows his seafood, visitors and locals alike flock to his places for oysters, Royal Red shrimp, and crab claws. The restaurateur, who has appeared on the Travel Channel's *Lonely Planet* and Bobby Flay's *Food Nation* on the Food Channel, serves only oysters from Bon Secour Fisheries and Alabama wild shrimp.

During the second weekend of October, more than 300,000 seafood lovers flock to *Gulf Shores's National Shrimp Festival* to eat shrimp, enjoy music, and look at arts and crafts, as well as fine art, created and presented by more than 200 artists. The Alabama Gulf Coast Area Chamber of Commerce produces this festival. Visit myshrimpfest.com for information. Speaking of shrimp, this is the place to walk into a seafood outlet, just after the fleet has docked, and buy your dinner fresh from coastal waters. Many area fish markets will ice-pack local seafood for travel.

The tiny fishing village of *Bon Secour,* located west of State Route 59 between Foley and Gulf Shores, is home to several shrimp-packing operations. At some of these, you can crunch your way through oyster shells to watch the unloading process and buy the day's freshest catch directly off the boat. Look for signs along Baldwin County Road 10 that lead to several of these markets with their colorful shrimp boats on the Bon Secour River.

During the late 1700s French settlers staked a claim here, naming the area Bon Secour for "Safe Harbour." While driving around, notice the lovely little church, Our Lady of Bon Secour, framed with Spanish moss in its tree-shaded setting.

After dipping into the Gulf of Mexico's foaming waves and basking in the sunshine, you may want to sally forth to other points of interest, such as historic *Fort Morgan* (251-540-7127; fortmorgan.org). Located at the end of a scenic drive 22 miles west of Gulf Shores on State Route 180, the fort—built to guard Mobile Bay—played a major role during the Civil War. At the Battle of Mobile Bay on August 5, 1864, "torpedoes" (underwater mines) were strung across the channel to stop the Union fleet from entering.

This strategy failed when Adm. David Farragut issued his famous command: "Damn the torpedoes—full speed ahead!"

Today's visitors can explore vaulted corridors and peer into dark rooms of this historic fort, named in honor of Revolutionary War hero Gen. Daniel Morgan. Designed by Simon Bernard, a French engineer and former aide-de-camp to Napoléon, the five-pointed-star structure pays tribute to the craftsmanship of men who labored from 1819 to 1834. As technology changed, the original fort continued to be modified and upgraded, said the curator. In the museum, exhibits cover military history from the fort's early days through World War II. Take one of the guided tours with a costumed guide to make history come alive. Be sure to put your fingers in your ears for the cannon-firing demonstration. Loud! Except for major holidays, the museum is open daily from 9 a.m. to 5 p.m., and the museum and fort are

Freakish Accident at Fort Morgan

If the walls of Fort Morgan could talk, imagine the tales they would tell. The old fort guarding Mobile Bay was the site of a freakish accident that visitors can learn about in the fort museum. It involves Charles S. Stewart, who died April 30, 1863. Born in New York in 1828, Stewart moved to Alabama and became a successful merchant in Mobile and married Julia Brown. When Alabama seceded from the Union in 1861, Stewart cast his lot with his adopted state and joined the Mobile Cadets No. 2 of the Confederate army, proving to be a daring leader in the battles of Shiloh and Corinth.

Promoted to lieutenant colonel in May 1862, Stewart was placed in command of Fort Morgan. He regularly wrote long letters home to his wife, some of which are displayed at the fort museum. Amid rumors of a powerful Union ironclad fleet preparing to attack Fort Morgan, Stewart decided to ready the fort, testing the its 33-pounder cannons.

On April 30, 1863, Stewart was standing by with other officers and his gun crew when one of the cannons was fired. Somehow by accident, the gun had been loaded with two powder charges instead of one. When the order to fire was given, the cannon exploded, spewing large pieces of metal.

Five soldiers were killed, including Stewart, who died instantly when a 200-pound fragment struck him in the head. Years later, Stewart's granddaughter placed a marker on the steps of Fort Morgan, at the exact spot where Stewart was killed. Tradition says that stains from Stewart's blood are still visible on the steps.

open from 9 a.m. to 5 p.m. Admission: adults $7, college students and senior citizens $5, military plus guest free, children $3 (ages 6 to 12).

After seeing Fort Morgan you may want to board the Mobile Bay Ferry for a visit to *Fort Gaines* on Dauphin Island. The ferry transports passengers and vehicles between the two forts at 90-minute intervals. Call (251) 861-3000 for specific times and current rates.

History buffs will get a charge out of exploring the *Fort Gaines Historic Site* (251-861-6992) at the eastern end of Bienville Boulevard. To learn more about this Renaissance-style fort that dates to 1821 or Dauphin Island's public parks, beaches, and campgrounds, check out dauphinisland.org. By the way, this barrier island is a birder's paradise.

alabamatrivia

Isabella de Soto planted America's first fig trees, which came over from Spain, at Fort Morgan.

Nearby, both big and little kids will enjoy seeing the marine life and interactive exhibits at the *Estuarium at Dauphin Island Sea Lab* (251-861-2141). Located at 101 Bienville Boulevard, this facility highlights coastal Alabama's key habitats from the Delta's swamps to the reefs of the Gulf of Mexico. (The seahorses are mesmerizing; I could watch them for hours.) The sea lab is open March 1 through August 31 from 9 a.m. to 6 p.m. Monday through Saturday and noon to 6 p.m. on Sunday. From September 1 through February 28, it is open 9 a.m. to 5 p.m. Monday through Saturday and Sunday 1 to 5 p.m. Admission: adults $10, senior citizens $8, children (ages 5 to 18) $6. To learn more about the fascinating programs offered here, visit estuarium.disl.org.

You can also reach *Dauphin Island* via State Route 193 South, which peels off I-10 south of Mobile. So set your GPS and go.

Don't miss nearby *Bellingrath Gardens and Home* (251-973-2217 or 800-247-8420), located at Theodore about 20 miles southwest of Mobile. Once a simple fishing camp, the 65-acre wonderland lures visitors year-round. Because of south Alabama's climate, you can expect gorgeous displays of blossoms here, whatever the season. Upon arrival you'll receive a map illustrating the layout of the six gardens linked by bridges, walkways, streams, lakes, and lily-filled ponds. (Be sure to wear your walking shoes.)

After exploring the gardens you may want to tour the former home of Bessie and Walter Bellingrath (he was an early Coca Cola executive). The house contains outstanding collections of Dresden china, Meissen figurines, and antique furnishings. The world's largest public exhibit of porcelain sculptures by Edward Marshall Boehm is on display in the visitors lounge. Separate admission fees for gardens and home: adults $20.50 for both or $12.50 for gardens only; children (ages 5 to 12) $12.50 for both or $7 for gardens only. The gardens are open daily from 8 a.m. to 5 p.m. Home tours are from 9 a.m. to 3:30 p.m. Visit Bellingrath.org to see what's in bloom.

Enjoy a sightseeing tour down the Fowl River or opt for a weekend dinner cruise. For more information call **Alabama Cruises** (251) 973-1244 or check out alabamacruises.com.

Save plenty of time for **Mobile,** a city famous for its magnificent live oaks, some reputed to be more than 400 years old. Trimmed in silvery Spanish moss, the enormous trees spread their branching canopies over city streets. Always magical, Mobile is especially so during spring, when masses of azaleas explode into vibrant pinks, reds, and magentas, making the Church Street area, DeTonti Square, Oakleigh Garden, Spring Hill, and other historic districts more beautiful than ever. March is the month to view the azaleas at their vibrant peak. During the annual **Azalea Trail Festival,** you can follow the signs along a 37-mile route that winds past lovely homes ranging in style from Greek revival and Italianate to Southern Creole. (Mobile's own "Creole cottage," adapted for the local climate, evolved from the French colonial form.)

alabamatrivia

Mobile is Alabama's oldest city.

Be sure to stop by the official welcome center, **Fort Condé** (251-208-7304) at 150 Royal Street, for some background on Alabama's oldest city. Mobile has been governed by France, England, Spain, the Republic of Alabama, the Confederate States of America, and the US. Built in 1711, Fort Condé was once home base for the sprawling French Louisiana territory, and a re-created version now serves as a living-history museum. Soldiers in period French uniforms greet visitors, guiding them through the complex with its thick walls and low-slung doors.

Costumed guides set the early scene for visitors and may even fire a cannon in the courtyard. Displays and dioramas tell the city's story. You'll see military furnishings typical of the times, photography exhibits, and arti-facts such as china and pottery shards, brass buckles, buttons, porcelain and bisque doll parts, dice, and gun barrels. Hours are 8:30 a.m. to 4:30 p.m. daily, and admission is free.

For a breakfast you won't forget, stop by **Spot of Tea** (251-433-9009; spotoftea.com) at 310 Dauphin Street, across from Cathedral Square. Now celebrating more than a decade of business, the restaurant offers much more than breakfast and tea. The property features an inviting sidewalk cafe, lovely gift shop, Victorian dining room, private Victorian Tea Room, New Orleans–style carriageway, and Léstradé Dinner Theatre in the rear.

Quench your thirst with the award-winning strawberry iced tea. Break-fast/lunch, served seven days a week, offers items such as bananas Foster French toast and banana waffles, as well as the signature breakfast choice, eggs cathedral (an English muffin topped with a crab cake, eggs, and sea-food sauce). Omelets, pancakes, eggs Benedict, soups, sandwiches, and salads are all included on the extensive menu. Hours are 7 a.m. to 2 p.m. daily. Economical to moderate.

Take a tour of the Lower Dauphin Street Area (LoDa) and follow your nose to the **A&M Peanut Shop** at 209 Dauphin Street (251-438-9374; ampeanuts .com) with its freshly roasted nuts, served warm from a 90-year-old roaster. The shop is open Monday through Saturday 9 a.m. to 6 p.m. Then saunter into **Three Georges Southern Chocolates** (251-433-6725; 3georges.com) at 226 Dauphin Street, a spot that has lured locals and visitors since 1917. Marble-based cases and original glass candy jars hold hand-dipped chocolates, pralines, divinity, and many varieties of fudge plus a rainbow assortment of jelly beans and rock candy. Scott Gonzales, who purchased the historic property in 1992 and later the H. M. Thames Nuthouse, now operates four sites. His dream "is to grow into a company that makes Mobilians proud while introducing some of our most treasured Southern delicacies all over the world."

Those who subscribe to the theory of eating dessert first because of life's uncertainty can savor a praline made with oven-roasted pecans while waiting for one of the weekday lunch specialties, like red beans and rice, jambalaya, or muffalettas, now available at this vintage sweet shop. Hours are 10 a.m. to 5 p.m. Monday through Friday.

When hunger pangs hit again, head for **Wintzell's Oyster House** (251-432-4605), which dates to 1938 at its historic downtown address, 605 Dauphin

Street. Wintzell's also offers its fried, stewed, and nude delicacies at other nearby locations as well as in Guntersville in the state's northeastern section.

"He was a bold man that first ate an oyster," wrote Jonathan Swift, the 18th-century satirist. If you're bold and enjoy oysters enough to attempt breaking the current consumption record—280 for women and 421 for men—declare your intentions at any of Wintzell's locations. The staff will then alert the restaurant's suppliers if you look like a serious contender. You have one hour, while seated at the bar, to consume oysters on the half shell. If you set a new record, your feast is free, and you receive a check for $25. Otherwise, well, you would have had to pay anyway.

If you prefer your oysters not nude, then order them steamed, fried, or in stew. Other delectable versions include oysters Rockefeller, Bienville, Buffalo, Monterey, Alfredo, and Parmesan. Try the yummy gumbo while reading Wintzell's signs (on life in general) as you dine. Hours at all locations are 11 a.m. to 10 p.m. Sunday through Thursday and 11 a.m. to 11 p.m. Friday and Saturday. Slither to wintzellsoysterhouse.com for more pearls of wisdom on these bivalves.

At the William and Emily Hearin **Mobile Carnival Museum** (251-432-3324; mobilecarnivalmuseum.com), you can dip into the magical world of Mardi Gras. You can't miss it. Look for an 1870 Italianate townhouse at 355 Government Street with two colorful 10-foot-tall jesters on the front porch.

Mobilians celebrated America's first Mardi Gras in 1703, and you'll get a great overview here, surrounded by a glittering array of memorabilia. You'll encounter a fire-breathing dragon float in the den (former carriage house) and can climb aboard the rocking float to enjoy a rollicking good time.

Volunteer guides, some affiliated with Mobile's mystic societies, share fascinating anecdotes with visitors. Exhibits showcase elaborate gowns with their flowing trains. These creations reflect intricate workmanship, and countless hours go into their construction. According to *National Geographic*, Mobile's coronations rival those of real coronations in Europe. Today's Mardi Gras festivities, which extend over a two-month period (with preparations going on around the calendar), feature many spectacular parades and magnificent balls. At last count 32 parading organizations and 55 nonparading organizations staged balls during the Mardi Gras season. Museum hours are 9 a.m. to 4 p.m. Monday, Wednesday, Friday, and Saturday. Admission: adults $5, children (ages 3 to 12) $2.

America's First Mardi Gras

After surviving a deadly scourge of yellow fever, a colony of French soldiers in Mobile decided to celebrate life. Painting their faces red, they feasted and drank. There is no historical record that they paraded. But this festive gathering has gone down in history as the first Mardi Gras celebration in America, a century before Alabama became a state. Today, it remains an important part of Alabama Gulf Coast culture.

It was not until years later, in 1830, that the parade part became popular in Mobile. On New Year's Day, a cotton broker named Michael Krafft and some of his friends gathered up some cowbells, rakes, and hoes in a local hardware store. They then proceeded to march through the streets of Mobile and called themselves the Cowbellion de Rakin Society.

They liked it so much that the Cowbellions decided to have an annual event tied into Mardi Gras. Some of this partying group carried their customs to New Orleans. In 1857 the Cowbellion de Rakins assisted the Big Easy in setting up a mystic society of its own, the Mystic Krewe of Comus, to this day New Orleans's most prestigious Mardi Gras society.

Mobile festivities grew until the Civil War, when celebrations were put aside. Even after the war, Mobile was under Union occupation and no one felt like partying. That's when Joseph Stillwell Cain decided that people needed to be happy and he was going to do something about it. On Shrove Tuesday in 1866, town clerk Cain dressed up in Indian regalia, called himself "Chief Slacabormorinico," and climbed aboard a coal wagon he had decorated. The defiant Cain rode his mule-powered one-float parade through the streets of Mobile, and single-handedly brought about the rebirth of Mardi Gras festivities to the depressed city.

By the time Cain died at age 72, he had founded a number of mystic societies, including the well-known Order of Myths. In Mobile's historic Church Street Cemetery, Cain's tombstone notes: "Here lies Joe Cain, the heart and soul of Mardi Gras in Mobile."

Every year on the Sunday before Mardi Gras, the Joe Cain Parade pays honor to the rebel. A "people's parade," the Joe Cain Parade is not filled with big floats. Instead, it is a time to decorate a jalopy, wagon, wheelbarrow, or bicycle and join the parade. Of course, there are always plenty of "Cain's widows" in the processional, weeping and wailing for their man.

Look for the *Malaga Inn* (251-438-4701 or 800-235-1586; malagainn .com) at 359 Church Street. A charming place to make your base, this quaint hotel started out as twin townhouses in 1862—the families of sisters shared a patio between their mirror-image houses. In 1967 the historic structures were joined by a connector and converted into a hotel.

Individually decorated rooms and suites are furnished with antiques or nostalgic reproductions. You'll enjoy relaxing in the inn's garden courtyard with its flowing fountain, umbrella-topped tables, and surrounding galleries of ornamental ironwork. The inn serves a deluxe continental breakfast. Guests also are served spiced tea and cookies. Rates range from standard to moderate.

Several mansions, including the *Richards-DAR House* (251-208-7320; richardsdarhouse.com), open their doors to the public not only during spring tours but throughout the year. Located at 256 North Joachim Street in DeTonti Square, this 1860 Italianate antebellum home is noted for its "frozen lace" ironwork that decorates the facade in an elaborate pattern. Be sure to notice the etched ruby Bohemian glass framing the entrance. Other fine features include a suspended staircase, Carrara marble mantels, and striking brass and crystal chandeliers signed by Cornelius. In the rear wing you'll find a gift shop. Except for major holidays, the home, operated by the Daughters of the American Revolution, is open from 11 a.m. to 3:30 p.m. Monday through Friday, 10 a.m. to 4 p.m. Saturday, and 1 to 4 p.m. Sunday. Admission: adults $5, children $2.

You may also want to tour the *Oakleigh Historic Complex* (251-432-1281; historicmobile.org) in its serene oak-shaded setting at 300 Oakleigh Place. The guides dress in authentic costumes of the 1830s to conduct tours through an 1833 antebellum house/museum filled with early Victorian, Empire, and Regency furnishings. Open Tuesday through Saturday from 10 a.m. to 4 p.m. Admission: adults $10, children (age 12 and under) $5.

To dip into more of the city's past, make reservations at the *The Kate Shepard House Bed & Breakfast* (251-479-7048) in the heart of historic Dauphin Way. Located at 1552 Monterey Place, this handsome Queen Anne Victorian home is listed on the National Register of Historic Places. Built by C. M. Shepard in 1897, it was designed by well-known architect George Franklin Barber.

"Guests can pull into the driveway and park under the porte cochere," says Wendy James, who with her husband, Bill, owns the home. "We have a dog that will bark loudly when you arrive, but will be your best friend in minutes." The couple, who lived in Hawaii for almost 15 years, searched the southeast for the perfect historic house and setting to establish their long-planned bed-and-breakfast. Captivating Mobile and this lovely home, surrounded by century-old magnolia trees, won their hearts. Along with 11 fireplaces, four original stained glass windows, and beautiful woodwork, the home came with a surprise—an attic full of treasures. Wendy shares stories regarding this lagniappe (something extra) with her guests.

Mobile's Changing Skyline

Mobile's downtown renaissance continues with a skyline that looks very different—just as it did when construction on Alabama's first skyscraper started here a century ago. Looming above its neighbors, the impressive *RSA Battle House Tower* can be seen for 30 miles—all the way up Mobile Bay. So again this city on the move boasts the state's tallest structure—a 40-story tower that stretches skyward. Companion to the historic, rejuvenated *Battle House Hotel,* the pair represents a fusion of past and present. Call me astonished when I swept into the Battle House lobby on a recent visit to Mobile. I wasn't the only one marveling as I checked in. "This is gorgeous," the woman behind me said to her husband. The two kept looking in awe at the magnificent ceiling. And so did I.

Once again, the Battle House dispenses classic Southern hospitality, which translates to plenty of pampering. Don't pass up a chance to unwind in the spa. Then dine on divine regional and continental specialties in the *Trellis Room.* (I'm still salivating over the chef's take on crème brûlée. Oh yes, and that Chilean sea bass.) The historic hotel is connected to the new RSA Battle House Tower by the 9,628-square-foot Moonlight Ballroom.

A hotel with a history—that's what I like. With its grand staircase (plus the whispering arches that heard goodness knows how many secrets), the Battle House served as the setting for countless debutante balls. Besides presiding over the social scene in downtown Mobile for a century, this iconic hotel played host to such American statesmen as Woodrow Wilson and Confederate president Jefferson Davis. The hotel's historic roots date back to 1852. For more information on the Battle House, a Renaissance Hotel & Spa, at 26 North Royal Street in downtown Mobile, call (251) 338-2000 or (866) 316-5957.

Five Rivers Run Through It

To launch a kayak or canoe outing through the country's second largest river delta, head to Spanish Fort, about 5 miles from downtown Mobile. *Five Rivers Delta Resource Center* (251-625-0814) marks the spot where the Mobile, Spanish, Tensaw, Apalachee, and Blakeley Rivers converge in Mobile Bay. Here, you can immerse yourself in the area's natural beauty, learn about its history, and set off on an adventure through scenic waterways, woods, and wetlands.

Swing by the Nature Center Complex, a trio of pile-supported buildings with wraparound porches and decks, overlooking the Delta. A favorite with visitors, the exhibit hall showcases some of the state's wildlife. You'll also find information on other nature-based attractions in this coastal area: Blakeley State Park, Dauphin Island Estuarium, Gulf State Park, and Weeks Bay Reserve.

Special Saturday programs offer canoe and kayak lessons, wilderness survival training, cooking demonstrations, and more. Located across from Meaher State Park on the Mobile Bay Causeway (US 90/98), the center is open daily from 8 a.m. to 5 p.m.

Shepard's daughters, Kate and Isabel, operated a private boarding and day school here during the early 1900s. Wendy, who continues to research the home's history, filled several glass-front cases with school memorabilia and framed several photos from that era. Moderate to deluxe rates. For more information, click on kateshepherdhouse.com.

No visit to the Port City would be complete without scaling the decks of the *Battleship USS* **Alabama** (251-433-2703), moored in Mobile Bay. This renowned vessel played the role of the USS *Missouri* in the movie *Under Siege*, starring Steven Seagal.

Now the focal point of the 155-acre park on Battleship Parkway just off the I-10 causeway, the USS *Alabama* served in every major engagement in the Pacific during World War II, apparently leading a charmed life throughout her 37 months of active duty. She earned not only nine battle stars but also the nickname "Lucky A" (from her crew of 2,500) because she emerged unscathed from the heat of each battle.

She also rode out hurricanes Camille, Frederick, and Ivan, but Katrina slammed in with a 12-foot storm surge and triple-digit winds, tilting the ship by eight degrees. Setting a structure of this magnitude—half the length of the

Empire State Building's height—upright presented quite a challenge. Waves swept over the ship's bow, 30 feet above sea level. As for the park's Aircraft Exhibit Pavilion, hurricane winds lifted and dropped military tanks and artillery exhibits, scattering parts across the grounds and severely damaging 14 planes. After $6 million in restoration costs, the iconic USS *Alabama,* the submarine *USS* **Drum** (which received no storm damage), and a new pavilion reopened to the public. Again, you can explore below and upper decks and roam through the captain's cabin, officers' staterooms, messing and berthing spaces, and crew's galley. Authentic touches include calendar girl pinups and background music, with such singers as Bing Crosby and Frank Sinatra crooning songs popular during the 1940s.

Anchored beside the battleship, the USS *Drum* gives visitors a chance to thread their way through a submarine and marvel at how a crew of 72 men could live, run their ship, and fire torpedoes while confined to such tight quarters.

Open every day except Christmas, the park can be visited from 8 a.m. to 6 p.m. April through September and from 8 a.m. to 5 p.m. October through March. Admission: adults $15, senior citizens $13, active or retired military free, children (ages 6 to 11) $6. For more information check out ussalabama.com.

Places to Stay in Southwest Alabama

CAMDEN

Roland Cooper State Park
285 Deer Run Dr.
(334) 682-4838
alapark.com/rolandcooper

EUTAW

Oakmont Bed & Breakfast
107 Pickens St.
(205) 372-2326

FAIRHOPE

Bay Breeze Guest House
742 South Mobile St.
(866) 928-8976

GULF SHORES/ORANGE BEACH

The Beach Club
925 Beach Club Trail
(251) 540-2500 or
(888) 260-7263

Island House Hotel
26650 Perdido Beach Blvd.
(251) 981-6100 or
(800) 264-2642
islandhousehotel.com

Meyer Real Estate
(for resort rentals)
1585 Gulf Shores Pkwy.
(251) 968-7516 or
(800) 487-5959
meyerre.com

Perdido Beach Resort
27200 Perdido Beach Blvd.
(251) 981-9811 or
(800) 634-8001
perdidobeachresort.com

MAGNOLIA SPRINGS

Magnolia Springs Bed & Breakfast
14469 Oak St.
(251) 965-7321 or
(800) 965-7321
magnolaisprings.com

MARION

The Gateway Inn
1615 State Rte. 5 South
(334) 683-9166

MOBILE

The Battle House, a Renaissance Hotel & Spa
26 North Royal St.
(251) 338-2000

Holiday Inn
301 Government St.
(251) 694-0100 or
(800) 692-6662

The Kate Shepard House Bed & Breakfast
1552 Monterey Place
(251) 479-7048
kateshephardhouse.com

Malaga Inn
359 Church St.
(251) 438-4701 or
(800) 235-1586
malagainn.com

Mauvila Mansion
1306 Dauphin St.
(251) 408-9478

Renaissance Riverview Plaza Hotel
64 South Water St.
(251) 438-4000 or
(866) 749-6069

MONROEVILLE

Best Western Inn
4419 South Alabama Ave.
(251) 575-9999 or
(800) WESTERN

Country Inn & Suites
120 Hwy. 21 South
(251) 743-3333 or
(800) HOLIDAY

POINT CLEAR

Grand Hotel Marriott Resort, Golf Club & Spa
One Grand Blvd.
(251) 928-9201 or
(800) 544-9933

FOR MORE INFORMATION ABOUT SOUTHWEST ALABAMA

Alabama Gulf Coast Convention & Visitors Bureau
23685 Perdido Beach Blvd.
Orange Beach 36561 or
PO Drawer 457
Gulf Shores 36547
(251) 974-1510 or (800) 982-8562
gulfshores.com
info@gulfshores.com

Alabama's Front Porches
Official website of Rural Southwest Alabama
alabamasfrontporches.org

Demopolis Area Chamber of Commerce
102 East Washington St.
PO Box 667
Demopolis 36732
(334) 289-0270
demopolischamber.com

Eastern Shore Chamber of Commerce
327 Fairhope Ave.
Fairhope 36532
(251) 928-6387
eschamber.com

Foley Welcome Center
104 East Laurel Ave.
Foley 36535
(251) 943-1300
visitfoley.org

Gulf Shores Welcome Center
3150 Gulf Shores Pkwy.
(Alabama Highway 59 South)
Gulf Shores 36542
(251) 968-7511 or (800) 745-SAND
gulfshores.com

Mobile Bay Convention & Visitors Bureau
150 South Royal St.
PO Box 204
Mobile 36602
(251) 208-2000 or (800) 566-2453
mobilebay.org
mbcvb@mobile.org

Monroeville Area Chamber of Commerce
86 North Alabama Ave.
Monroeville 36461
(251) 743-2879
monroecountyal.com
info@monroecountyal.com

Selma/Dallas County Chamber of Commerce
912 Selma Ave.
PO Box 467
Selma 36702
(334) 875-7241 or (800) 457-3562
SelmaAlabama.com
info@SelmaAlabama.com

SELMA

Hampton Inn
2200 West Highland Ave.
(334) 876-9995 or
(800) HAMPTON

Holiday Inn Express Hotel & Suites
2000 Lincoln Way
(800) 876-9995

Quality Inn
2420 North Broad St.
(334) 874-8600

St. James Hotel
1200 Water Ave.
(334) 872-3234
historicstjameshotel.com

MAINSTREAM ATTRACTIONS WORTH SEEING IN SOUTHWEST ALABAMA

The *Gulf Coast Exploreum, Science Center, and IMAX Theater,* 65 Government Street at exit 26B off I-10, Mobile, features fascinating exhibits from the world of science, and that's not all. Throngs of visitors find the three permanent galleries exciting with more than 150 hands-on science adventures --Hands On Hall, the Wharf of Wonder, and MyBodyWorks. The center also hosts traveling exhibits. To check the current schedule, call (251) 208-6873 or (877) 625-4FUN or visit www.exploreum.net.

Adjacent to the Gulf Coast Exploreum, at 111 South Royal Street, the *History Museum of Mobile* offers a treasure trove in a National Historic Landmark building that dates to 1857 and occupies a portion of the Southern Market/Old City Hall. From the entry's 1936 WPA murals depicting the history of Mobile to the hands-on Discovery Room and Special Collections Gallery, this museum offers something for all ages and interests. You'll see a dugout canoe from the 14th century, relive the atrocious passage on an African slave ship, hear stories of Civil War soldiers, and learn about disasters like hurricanes, yellow fever, and fires that have impacted the area. The Themes Gallery puts the spotlight on Hank Aaron, Satchel Paige, and other sports figures from this city, known as a "baseball mecca." Check out museumofmobile.com or call (251) 208-7569.

Don't miss the stunning *Mobile Museum of Art.* Established in 1964, the museum moved in 2002 from its former quarters on Civic Center Drive to its present setting at 4850 Museum Drive in Langan Park. The grand lobby's commanding glass entrance hall overlooks a lake and makes the outdoors seem part of a sweeping landscape. The handsome building is home to a permanent collection of more than 6,000 works of art, which span 2,000 years of cultural history, and is particularly strong in American paintings of the 1930s and 1940s plus works by Southern artists, art of the French Barbizon School, and contemporary American crafts. For more information click on mobilemuseumofart.com or call the museum at (251) 208-5200.

Places to Eat in Southwest Alabama

CAMDEN

Gaines Ridge Dinner Club
933 State Rte. 10 East
(334) 682-9707

DAPHNE

Cousin Vinnie's/ Guido's Italian Restaurant
1709 Main St.
(251) 626-6082

DEMOPOLIS

The Red Barn
901 US 80 East
(334) 2890595

FAIRHOPE

Mary Ann's Deli
7 South Church St.
(251) 928-3663
maryannsdeli.com

FAUNSDALE

Ca-John's Faunsdale Bar & Grill
35558 State Rte. 25
(334) 628-3240
ca-johns.net

FOLEY

The Gift Horse
209 West Laurel Ave.
(251) 943-3663 or
(800) FOLEYAL
gifthorserestaurant.com

GULF SHORES/ORANGE BEACH

King Neptune's Seafood Restaurant
1137 Gulf Shores Parkway
(251) 968-5464
kingneptuneseafood restaurant.com

Lulu's at Homeport Marina
200 East 25th Ave.
(251) 967-5858
lulubuffett.com

Shipp's Harbour Grill
27842 Canal Rd.
(251) 981-9891
shippsrestaurant.com

Villaggio Grille
4790 Main St., F108
(251) 224-6510
villaggiogrille.com

LAVACA

Ezell's Fish Camp
166 Lotts Berry Rd.
(205) 654-2205

MAGNOLIA SPRINGS

Jesse's Restaurant
14770 Oak St.
(251) 965-3827
jesserestaurant.com

MOBILE

Spot of Tea
310 Dauphin St.
(251) 433-9009
spotoftea.com

The Trellis Room
Battle House Hotel
26 North Royal St.
(251) 338-2000

True Midtown Kitchen
1104 Dauphin St.
(251) 434-2002
kitchen.truedine.com

Wintzell's Oyster House
605 Dauphin St.
(251) 432-4605
wintzellsoysterhouse.com

Zea Rotisserie & Grill
4671 Airport Blvd.
(251) 344-7414
zearestaurants.com

POINT CLEAR

The Wash House Restaurant
17111 Scenic Hwy. 98
(251) 928-4838
washhouserestaurant.com

SELMA

Tally-Ho Restaurant
509 Mangum Ave.
(334) 872-1390
tallyhoselma.com

Index

Already "Been There, Done That"? Then Get Off the Beaten Path!